AGAINST THE THIRD REICH

AGAINST THE THIRD REICH

PAUL TILLICH'S WARTIME ADDRESSES TO NAZI GERMANY

TRANSLATOR: MATTHEW LON WEAVER

EDITORS: RONALD H. STONE AND MATTHEW LON WEAVER

WESTMINSTER JOHN KNOX PRESS
LOUISVILLE, KENTUCKY

Scripture quotations from the New Revised Standard Version
of the Bible are copyright © 1989 by the Division of Christian Education
of the National Council of the Churches of Christ in the U.S.A.
and are used by permission.

Book design by Jennifer K. Cox
Cover design by Kim Wohlenhaus

First edition
Published by Westminster John Knox Press
Louisville, Kentucky

This book is printed on acid-free paper that meets the
American National Standards Institute Z39.48 standard. ∞

PRINTED IN THE UNITED STATES OF AMERICA
98 99 00 01 02 03 04 05 06 07 — 10 9 8 7 6 5 4 3 2 1

Library of Congress Cataloging-in-Publication Data

Tillich, Paul, 1886–1965.
 Against the Third Reich : Paul Tillich's wartime addresses to Nazi Germany /
editors Ronald H. Stone and Matthew Lon Weaver ; translator Matthew Lon
Weaver. — 1st ed.
  p.   cm.
 Includes bibliographical references.
 ISBN 0-664-25770-4 (alk. paper)
 1. Tillich, Paul, 1886–1965. 2. Radio broadcasting—United States—
History—20th century. 3. World War, 1939–1945—Propaganda. 4. Propaganda,
American. 5. Jews—Persecutions—Germany. 6. Radio addresses, debates, etc.—
United States—History—20th century. 7. National socialism. 8. Propaganda,
Anti-German—United States—History—20th century. 9. Anti-Nazi movement—
United States. I. Stone, Ronald H. II. Weaver, Matthew Lon. III. Title.
D810.R33T55   1998
940.54′88′973—DC21   97-47376

CONTENTS

CONTENTS

CONTENTS

ACKNOWLEDGMENTS

The editors express their gratitude to Dr. Mutie Tillich Farris, executor of the Paul Tillich estate, for her encouragement on this project and her permission to publish the translations of Professor Tillich's radio addresses. Walter de Gruyter and Company, the holder of the rights to the German publication, has also generously granted permission for the translation and publication of the addresses. The editors have also been assisted by Gene McAfee, assistant in Manuscripts and Archives of Andover-Harvard Theological Library, who assisted us in acquiring the microfilm copies of all of Paul Tillich's German addresses. Mrs. Sheryl Gilliland's work was essential to the project, and we delight in her generous and efficient work. Finally, we express our thanks to Pittsburgh Theological Seminary's support, which made this project possible.

INTRODUCTION

Paul Tillich prepared 112 five-page addresses in German for broadcast into occupied Europe from March 1942 through May 1944. Even his closest friends in the United States did not know of his secret work for the Allied cause. These addresses have been largely unknown in the United States, except by specialists in Tillich scholarship. The decision to translate and publish them in English is to make a contribution to the debate over German guilt for the Nazis' extermination campaign and to reveal Paul Tillich as a political theologian. The essays are among the most concrete and passionate of his political writings. They also show that Tillich, who could announce the end of the Protestant Era and castigate Protestantism so thoroughly, was also a German Protestant theologian who saw the demonic, named it, and did what he could to denounce it. The reader of these essays will learn that Tillich's analysis was not only profound, powerful, and polemical but also true. These radio speeches are the raw data of a theologian at war from 1942 to 1944, following the daily events and analyzing them theologically. These are not works from hindsight but represent engaged, political, and theological risk taking.

The many individuals who were recruited to write for the Voice of America were not expected to create propaganda in the popular sense of the word. The Voice of America was the strongest section of the Radio Program Bureau of the U.S. Office of War Information (OWI). It was forbidden to use falsehood in its efforts. Another agency—the Office of Strategic Services (OSS)—was specifically mandated to serve as a subversive tool of the military. It was unabashedly engaged in psychological warfare. The OWI, in contrast, was committed to the truthful dissemination of information in the domestic and foreign sectors—a truth admittedly steeped in New Deal liberalism.[1]

Did Tillich's service to the OWI nevertheless make him a propagandist? The fields of propaganda studies and communication research flowered in the years between the two world wars. While propaganda studies focused on the truth or falsehood of media messages, communication studies concentrated on the impact of these messages on the hearers. The political scientist, Harold Lasswell, came to the conclusion that propaganda was "no more moral or immoral than a pump handle." Its truth or untruth was irrelevant to its function. In his eyes, it had become a necessary tool for moving the masses in the modern, technological era.[2] Jacques Ellul a Protestant, French theologian, later pointed out the inherent risk contained within a modern situation in which propaganda becomes technological civilization's weapon against the autonomy of the individual.[3]

Tillich certainly understood the ambiguity of his situation. One could hardly imagine his participation in activity that bore any resemblance to the crude propaganda of Nazism. He certainly had no illusions about the purity of the American system; he presaged Ellul's concerns in his own thought. Neither shamelessly untruthful nor blind to Allied shortcomings, his speeches offer a relentless confrontation of the truth and its undeniable consequences. Tillich's addresses are about Germany of the past, the Nazi–occupied Germany of his present, and a liberated Germany of the future. The past Germany and the future liberated Germany are used as hammer and anvil to beat Nazism out of the present Germany. If propaganda is the perpetuation of falsehood or the effort to persuade by concealing the truths about one's opponents, Tillich was not a propagandist. If it is a "means of persuasion," in the manner of Aristotle's *Rhetoric*, it could be argued that Tillich was writing propaganda.

Tillich's address writing began at an Allied low point in the war, moved through the Axis defeats of 1942, and concluded before D day in mid-1944. Throughout this period, Tillich optimistically trusted in the ultimate Allied victory. The United States and the Soviet Union were both stronger than Germany. With the empire to draw on, Britain's strength was certainly as great as Japan's, and the lesser nations of the world were drawn into functional alliances with the Allies. Tillich regarded the outcome as certain, but to be achieved through much suffering and hard fighting. In terms of population and industrial production, the Allies were too strong for the Axis powers. The military skills of the democrats and the Communists were to be proven as in no way inferior to those of the Nazis, Fascists, and Japanese militarists. Tillich portrayed Adolf Hitler as a gambler who had taken a contest at bad odds. Having lost his gamble, Hitler compulsively tried to repair his losses; but when defeated, his actions turned into an orgy of German self-destruction.

Should we regard Tillich as too optimistic? Probably not. Most Americans of Tillich's generation with whom we have spoken also regarded the outcome of the war as a foregone conclusion. After all, Pittsburgh itself would outproduce the Ruhr Valley. Once U.S. production was geared up, more aircraft and ships would flow from North American mills on the invulnerable continent than the Japanese could destroy. In addition to population, material, and military intelligence, will was needed to defeat the Axis. Both Japan and Germany, in their terrible barbaric excesses, aroused the will to fight in both communists and democrats.

Tillich's judgments were shrewd, formulated from experience in the trenches of World War I. It is worth remembering that his rank in World War I was higher than Hitler's. By the time of his writing, Hitler's and Japan's mistakes had doomed their regimes. Hitler's Barbarossa invasion of the Soviet Union might have had a chance in 1941 — if Japan had struck the Soviets in the East. But Japan's foolish attack on the United States and Hitler's declaration of war on the world's strongest industrial power sealed their fate. If Joseph Stalin, in the sure knowledge that Japan was committed elsewhere, had not been able to shift thirty-two divisions from the East to thwart the Nazis at the gates of Moscow in the first winter, things might have been different. But by March 1942, Tillich could anticipate the Nazi defeat. The turning points for Germany came in North Africa in 1942 and at Stalingrad in early 1943.

Tillich, for his part, was trying to divide the will of his German listeners from the mania of their Nazi rulers. Again and again he struck the theme Nazism is doomed and that listeners should abandon it. He tried to persuade Germans to stop cooperating with their rulers. This attempt, of course, confronted the obedient character of the good German. Just by listening to his broadcasts, a German or other European was engaging in resistance. As Jakub S. Trojan, a Czech theologian put it to me in 1995, "The broadcasts of the Voice of America were very important to us, but we could be executed for listening."[4]

Resistance to Hitler was not widespread. Those who engaged in resistance in public were executed, assassinated, or imprisoned. Given the nature of totalitarian rule, resistance had to be in secret if it were to be sustained. Tillich finished writing his addresses before the July 20, 1944, attempt on Hitler's life brought the deadly reprisals against the plotters. Tillich's hopes for Germans taking their fate and liberation into their own hands by overthrowing Nazism were too grand for his suppressed audience.

To call anti-Nazi activities within Hitler's Germany a resistance "movement" would be overstatement. Such a description implies a cohesiveness among those involved that simply did not exist. Most resistance that occurred was undertaken by courageous individuals. Their actions ranged from providing sanctuary for those fleeing the government, to reading illegal literature, to listening to forbidden radio stations. While seemingly minor, all of these were capital offenses.[5]

Individuals such as Georg Elser and Kurt Gernstein went beyond this. Elser acted alone in his attempt to assassinate Hitler in 1939. Gernstein worked within the system to slow the flow of Zyklon-B to the death camps. Elser was executed. Gernstein's ambiguous position led to his imprisonment in postwar France, where he committed suicide.[6]

The futility of individual resistance led to small-scale collective resistance. Discussion groups such as the Wednesday Club, the Solf Circle, and the Kreisau Circle sought to neutralize the oppressive impact of Nazism and plan for a post-Nazi Germany. Subversive journals such as *Resistance* (published by the Communist Ernst Niekisch) and *Information Journal of the Central Conservative Association* (published by Ewald von Kleist-Schmenzin) were banned in the first years of Nazi rule. Communist resistance began with Hitler's betrayal of the Ribbentrop-Molotov Pact. The Red Orchestra was perhaps the most notorious of the Communist groups; fifty-five of its members were executed when German authorities discovered their shortwave radio signals to the Soviets.

The Edelweiss Pirates and the White Rose were youth resistance groups. The Pirates damaged Nazi property; at the same time, they assisted in rescue and firefighting efforts in bombed-out German cities. The White Rose, composed of college-aged young people, wrote and distributed pamphlets. Its leaders, Hans and Sophie Scholl, were caught dispersing their material in Hitler's stronghold of Munich in 1943. They were arrested, tortured, and executed soon thereafter.[7]

These scattered collective activities kept hope for change alive among their participants yet lacked the leverage necessary to effect real change. Such leverage could be found only in the German institutions, particularly the civilian government, the Foreign Office, the Abwehr (the Nazi intelligence and counterintelligence branch), the church, and the army. Each institution had figures who acted heroically against the Nazis. Former Leipzig mayor Carl Goerdeler and Social Democratic Party member Julius Leber worked with others to plan for German rule after Hitler. In the Foreign Office, Secretary of State Ernst von Weizsaker created a haven for resistance work. At the Abwehr, Admiral Wilhelm Canaris used his organization to curb Nazi extremism. Under his watch, Hans Oster and Hans von Dohnanyi assembled extensive evidence of Nazi criminality dating back to the beginning of the regime, all of it destroyed at the time of their arrest. Theologian Dietrich Bonhoeffer (Dohnanyi's brother-in-law) became active in resistance through the Abwehr; along with Berlin pastor Martin Niemöller, Bonhoeffer represented one of the very few bright spots in the Christian church's relationship to Nazism.

The army—the one institution with the organization and the power to overthrow Hitler—was overseen by members of a ruling class prone to support strong leaders. Out of two thousand generals, only twenty-two of them (often retired) had any role in resisting Hitler. Therefore, it was "the colonels," rather than "the generals," who took significant action. Most prominent among them was Colonel Claus von Stauffenberg, a latecomer whose July 20, 1944, assassination attempt on Hitler was the "movement's" closest chance for success.[8]

Through his speeches, Tillich appealed to people like these to muster the necessary courage to stand against the terrorizing police state of Nazism.

Tillich did not last long under Hitler. He was among the first professors whom the Nazi regime dismissed from the University of Frankfurt in 1933. All the others of this first group were Jews. His publication of "Ten Theses: The Church and the Third Reich" in 1933, combined with his support for Jews, his religious socialism, and his actions as Dean at Frankfurt to expel rowdy Nazi students, earned him his quick dismissal.[9] He urged in Thesis Seven that Protestantism set "the cross against the paganism of the swastika," and he testified that the cross was against the " 'holiness' of nation, race, blood and power." Narrowly missing arrest, he was allowed to emigrate in response to invitations from Union Theological Seminary and Columbia University. From his safe haven in New York, he would direct his programs of Self-Help for Emigrés from Central Europe and the Council for a Democratic Germany and write the addresses collected here.

Tillich's great distance from the Confessing Church in his rejection of Nazism derived from two aspects of his theological life. First, he was closely associated with Jewish friends, intellectuals, and causes. Second, his theology was political. The Confessing Church, at Barmen and later, was relatively apolitical and concerned primarily about the freedom of the church. For Tillich, Nazism was not to be submitted to even in matters of the state; it was to be defeated. Christianity was grounded in and depended on its Jewish roots, and to be anti-Jewish was to be anti-Christian. The Nazi fight with Judaism was of the movement's essence, necessary to the blood-bound folk paganism of Nazism.

His resistance to Nazism also had its personal loyalties in his friendships with Jews from Berlin, Frankfurt, and New York. Adolf Löwe and Eduard Heimann, members of Tillich's circle at both Berlin and Frankfurt, eventually would join him in New York, as would the Frankfurt philosophers Max Horkheimer, Herbert Marcuse, and Erich Fromm.

Tillich's first political speech in English, in a rally at Madison Square Garden in 1938, attacked Hitler's anti-Semitism. Tillich appealed for unity between Jews and Christians on the foundation of prophetic religion. He opposed Nazi ideology with references to the universalism of German classicalism and argued how dependent German thought was on Jewish contributions. He urged solidarity with Jews and opposition to Nazism. Many of the themes of 1938 would reappear in the addresses of 1942–1944. By mid-1942,

Tillich had joined with Reinhold Niebuhr in supporting a national homeland for Jews. They and three others composed the executive committee of the Christian Council on Palestine, which promoted Zionist understanding and encouraged American clergy to support a homeland for Judaism.

The first speech to "my German friends"—as Tillich began each of the Voice of America broadcasts—was against anti-Semitism. This address sets the theme for the selection of fifty-five addresses in this book. It was logical for Tillich to begin his speeches with "the Jewish question," both existentially and intellectually. Nazi atrocities against Jews had begun prior to his exit from Germany in the early 1930s.[10] They were a fact of life that had to be confronted. Further, the historic identity of the Jewish people had a significant place in Tillich's theology, as well as in his philosophy of history. Theologically, the Jews are the inspiration for his notion of the Protestant principle, that element of perpetual critique that stands against the ever-present threats of idolatry and utopianism.[11] Historically, Jewish prophetism is the vehicle for his argument of the dominance of time over space as the necessary prerequisite for the existence of justice.[12] Tillich began his speeches at this point because the Jewish question was central to his thought.

Before 1942 was over, Tillich was speaking of the Nazi actions of extermination of the Jews (September 12, 1942, and November 12, 1942). In December 1942, he was telling Germans of the trains of death, of the machine-gun executions of Jewish children and women, and of German physicians who joined in the slaughter in the camps. The Nazi guilt was a burden to the country that had become the tool for Nazism. The essays from March 1942 to May 1944 detail the guilt of all responsible Germans, and Tillich's own guilt fuels the passion of his writing. He does not ignore guilt for the breakdown of German democracy attributable to other nations, but he focuses the guilt for the horror of the war, the extermination campaigns, and the assault against humanity on Germans themselves. The faults in Germany are deep, and he expounds on German character, myth, and history. But responsibility rests on those who allowed themselves to be enslaved by Hitler. The majority of the addresses urge Germans to act to liberate themselves from the Nazis. Historically, the Germans could not liberate themselves, and the Soviets had to bear the brunt of that liberation struggle. But though Soviet communism brought liberation from Nazism, it also brought a new tyranny to millions of Germans. The united, cooperative Germany that Tillich hoped for after the liberation had to wait until the 1990s.

The addresses are theology of culture. The culture is terribly evil, and though many are guilty, the Nazis utilizing the Germans are particularly guilty. Redemption could come if the Germans could liberate themselves, but it becomes apparent that they cannot. In fact, as the war closes, the conquest of Germany by the Allies promises only a partial liberation. Tillich's own political leadership in the German émigré organization the Council for a Democratic Germany falters on the clash between the democrats and the Communists who will divide and oppress much of Germany. World War II was, for Tillich, a war to liberate Europe and Germany from the Nazis; one could say it was a war to *save* Germany and Europe from the Nazis. But the results of the war of liberation turn out, as they almost always do, to be ambiguous.

The reader will probably recognize in these pages the theology of prophetic religion more than a christological theology. It is a theology for very troubled nations upon whom judgment has come or is coming in its historically ambiguous character. The author recognizes the hope for self-liberation, but it has not been historically realized. Judgment and retribution upon evil are more sure than liberation in this theology.

The question of Israel's salvation is also close to the center of the story. Can poor Israel, crushed beneath the superpower, be liberated? For Tillich by 1942, not much of European Israel would be saved, but a remnant for a restored home in Palestine was at least a hope. Even so, the plagues of Egypt that forced the freedom of Israel are compared to the scourges to come upon Germany in its oppression of Israel (September 1943).

The addresses in this volume, which represent approximately half of the original broadcasts, are arranged chronologically, with brief notes explicating historical context. The one exception to this chronological order is the final entry, which is a summary address that was given two months before the end of the lectures. Because each speech is a separate work, some ideas are repeated; rather than edit these repetitions out, however, we have allowed the themes to stand in their historical context.

In the final address, "One Hundred Speeches on Liberation from Nazism" (March 7, 1944), Tillich tells his listeners that he has tried to encourage them to separate from Nazism. He affirms that he speaks for Germany to find liberation from Nazism—or, in a cautionary note, at least from the spirit of Nazism. Expression of support for Germany while opposing Nazism would not be easily understood by American bureaucrats. Before the war ended, Tillich would be blacklisted by the U.S. Army as pro-German. Indeed, he was deeply pro-German—and, as the following pages reveal, deeply pro-Jewish and totally anti-Nazi.

NOTES

1. Lawrence C. Soley, *Radio Warfare: OSS and CIA Subversive Propaganda* (New York: Praeger Publishers, 1989), 69, 71; Holly Cowan Shulman, *The Voice of America: Propaganda and Democracy, 1941–1945* (Madison: University of Wisconsin Press, 1990), 9, 25; and Clayton D. Laurie, *The Propaganda Warriors: America's Crusade against Nazi Germany* (Lawrence: University Press of Kansas, 1996), 7, 119, 123.

2. Harold D. Lasswell, "Propaganda," in *Encyclopedia of the Social Sciences,* ed. Edwin R. A. Seligman (New York: Macmillan Co., 1937), 12: 525, 526.

3. Clifford G. Christians and Michael R. Real, "Jacques Ellul's Contribution to Critical Media Theory," *Journal of Communication* 29, 1 (winter 1979): 86, 87; and Jacques Ellul, "Between Chaos and Paralysis," *Christian Century* 85 (June 1968): 749.

4. Professor Emeritus Eberhard von Waldow of Pittsburgh Theological Seminary recalls his father Bernd Bastian von Waldow, a pastor in East Polmerania, actually hearing Paul Tillich's wartime broadcasts. Prof. von Waldow remembers standing outside to be sure that no one was approaching his family's home while his father listened to the BBC. (The "Voice of America" negotiated with the BBC to have its programs broadcasted over the BBC's medium- and long-wave transmitters. These were much clearer than short-wave broadcasts transmitted directly to the European continent from the United States. Shulman, 26.)

5. Anton Gill, *An Honourable Defeat: A History of German Resistance to Hitler, 1933–1945* (New York: Henry Holt, 1994), 23–24.

6. Ibid., 129–31, 151–55.

7. Ibid., 24, 43, 66, 67, 160–61, 175–79, 183–87, 192–94, 197–98.

8. Ibid., 2, 31, 47–55, 75, 80–86, 127, 161, 219, 233, 242–46, 250, 276 n. 2.

9. Paul Tillich, "The Church and the Third Reich: Ten Theses" in Leopold Klotz, *Die Kirche und das Dritte Reich* (Gotha: Klutz, 1932) trans. Andrea Böcherer in Mark Kline Taylor, ed., *Paul Tillich: Theologian of the Boundaries* (London: Collins, 1987), 117–18.

10. Wilhelm and Marion Pauck, *Paul Tillich: His Life and Thought* (San Francisco: Harper & Row, 1976), 127–30.

11. Paul Tillich, "The Protestant Principle and the Proletarian Situation," in *The Protestant Era* (Chicago: University of Chicago Press, 1948), 161–81.

12. Paul Tillich, "The Struggle between Space and Time," in *Theology and Culture* (London: Oxford University Press, 1959), 31, 32; and idem, *The Socialist Decision* (Washington, D.C.: University Press of America, 1977), 6, 20, 22.

1942

The radio speeches to the German opposition, broadcast over shortwave radio, began on March 31, 1942, with the topic of "the Jewish Question." This, for Tillich, was the fundamental issue. In the very next address, and throughout the year, he would tell the Germans of the forthcoming defeat of Germany and urge them to abandon their Nazi leadership. The Nazis had been educated for death, and the Germans had to leave them in their death to find life.

Barbarism had rushed in to fill the spiritual and cultural void created by the breakdown of Europe in the 1930s. Nazism crushed the independent centers that might have nurtured a rebirth beyond the emptiness of modernism and reduced all to the totalitarian-racial-military state. Tillich wrote of the spiritual-cultural collapse of European civilization in 1942.[1] Nazi aggression aimed for world revolution. In the Axis alliance, Hitler saw forces from a Japan undefeated in three thousand years; from a historically powerful Italy; and from a seemingly invincible Germany.[2] Tillich saw these forces react to the weaknesses of the rational middle-class democratic societies. He could not see or call forth the new spiritual-cultural renaissance that would renew the Allies, but in 1942, when he began his radio addresses, he could foresee the defeat of the Axis revolution. Tillich recognized that an Allied victory would not renew civilization, but it could at least permit the renewal to begin.

The events in Europe during 1942 and beyond were shaped by the Japanese mistakes of 1941–1942 in the Pacific. The Japanese decision in 1941 to attack the United States, and not the Soviet Union, enabled the Soviets to transfer thirty-two divisions from the East to save Moscow in December 1941. Moreover, the entry of the United States into the war meant the Axis was decisively outnumbered and outproduced. The failure of the Japanese attack on Pearl Harbor led to the shattering defeat at Midway in 1942, which broke the Japanese fleet. The prospects of stalemate and negotiated peace, if they ever existed, were lost at Pearl Harbor and at Moscow in December 1941; 1942 thus became the turning point of the war. By December 1942, the Stalingrad campaign was stalled, and in 1943, it ended in German defeat. In November 1942, German field marshal Erwin Rommel, despite Hitler's frantic commands that he stand his ground or die, retreated in northern Africa.

Tillich's perspective in his weekly radio talks did not shift from event to event. He saw, and said repeatedly, that the Axis powers could not prevail.

1.
THE QUESTION
OF THE JEWISH PEOPLE

MARCH 31, 1942

MY GERMAN FRIENDS!

As a Protestant theologian and philosopher of history, I want
to speak to you today about a question that, compared with the
great events of history through which we are now living, might
seem to be of lesser significance but that, in truth, is of decisive
significance for our spiritual and political destiny: the question of
the Jewish people. I am speaking especially to Protestant Christians, therefore, to people who cannot avoid these facts: that their
religion was prepared in the womb of Jewish history; that he in
whom they see the presence of God in the world was of Jewish
lineage; that the Old Testament is also part of the Christian Bible;
that the achievement of the [Protestant] Reformers took place in
the spirit and in the name of the Jew, Paul; and that for two thousand years, Jews and Christians have drawn religious strength
from the same commands of the law and the same promises of
the prophets and the same words of prayer from the Psalms. We
could renounce our claim to being Christians, but as long as we
want to remain Christians, we cannot renounce that we live out
of the same religious roots from which the religious Jew lives.

Every judgment by Christians concerning the Jewish question
must proceed from this presupposition. Every attempt to impugn
this particular foundation of Christianity renders destruction to
the foundations of Christianity. People may want to do that, and
there are many in Germany today who not only want to do it but
say that they want to do it. This is a clear and firm attitude. It
would be good if all Christians who represent the opposing side
were displaying an equally clear and firm attitude.

Then it would be clear that the Jewish question is a question of the religious understanding of universal history, that it refers to the meaning of our historical existence as people and as Christians. The Jews are the people of history. They have lost their geographic place, yet they live. They have been persecuted by nations that live within boundaries, but they have survived it all because they serve God, who is the Lord of time, who creates and guides history and brings it to its goal. They are being persecuted at the present time as never before, yet they will survive, because they have a vocation without which the vocation of the human race cannot be fulfilled: the Jewish people are called to bear witness to the God of justice and to the oneness of all people and to the God who alone is God, beyond the gods of nations, beyond all national values and ideals.[3]

We know that the Jewish people have again and again forgotten and betrayed this vocation of theirs—and no one knows it better than the Jews themselves, and nowhere is it more evident than in the Old Testament as a whole. But we also know that their vocation stands and cannot fall, as long as there is history, as long as people are able to look beyond limited national space to the reign of God that shall come to us and in whose shadow all nations shall dwell. As long as we believe that universal history has a meaning, that its meaning is judgment and promise, we must understand and appreciate the Jewish people in the light of this meaning.

We cannot understand the Jews if we regard them as one national minority among others. They are a minority and share the fate of all minorities: to become an object of fear and hatred and distracting propaganda if the majority or if the leaders need a sacrifice. That is an outrage, but it does not strike at the depth of the Jewish question.

And we cannot understand the Jews if we regard them as one religious group beside others. They are this also, and this has brought them suffering like many other religious sects that have become the victims of ecclesiastical lust for power and religious fanaticism. This is an injustice, but it does not strike at the depth of the Jewish question.

The depth of the Jewish question is that the Jews are the people of history, the people of the prophetic, future-judging spirit. This means that we ourselves sin against the meaning of our own history if we bear guilt against the Jewish people. And the German people have become guilty, offering resistance to be sure, and this under the pressure of the most dreadful terror, but they didn't put up that resistance which would have been possible and which would have frightened off the rulers. What happened? The German people assumed to be true what the Jewish prophets fought against to the sharpest degree: Jewish nationalism. That which those carrying out the Jewish vocation within Judaism opposed, that for which God rejected and abandoned the Jews to a tragic fate, that has now become the German belief, and—since that belief should be otherwise—it has become the German curse! And the great achievement in Judaism, the prophetic message, whose full sharpness is directed against Jewish self-confidence—as it is against every other national self-confidence—that prophetic message is being rejected and combated! In their struggle against Judaism, the combatants have become fools: they seek to destroy what is great and divine and unique in Judaism, and they mock what is small and human and common in Judaism. They term "the Jewish spirit" that which is the worst in their own spirit and seek, in this way, to disguise that they and others actually want to destroy the best in themselves, in the German people, and in humankind.

The Jewish question is not one of political tactics or technical expediency. It can never be answered in this way. And if all Jews should vanish from the earth, the Jewish question would remain as the Christian question, as the question that inquires about the place the prophetic spirit and the spirit of Jesus on earth have and should have. And it would remain as the human question, as the question of whether human beings should remain bound to their limited space, to blood and to nation, or if the meaning and value of human existence is to reach out over such boundedness to a realm beyond nation and beyond every limited space. This question cannot vanish as long as there are people, and on that account the Jewish question cannot vanish. The Christian church bears witness to it through its existence. The human heart bears witness to it when it beats for that which is greater than itself.

For this reason, wake up to the truth of your Christian—your human—essence, and grasp what the persecution of the Jewish people means! Not only does it mean human misery, not only shame for all Germans—whether or not they want to feel it—not only a curse that redounds on those who have hurled it. Moreover, it means hostility against the spirit, against human dignity, and against God. As a famous theologian recently wrote, "Anti-Semitism is a transgression against the Holy Spirit." If the entire German nation had committed this transgression, likewise as a whole it would have lost its way. It would have been unable to find its way back again. It would have ripped—so to speak—the human heart out of its body. We know that this is not so. Countless Germans are hiding themselves in shame, countless are shivering in indignation. Many are offering opposition through deed, some through word. But all this is not enough to atone for the sin that the entire nation has brought on itself. Many in Germany, nearly all, know this. I will never forget the word that a friend said to me in the spring of 1933, after the persecution had begun—a friend who at that time was leaning toward this new thing but who nevertheless said—"Their blood will come upon us and upon our children." Today, this statement has already become an accomplished fact. It will become an even more accomplished and more frightful truth. However, that is not the most important thing. What is important is that the eyes of the German people be opened, that the German people realize this: the Jewish question is the question of our own existence or nonexistence as Christians and human beings. It is the question of our redemption or our judgment.

2.
THE DEATH AND RESURRECTION OF NATIONS

APRIL 1942

MY GERMAN FRIENDS!

It is an ancient, profound notion that not only nature and not only humankind but also the godhead dies and rises up again. Out of the most ancient times, this myth rings into our present time; the Christian church adopted it; and today the peal of Easter bells in all Christian lands brings it to our ears and—perhaps—even to our hearts. If the godhead itself must die in order to rise again, how much more is this great law of life true for us as human beings, individuals, and nations. I want to speak to you today about the death and resurrection of nations, and of the German nation in particular.

There are two ways in which people attempt to elude the law of death and resurrection. In the first way, people want to avoid death, and in the other way, people deny resurrection.

It was a dangerous thing for the nineteenth century and the entire bourgeois culture to repress and forget the law of death. People settled down into the world and into life. People made a comfortable home out of earth. People had no time for that which lay beyond the limits of their temporal horizon. They knew that there were limitless tasks to perform beyond this temporal horizon, rewarding tasks whose fulfillment furnished pride and security for humanity. But they thought, "Why think over and beyond the temporal? Its horizon is infinitely wide; infinite progress is possible within it; the house of the earth can be limitlessly expanded and improved. Death lies on the boundary; but why think about the boundary when so much has to occur in the middle?" It was neither dying nor resurrecting but rather making progress that was the catchword. Even in the nineteenth century the Protestant churches celebrated Good Friday as their highest feast day. Even then, the individual was reminded of the great law of life: death and rebirth. Never was it possible, and never will it be possible, to eliminate death from life completely. It is not to be eliminated; it can be concealed only for a time. But all of a sudden it is there, and everything looks differently than before. And the Good Friday story was understood at that time as well. But it was not understood that it is true for nations and cultures as well. They appeared to be long-lived, like the Greek gods, indeed, immortal. The principle of progress itself seemed to guarantee their imperishability. People still remembered that nations and cultures perished in the past. But they could not conceive that this could be true for the bourgeois Christian culture and for the nations that bore it. Toward those who, since the turn of the century, predicted the catastrophe, they acted as Peter did to Jesus when he predicted his passion: they snapped at them, because they could not bear it.[4] Today there are only a few places in the world where people believe they can get around the last judgment, the great Good Friday of humankind that we are living through, the death of an age of the world. Europe certainly doesn't belong to that group, least of all Germany. In Germany, despite many outward victories, people know what the Good Friday of a nation, what the death of a world, means.

Today, people in Germany know what death is. But do they also know what life is? They have learned the first part of the law of death and resurrection, death, but they have lost the second part, resurrection. They no longer know that there is such a thing. Symbols of death dominate the life of the entire nation. An American pedagogue who was active for years in Germany received permission to visit many German schools and youth centers shortly before the outbreak of the war. He wrote a book under the title *Education for Death*[5] that aroused horror in everyone who read it. In countless examples, it shows how the German youth from early on are trained to that end: to seek the meaning of life in death. The desire for life, which is natural for every person, is bent back into the desire for death, first the death of one's opponent and then one's own death. The symbols of life are given a new interpretation as symbols of death. The community, which should bestow life, turns into a community that, in word and song and deed, prepares for death. Education, which should convey the wealth of human experience and—through it—mold the human nature of the young generation, turns into an implement of battle against all the greatest achievements of the past. It turns into an education against humanity, against the form, against the meaning of life. Perhaps you will say that the death of the individual for the sake of the life of the nation should serve for the resurrection of the nation. But what does the nation signify when everything that belongs to it perishes for its sake? Has it not, then, itself perished, physically or—what is worse—spiritually? Can the spiritual destruction of the German youth through this education for death be offset by any increase in the power of the German nation? And if it should win the entire world, will it not have suffered irreparable damage to its soul? And is not the desire for death the most frightful symbol for that? Do not nations die, just like individuals, when the desire for death has gripped them?

The past age wanted Easter without Good Friday. But it was not a genuine Easter; it was not a resurrection because it bypassed death. Present-day Germany wants Good Friday without Easter. But it is not a genuine Good Friday because it does not know the secret of life, that death is not the end. Permit me to express some thoughts about that to you. You and I and many precious people in the lands of your enemies want the death spell of this time to be broken through a resurrection of humankind and of all nations within it, even, and above all, the German nation. How is such a resurrection possible? Only if death is genuinely death, the death of that which is subject to death, so that that which triumphs over death can live. To be sure, this looks different from what your preachers and teachers and leaders of death are saying to you and doing with you.

When it is solely life that dies, the spirit is born. The spirit is the fruit of that life which sacrifices itself. It is the new that triumphs and hasn't fallen to death. The spirit is creative; it looks out beyond the limits of life; it is the truth that breaks through the chains of propaganda, falsehood, and fanaticism. It is the justice that tears apart enslavement beneath will-to-power and hatred and arbitrariness. When the individual life sacrifices itself, the spirit is born that seeks the universal that is greater than the individual person and the individual nation, that is, the human and the divine that overcomes death. For this reason, those who hate the spirit want to lead you to death. They persecute and—what is more dangerous—distort the truth. They destroy and—what is more dangerous—deface justice. They seek to make everything subject to death, and because they are unable to do it as long as the spirit lives, they seek to kill it. Save the spirit within you, within your nation, so that out of your death, resurrection can arise. If the educators of death are successful in destroying the spirit, then everything is destroyed; then you will remain in that death which its harbingers are preparing for you. But if it is life alone that dies, love is born, which is the innermost part of the spirit. It is the most mature and most precious fruit of the life that sacrifices itself. Love breaks out of the prison of individualism and nationalist stupidity. Love goes to another person, even one with a different language or of a different race, and returns from him richer. There is another way to break through the limits of power and oppression: the path of those who are training you for death. This path also meets with "success," but when you take this path to another person, you return from him poorer, just as you are experiencing it now with all defeated nations. It is the path on which hatred is sown and hatred is reaped. It is the path at whose end death stands, to which you shall be led. Tear yourselves loose from these leaders, take the other path, the path of the spirit and of love, the path through death to resurrection: that is what the Easter bells are calling out to you.

3.
Internal and
External Freedom
April 20, 1942

MY GERMAN FRIENDS!

In classical German poetry, no word has a stronger ring to it than the word *freedom*. And among the writings of the greatest German, Martin Luther, nothing is more noble in spiritual power and religious depth than that concerning "the freedom of the Christian person." And Germany's most powerful thinkers— Kant, Fichte, Hegel—recognized freedom as the essence and innermost core of being.[6]

Among few other peoples is the idea of freedom as deeply rooted as it is among the Germans, and at the same time, among few other peoples has there been true freedom as rarely as there has in Germany. Luther, the prophet of religious liberation, needed the existence of subjugation to German princes to accomplish religious liberation. German poets created their realm of freedom in the land of fantasy but not in the land of real life. German philosophers fell back on internal freedom without making serious efforts toward external freedom. Freedom in spirit, bondage in life: this contradiction rests as a curse over German history.

Protestantism has not been able to defeat this curse. The freedom of a Christian person—the right, in the name of God, to protest against ungodly authorities—was surrendered in favor of subjugation to a new tyranny, that of doctrine. And the freedom of a Christian person was not understood as political freedom. The godly right to protest against ungodly political authorities was never recognized. As diabolical as they may be, even the diabolical is ordered by God, if it proceeds in the name of the government:

[21]

Christ subjugated himself to it. This doctrine is one of the bases for German bondage. It is one of the reasons why the present authorities came to rule and to set up a tyranny to which the darkest periods of world history can be compared. German poets managed to bring German freedom down out of the land of fantasy into that of reality with the same infrequency. Not once did Schiller—whose freedom dramas are banished from German theaters today—bring the German freedom struggle from the stage onto the street.[7] He remained on the stage, and now the street has captured even the stage and has without assistance repressed even the false freedom of drama. And the philosophers were not capable of changing internal freedom into external freedom and of making free people out of thinkers of freedom. And because there were no—or too few— free people in Germany, the thinkers of freedom were also expelled or oppressed, and the young generation is being brought up today by thinkers of bondage. Internal freedom without external freedom cannot propagate itself and withers. That is the lesson which the German people have to learn in this age of the most frightful catastrophes. The conflict between inner freedom and outer bondage, which became a curse for the Germans, has now become a curse for Europe and for the whole world through them. The vast powers—which have developed through spiritual, internal freedom in Germany—have been put into the service of the external servitude of Germans and many other nations. And internal freedom was defenseless, because it found no one to fight for external freedom.

Above all, I wished that German Protestants would have been willing to learn from these events. They offered resistance only when the church itself was being attacked.[8] But even as great as the church's struggle was, and as greatly as it aroused the admiration of the entire world, and as greatly as it served the reputation of Christianity, the resistance came too late. It ended with no victory, although it prevented a more complete defeat. There are moments in history in which the struggle for external freedom takes the form in which one must suffer for the gospel. The evangelical churches had to learn that in the age of religious wars. They must learn that anew today. The present upbringing for bondage, for hostility toward Christianity, and for the negation of that which is human in the person—is that really a lesser reason for the struggle against a tyrannical government than assaults on churches and ministers? Is the soul of the children of lesser worth than the church organization? And it is a question of not only the soul of the children but the soul of the entire nation, including those belonging to the church. Can inner freedom be set free if the bondage is not only external but if even minds and souls are being cleaved, conquered, and enslaved? Protestant Germans! Free yourselves from the belief that internal and external freedom, that religious and political freedom can be separated! Cast away this false inheritance that the churches—and with them, the poets and philosophers—have dragged through the centuries: the belief that freedom would not depend on political freedom. The last ten years are the major rebuttal to this fact. They may also signify a turning point in the history of the German people, that they are learning once and for all: without political freedom, without freedom from tyranny, in the long run, religious and intellectual freedom is impossible.

When the Western nations began their freedom struggles, it occurred in their thought that all aspects of life—religious, intellectual, human—were threatened by the tyranny of particular ruling groups. People fought in Holland for the freedom of Protestants, in England for the freedom of the Reformed churches, in America for the freedom of a New World, in France for the freedom of human reason. These peoples went to death not for constitutions or parliaments but rather because they experienced what freedom means. In the course of the last centuries, they have sinned against the freedom for which they fought a thousandfold. They have betrayed it for all ends, above all in the service of profit and exploitation. They have atoned for this, and many of their leaders have understood this. Today, these leaders are fighting a double battle: for the restoration of genuine freedom inside their own countries and for the restoration of freedom in every single nation. It is a difficult struggle in both directions, but it is a struggle on whose outcome hangs not only the fate of their own nations but also that of the German nation. It is not a battle for the restoration of a corrupted and weakened freedom, which became an easy victim of tyranny. On the contrary, it is the struggle for a new freedom, namely, the sort that means freedom for every person and every nation and—consequently—that contains security. It is called freedom from want and from fear. Tyranny seems to make the individual secure, but it is unable to do so, because tyranny is arbitrariness, and arbitrariness is insecurity. Fear and want proliferate in perpetually new forms on the soil of tyranny. There is much fear in German hearts, not fear of dying but rather fear on account of a life that has lost its meaning, because it has lost its freedom. This fear is missing in the countries in which there is still freedom. And therefore, these countries will triumph. Where freedom is, there the will to live is. For human nature is so constructed that it cannot breathe in the air of bondage. Why do countless people struggle for freedom in conquered lands? Perhaps the bondage offered them more good things, more security. But for them that is not the point. They wanted to be free, and for that no price is too high. They are dying in the thousands, and new thousands are walking in their place. The German people should continually think about the fact that daily people sacrifice themselves for that freedom which is taken from them by the Germans. From Norway to Greece, people fight and die for nothing else but for freedom. The Germans should have two feelings in relation to that which has taken place. They should fear this rebellion against servitude. Every new martyr should weigh heavier on the German soul. A wholesome fear should come over the Germans: the fear of being called to account as murderers of freedom. This fear is justifiable; but fear is only one feeling that you should derive from this struggle for freedom. The other is hope: if it is truly freedom for which these nations are fighting, then the freedom of the Germans must also be demanded and preserved. Some leaders with whom I've spoken understand this and do not want a slave nation to be created in the middle of Europe. Today, they understand that the bondage of one nation threatens the freedom of all nations.

For the sake of this fear, for the sake of this hope, enter into this freedom struggle yourselves. Throw off the tyranny that desires to destroy the internal freedom—the human and the divine—within you. Allow the Protestant protest to become strong among you, as it did among your fathers in their time. Internal and external freedom have proven to be one. The struggle for both is what your time requires of you.

4.

JUSTICE
AND HUMANITY

MAY 11, 1942

MY GERMAN FRIENDS!

An astonishment went through the countries in which human rights are still highly valued when the German Führer demanded and obtained new powers from the Reichstag. They are powers that set aside the fundamental right of every human being to be considered as a person. They are powers that now do away with even the principle of justice as a basis for civil law, after it was long ago done away with as a basis for constitutional law. Something is coming to pass, thereby, that so deeply touches the foundations of human existence that every individual must understand it. The annulment of justice as unconditionally valid is an annulment of the human being as human being, as an entity with a particular dignity, particular strengths, and particular rights.

Even the present rulers perceive this. Therefore, they have walked along the legal path to abolish justice. It has provoked universal astonishment that someone who already had all authority was permitted to have new powers. It has been asked, why was the introduction of unlawfulness being legally sanctioned, why was the Reichstag being bothered with something that plunged the existence of every single one of its members into complete uncertainty? This question is easy to answer: it is the silent recognition of authority by those who are setting it aside. They remember that without the many legal cloaks with which they have clothed themselves, they would have never come to power; and afterward, even if they did cast off each of these cloaks and displayed the shape of the brutal power behind the apparent justice, surely they did this only to clothe themselves in other justice cloaks for other power aims. So, also, this time. That seems completely insignificant, but it is not. So deep is the justice consciousness of humanity that even the destroyer of justice must do his obeisance to justice in order to be able to destroy it. Even in foreign policy it is so. There are no longer aggressors, because every aggressor explains that he has been attacked. Why? Because he must acknowledge that there is an ideal of justice that forbids attacks and that he must lay claim to himself. Justice is so deeply rooted in the human soul that it cannot be pulled out. Only in the name of justice can one successfully be unjust. That is the significance of the demand made of the Reichstag, by a leader with unlimited power, a demand which contradicts the fact that no law can give authority that is both limited and total. Practically, it means that from now on, every German can be robbed in every moment of all vested rights, without a new statute and without legal proceedings and without being seen as a public enemy. In every land, precise rights can be set aside by precise statutes—living justice requires that; and in every land, the enemy of the state and the criminal stands under a separate justice. But in no just state is the protection of the law taken away altogether. That is something new or—perhaps—primeval: the return to prehuman forms of existence.

It would be a great falsification and an affront to German antiquity for anyone to maintain that there would have been no authority by which the power of the leader would have been restricted. On the contrary, it was one of the features of German antiquity that the rights of free people had to be respected by every leader.[9] The freedoms of which there is so much discourse in German history were the diverse rights that protect the individual, giving him his dignity, security, and inner autonomy. These freedoms are German legacies. The instinct for justice that erupts so passionately and devastatingly in a Michael Kohlhaas is an ancient German instinct.[10] Did something of it stir in you as, step by step, guaranteed rights that are the foundation of freedom were being taken? And that in the name of the German race and its greatness? What is now taking place? The right, and with it the freedom, of each one is taken and transferred to one individual who alone has authority, who alone is free. The great German philosopher has said that it is the mark of despotism that only one is free and all others are without freedom, without rights. He has further said that it is the mission of the German tribes in world history to translate freedom into full reality.[11] At present, it looks as if the Germans have taken possession of the mission to destroy freedom—which was already gained—in favor of a new despotism.

The belief in justice is not only indestructible in the depth of the human heart; it is also borne by religion. Every higher religion has had gods whose special, holy task it was to give laws and protect justice. But nowhere is the thought of justice more closely connected with the idea of God than in the religion of the prophets.[12] For them, God is first, and above all, the God of justice. The unjust judges who pervert justice in accordance with the will of the ruling powers, the king who despotically misuses his power against his subjects and takes from them what is their due, the official who decides arbitrarily and not in accordance with justice—they all were placed under divine judgment and repudiated by the prophets with powerful words. God's holiness takes effect in his justice, and no one is more repugnant to him than the one who destroys justice. That is certainly one of the bases for the present rulers' hatred for the Old Testament. Whoever destroys justice is an enemy of the God of the prophets, and this God is his enemy because he is the God of justice, the true God.

This is so because justice makes human beings human. What do we lose when we lose our justice? What did the German nation lose when justice was taken from it by its rulers? Much, in every way! First, we lose ourselves when we lose our justice. We cease to be a person when our justice is taken from us; by person, I mean a special, unmistakable essence, with special possibilities and special duties. Our justice, in which we exist, is the acknowledgment that we demand as a person. Whoever is deprived of rights, as the German people now are, has become a thing with which one can do what one desires. He has lost his dignity. He has become an instrument for strange ends, a slave of tyrants, a tool of arbitrariness, and an object of violation. Your rights are the acknowledgment that you are a person, that you have a dignity that is inviolable, that you are a uniquely irreplaceable self. They are the acknowledgment that you are human. Deprival of justice is deprival of humanity. Human dignity is one with its justice. Without dignity, representatives of the German people have dispensed with their rights and, with that, have surrendered the dignity of the nation and of every single individual. Reclaim your rights again, German people, and with it yourselves!

And whoever loses justice loses the other person, loses the other nation, loses humanity. Whoever surrenders his own dignity does not acknowledge the dignity of others as well. He is no longer in a position to see in others the human, the unique, the person: he sees in others the instrument for his aims, the object of his fear or his hate. A nation that is undignified—because it has come to be without justice—sees in another nation the strange, the hostile, a power that must be met with power, but not a person who must be met as a person, that is, whose rights must be acknowledged, as one desires to have one's own rights acknowledged. The rights of others, of individuals and of nations, are the foundation of their dignity, and whoever destroys these rights debases them, as he has debased himself. Look up at the innocent, the attacked, trampled-down nations round about Germany! The German conquerors have taken their rights, have destroyed the justice that was growing among these nations, have trampled human thoughts with their feet. And therefore, the other nations and the humanity of the Germans have been lost. When they destroyed justice, they lost themselves and their humanity.

And finally; whoever destroys justice loses God. All talk of divine providence is meaningless if God's justice is forgotten. God is only one God, because he is a just God. The God who rejects his own people on account of their injustice is the God of all people, the God of humanity. The German rulers have fought against this God. They must dispose of him so that they can destroy justice. They must invent a god who protects the injustices of his people, who is bound to his people: the German god. But this god is an idol, and he will be smashed by the God of righteousness and of justice.

5.
GOETHE ON REVERENCE

MAY 1942

MY GERMAN FRIENDS!

A few weeks ago was the 110th anniversary of Goethe's death.[13] In all likelihood, the day passed by uncelebrated by you, because Goethe's heritage doesn't fit into the range of ideas of your present leaders. They know that his image of the world and of humanity threatens their rule. Goethe's attitude toward life and toward the world was full of faith and reverence. That of your present leaders is cynical. Goethe loved people. Your present leaders despise people: not only the enemy that they fight but all of you. They see you only as a means to their power and as objects of their commands. They watch over you in all of your life's movements, just as prisoners and criminals are guarded. This disdainful outlook on life has alienated the people in Germany, one from another. Trust is destroyed. And it is becoming more and more lonesome and cold for you. Every victory that gains you new territories in Europe carries this disturbance of all human relationships further. For that reason, ever fewer people in Germany can be pleased with these victories. You sense that they will bring you no solution but that they are leading you onto paths of ever deeper error. Your soldiers return home from their victorious advances silently and reflectively. They have come to know that life ends when they arrive at the front, and that it ends for themselves as well, when they've been unsuccessful in laying down their weapons to become reconciled—that is, unsuccessful in making friends out of enemies. They are beginning to grasp that the "new order" in Europe is an order of death. And the question "Why is this so?" lies heavily on many young hearts. Whether they can find the answer to that I do not know, because your present rulers have carefully cut your youth off from the influence of all those spiritual leaders of the German past who could give them an answer to this question. Goethe is one of these leaders who could open the eyes of the young people who have begun to ask. He could say to them that life dies and that the relationships of people are destroyed when disdain and cynicism—instead of reverence—are the basis of all thought and action.

For this reason, I want to speak to you today of Goethe's thoughts on reverence. It was not only the deepest root of his own attitude toward life, but it was also the essential part of his pedagogy. In his novel *Wilhelm Meister's Apprenticeship and Travels,* in the description of the pedagogical province, he disclosed the development of reverence as the ultimate and deepest secret of his education of the new person. The educators in this province of education prepare their pupils for life in that they instill in them the reverence for those who are superior to them, the reverence for those who are equal to them, and the reverence for those who are beneath them. These educators consider reverence to be so central that they drive it home for their students not only in their lectures and not only in metaphors but daily and hourly in the symbolic form of the gesture of greeting. The youngest pupils greet those above them by crossing their arms over their chests and looking to heaven, in testimony to the respect for the Divine above us. The intermediate pupils fold their hands on their backs and look to the earth in greeting, to show that unspeakable joy and suffering spring from the earth. At the last stage, the pupils are obliged to greet by placing themselves in rank and file with their comrades and looking at them, in order to bring to expression reverence for their companions.[14]

You all know how much the educational ideal of your present rulers is set against this education for reverence. They have to suppress the reverence in your youth so that they can prepare them for their duties as executioners, a duty that keeps your leaders in power. They know that where reverence for one's fellow man is still awake, one struggles against abusing and degrading innocent people, one offers resistance to driving them from their homes and taking their property, one rebels against handing them over to the torments of concentration camps. Your leaders need your hatred, your contempt, your cruelty in order to deaden all of the impulses in you that permit you to acknowledge your victims as human beings, just as you yourselves are. Your leaders know that they will be most successful in suppressing reverence for those who are at your side if they snatch out of your heart the reverence for that which is superior to you. They have clearly acknowledged that the strongest threat to them comes from Christianity, which derives the reverence and love for human beings from the love for God. For that reason, from the very beginning, your leaders declared war on Christianity. At no time in German history has a government persecuted the churches as have your present leaders. People who have committed no sin other than that they wanted to obey God more than humanity, by confessing him as the highest leader,[15] have had to atone for this with humiliating imprisonment. Their children have been methodically alienated from the churches and Christianity, and when their parents' homes have not prevented it, they have grown up without reverence for that which gives life its deepest meaning. With the removal of reverence for the deepest life-reference,[16] the reverence for that which is beneath us is deprived of its essential foundation. No religion has grasped and established the reverence for the sick and weak as deeply as has Christianity. The cynical cruelty and indifference of your present leaders toward everyone who is weak and sick is connected most closely with their lack of understanding in respect to the religious dimension of our life. It is a burdensome fate to become old and sick in Germany today. It is a more burdensome fate to be born weak and crippled, because reverence for the troubled and burdened has no place in the hearts of your present leaders, and they don't want it to hold a place in your hearts. But the number of those who are becoming mourners today in Germany is growing, day by day. Every hour increases the number of the crippled and sick, the starving and impoverished, the widows and orphans. But the number of those who can console has become small, because the ultimate appreciation of pain and grief is missing where one has burned reverence out of life. It is for that reason that such a deep despair lies over many German people. They sense that not only were the immense sacrifices that they have offered for many years sacrifices of life and property but that they have been cheated of the meaning of their existence. For life remains meaningful only when it relates reverently to that which is above us, that which is beneath us, and that which is beside us. For that reason, find your way back to the followers of those leaders of the German spirit who know about such reverence. Goethe is one of them.

6.
THE NINTH ANNIVERSARY
OF GERMAN BOOK BURNING
MAY 18, 1942

MY GERMAN FRIENDS!

On May 10 was the ninth anniversary of the German book burning, that event which stands like a sign at the beginning of the great disaster that struck Germany, Europe, and the world. It is good to recall this day. None of us knew at that time what it meant. Only a few suspected that it was the beginning of the burning of Germany and of Europe. Today, we understand that this suspicion hit on the truth. A pair of books were the first victims. Millions of people followed, and are following, the books into annihilation. With the destruction of nations and cultures, the curse that lay concealed within the smoldering books will come to an end. Therefore, when we think back on that event today, we can understand it in the gloomy light of the present world conflagration, just as we can understand what is happening today in the dazzling light of the burning books.

Many of you still have a picture of the events of that day. I experienced them in a particularly opportune place and want to tell you how they impressed me: meaningfully, awfully, unforgettably. It was in Frankfurt am Main. We stood at a window of the *"Römer,"* the old royal residence of the German kaisers. [The *Römer* is now the venerable city hall with its imperial chamber from the Holy Roman Empire. It was rebuilt after World War II.] In the medieval square the masses thronged, restrained by brown-and blackshirts. A woodpile was stacked. Then we saw columns of torchbearers pouring forth out of the narrow streets, an endless line, in student and party uniforms. The light of the torches flickered through the darkness and fantastically illuminated the gables of the houses. I was reminded of paintings from the time of the Spanish Inquisition. At the end, a cart drawn by two oxen lumbered across the square. It was loaded with the books that were chosen as sacrifices. The pastor of students was striding behind the cart. When he had arrived before the funeral pyre, the pastor climbed onto the cart and delivered the speech of condemnation. He threw the first book onto the now ignited piles. Hundreds of other books followed. The flames leaped up high and illuminated the vision that was certainly present. Time had run backward about two hundred years.

Book burnings are as old as books. From the beginning onward, books were a power that was dangerous for the existing authorities. In the letters and sentences of a book, an explosive can lie hidden that destroys a world, and there can be locked up within it a spiritual force that constructs a new world! For this reason, books are sinister for all who want to maintain the old at any cost. For this reason, books are sinister for all who have a reason to fear the truth. For this reason, tyrants are enemies of books, just as they have dread before thought-furrowed faces. Behind these furrows and behind the lines of books they smell the spirit of rebellion that they can dispel no longer, once it becomes word and letter. For this reason, books are sealed, suppressed, and burned—sometimes with those who have written them, sometimes without them. But again and again, the books are victorious. The thoughts that have become embodied within them rise up out of their ashes, more powerful than before. The resurrection of thought through the fire of the spirit follows the destruction of the book through natural fire and burns the fire starter. For tyranny cannot withstand thought. It is built on lie and pretense and deceit and will be exposed as lie by thought. A period of time is given to the pretense, and the tyranny that exists by pretense, when it can rule, persecuting thought and burning books. But when this interval has elapsed, the thought returns and the book becomes alive. Already today, you sense that the time will soon have elapsed in which the German tyranny will be able to burn books and to persecute thoughts. It has not yet elapsed. Thought must still be concealed, completely on the inside of the individual or within one's closest community or in words that point to something other than what they are saying. The great skill of earlier centuries—in which books concealed as much as they were permitted to say—has again come to life. Once again, there is much to be said that cannot be said. But of course, thought cannot obtain a body in this way; it remains a spirit that has lost its way, that seeks a body for itself. Only when it has become word and letter has it become full reality and can it change reality. For this reason, space must be furnished again and again for word and book. For this reason, the thoughts that move about in the depth of your soul and that push to be given form must again be given the possibility to embody themselves. When the German tyrants burned the books on May 10, 1933, they knew what they were doing: they were taking the body from thought and keeping it from finding a new body, in order to be safe from it.

But they will be safe from it for only a short time. Everywhere, thought is beating on the doors of the world cordoned off by the tyrants. It wants admittance, it seeks embodiment, and already it is finding it here and there: in the hearts of the oppressed and the disillusioned and in those who enthusiastically joined in [with the tyrants] and who, now, are turning away with disgust. With them the forbidden thinking is finding admittance, here and there, embodied in the word of an unfamiliar wireless, in the lines of a pamphlet, in intimate conversations. Sparks are spraying out of the ashes of books burned long ago, sparks of the spirit and of rebellion. Soon thought will have found its body again. Soon it will have again become word and book, reality and power.

But it will not look like it did before. Not all that was burned will rise again from the dead. Much has justly come to ashes, because it was not thought but babble, not depth but temptation. The truth must prove its worth through fire. What is false must burn. And much of that which was thrown from the oxcart into the fire has no right to a resurrection. It was invalid even before it became ashes. In all of us was much nothingness that had to be burned away. In the entire world from which we came, there was much that was worthy only of rising up in flames. We all are implicated in the book burning because we had built up so much that became easy prey for the flames, much falsehood, ambiguity, lack of seriousness. That is the reason why the book burning became a symbol for the decline of the age. And that applies not only to Germany but to the entire world. The world conflagration, whose first leaping flame was the German book burning, is the judgment on a time period, a social order, a human outlook. For that reason, when we fight against the authors of book pyres, openly or silently, that does not mean that we are fighting for that which was before.[17] Today, there are people in Germany and in all of the world who want back that which was before the book burning. These are the same ones who were not at all alarmed when the report went through the world of the attempt to stamp out critical thinking. They themselves would have gladly thrown some of the books from the oxcart onto the woodpile, books in the English, French, or Spanish languages. They were not fond of the brutal, medieval form in which it took place, but they loved the cause itself, the repression, the eradication of thought and of the critical spirit. From these people, even when they are fighting today against German fascism, there is nothing to anticipate. They want to go backward, not forward. They have not understood what the ordeal by fire of the present age means. They don't know that the way through the fire is the way of the spirit, that that which was reckoned to be evil by those who did the burning became a blessing for many who were victims of the burning. For them, it became the fire of rebirth.

Can we comprehend the book burning, the destruction of Europe, and the conflagration of the world in this way? Can we comprehend it as rebirth? Is a new world in the making, for which even the book burners in Germany and in the whole world were instruments, contrary to their knowledge and will? They wanted to repress thought, truth, and criticism. They wanted to wipe it out, but they only strengthened it—because they wiped out what could not withstand the fire and hardened what is lasting and indestructible.

It is in this sense, today, that we want to look back on that sinister event in which thought burned and the spirit should have been driven out. It was one victory over the spirit, which was followed by many further victories. But in this victory, the victor created the weapon that will bring him down, the thoughts refined by fire, the will steel-hardened by tribulation.

7.
GUILT
AND INNOCENCE

JUNE 8, 1942

MY GERMAN FRIENDS!

You know that at present, almost daily, innocent ones are dying, for whose death Germans are responsible: hundreds have died in France—as hostages, it is reported. Many in Holland and Norway, countless in Poland, where it looks as if an entire crowd of people was exterminated. Of the suffering and dying innocent Jews in all parts of Europe I don't need to say anything. For years, the nations of the world have been looking upon that which has taken place with horror. In recent days, many innocents had to die because of one person whom they called the executioner, Gestapo chief Heydrich, who fell into the hands of an equitable court of justice. This man, who was responsible for the death, the torture, and the misery of countless people, is now taking hundreds more innocent people with him in his death. He was a German, and there are Germans who worked as his torturers and who continue to do so even after his death. There are Germans who work today throughout Europe as executioners of innocents. The ruling group in Germany has become, more often than ever before, a group of murderers and torturers, whose victims are the innocents.

Now it is very difficult—indeed, often impossible—for a refined, sensitive person to slay a guilty person, because a refined, sensitive person accommodates himself to others, and what he must do to others, he does to himself. And it is difficult for a refined, sensitive, humane person to slay the enemy on the battlefield, because he has a sense of him as the son of a mother or as the husband of a wife or as the father of children. If that is sentimental, then the best and bravest soldiers of the previous war were sentimental. All those whom I observed in the four years of my existence at the front, the ones whose letters and reports I heard and read, didn't want to kill, and they weren't sentimental but rather courageous and strong. Something of this noble tradition still lives in the German army, although certainly, it is often corroded away. Nothing of it lives any longer within the ruling party and its commissioned executioners. Not only the guilty, not only the enemy, but also the innocent are being murdered, brutally, without restraint, often with primitive bloodthirstiness. Whoever does not go along with this, whoever is dubbed sentimental, indeed, is in danger of becoming a victim himself.[18]

We know that it is often difficult to distinguish guilty ones from innocent ones. Here, there is no entirely clear separation. Who in Germany is completely innocent with respect to that which is now taking place?[19] Certainly not the ones who, out of folly, presumably in their own interest, propped up the ruling party in their struggle for power and then changed positions, disillusioned and disappointed. They are more rather than less guilty. They left the struggle to others while they themselves remained in the background in order to be beneficiaries of victory one day. And they also are accessories who stood aside and did nothing but greeted what was happening with hidden or open sympathy, out of political misunderstanding, out of narrowness based on nationalism, or out of class-based and race-based prejudice. Without them—the masses of spectators in the great struggle—victory could never have fallen to those who have brought the present disaster. They themselves are not innocent who saw what came with objection and horror and still did not begin to do everything in a timely way to prevent its coming. We who belong to this group, and who perhaps suffer because we belong to it, shall not exonerate ourselves of guilt. Yes, and what is more, the few who decided to do battle and who led it to the bitter end shared in the guilt: they led the struggle, but they did not lead it with a spiritual strength and depth and with the human greatness that alone would have been able to prevail over the frightening forces of opposition. Thus they are all guilty who could have turned around fate in those critical years and who did not. However, not only the Germans are guilty. And what I am saying has nothing to do with the wishes of the many German-haters who would annihilate or subjugate all Germans. They forget that they and their nations are also included in this universal guilt: not only that they drove Europe into disorder and Germany into despair through the false peace after the First World War, but also that wide circles within England, France, and the smaller countries behaved just like the Germans themselves. Partly, they supported the movement—as long as they themselves were not attacked by it—because they expected the same advantages from it as the German upper classes did: repression of the workers, conflict with Russia. Partly, they observed what was happening with a mixture of horror and sympathy: in part they rejected it, but they did nothing to help those Germans fighting the movement.

On the contrary, they abandoned one victim after another to the evil authorities and attempted to protect only themselves. They are all guilty; and it is useless to search for anyone who is completely innocent in the present calamity. The lament of the great apostle that there is no innocent person, not even one,[20] is once again dreadfully confirmed by what has taken place in our days.

Guilty parties and innocent parties are inseparable. And yet, in every moment of life—also of the life of nations—there is one who is guilty and one who is not guilty. We are all guilty in the offense of the criminal, because we are accessories to the social conditions that fostered his becoming a criminal. And yet, he remains the guilty one, bearing the responsibility and suffering the punishment. And that is justly so, because he gave himself up to be the tool through which the guilt became act and actuality. So it is with the German rulers and their executioners and torturers. They chose to be instruments of the guilt of all. And therefore they are the guilty parties, and in proportion to them, the others— Germans and non-Germans—are innocent.

But above all, they are innocent who became their victims. No doubt: even they, even persecuted Germans and non-Germans, shared in the responsibility of all. No prophet and no apostle and no martyr ever maintained that he did not share responsibility for the collective guilt, even for the guilt of those who persecuted him. No subtle conscience, no person of depth, will entirely exonerate himself from the responsibility for that which happened to him by way of injustice. But after he has done that, after he has placed himself and all the persecuted with him beneath the collective guilt, he will give testimony relating to the persecutors, with respect to his innocence, and, now, with clear, good conscience. Compared to those who have dispersed us, robbed us, injured us, or slain us, we are innocent. Compared to the German rulers' torturers, their victims are innocent, their German and non-German victims. And their suffering and dying—which happens a thousand times every day behind the battle lines in present-day Europe—is a monstrous indictment from which no one can exonerate the perpetrators.

But you, you should beware of becoming accessories for the second time. I don't know if you can imagine what consequences the murder of hostages has. First, it has an incalculable effect on the nations whose innocent countrymen are being slaughtered. If you knew, for example, how the mood in France—which was half-friendly toward Germans—toppled over into hatred and strife after their defeat, you could comprehend what the German torturers are doing to the German people. A further consequence is that the exact opposite of that which should have been achieved was achieved by the executioners. Every slaughtered innocent creates the resolve for vengeance in a few and an undying hatred in everyone. And from this hatred, something worse than hatred is being born: the moral death notice of their enemy. We have reports that German soldiers and officers are driven to suicide when they've met a mental wall of indifference in Norway, Holland, and other occupied countries, a wall through which they could not penetrate, neither for evil nor for good. They could not bear it that they were being looked through, as if they were empty space and not living people. In the hostility that is displayed there is still the acknowledgment of the enemy as person. In silent disregard there is the deepest rejection that a person can experience. And it is being experienced today by many German soldiers who—though innocent themselves—make themselves guilty as accomplices of the German torturers.[21]

But perhaps the deepest and most horrible consequence of the assassination of innocents is the spiritual decay—with all that it brings in its wake—in which the German soldiers have directly or indirectly participated. Even if one's consciousness resists, one's soul knows that something horrible has happened that can never be repaired. The soul of the individual knows it, and the soul of the nation knows it. It is as if one has lost his freedom and now, as under a curse, is continuously being driven from act to act, increasing the guilt and making it more inescapable. There is something hopeless in all of these doings. And I think this is the deepest cause of the hopelessness: not that the war is lost—that also plays a part—but possibly that the guilt has become overwhelming and inescapable. The screams of the innocent ones being tortured and the groans of the innocent ones being murdered resound within the soul of the German people, even if the rulers want to drown out these sounds with cries of victory and cries of hatred. On the surface, they can be fended off; within the depth, they cannot. In the depth, they are uttered by the death of the innocent, by guilt and judgment.

8.
THE TRAGIC IN THE EVOLUTION OF HISTORY
AUGUST 14, 1942

MY GERMAN FRIENDS!

The last weeks have brought events that need to be detailed and whose religious-ethical meaning must be worked out, for you and for us. I am thinking of two things: the independence movement in India, which has led to the arrest of Mahatma Gandhi and his coworkers, and the German successes in Russia, which have devastated a further, large portion of Russia. It is not my purpose to speak about the military significance of these facts. That is occurring from another source. It is my purpose to come to a deeper understanding with you about what has actually happened with all of this, no matter what military consequences it will have in the next epoch. Such an examination, to be sure, cuts short the movement of our thoughts about the future organization of the world, but at the same time, it gives these thoughts a deeper foundation and for this reason can also be beneficial, serving as the most important aim of these thoughts.

When I reflected on the events in India and Russia, I came upon something that they all have in common, and not only they but also this entire war: the tragic in the evolution of history. Many of you will immediately understand what I mean. For German education has taken care of this for the last century. And much of the best and most profound that the German intellect has brought forth—but we must admit, even some of its most dangerous features—stem from this understanding of the tragedy of life and of history. There is something remarkable about the German melancholy that repeatedly breaks through even the most triumphant figures, such as Luther and Goethe; that has shaped the religion and art of Germans; and that draws ever new nourishment from the countless tragic turning points of German history. But whatever its dangers may also be—for example, a self-isolation from the rest of the world and, at the same time, a longing to match the rest of the world—one thing it gives those Germans who want to know the truth about their situation today: it gives them the possibility of understanding what went before. It gives you—and those of us who think and sympathize with you—a glimpse into the depth of that which is taking place now, its tragedy, and the hope that looks out beyond the tragedy.

No one in the world, not even in England, who has an ethical-religious sensibility today has doubts about the fact that in the relationship with India, England has brought upon itself an immense abundance of tragic guilt: that is, a guilt that is not created maliciously but that is inseparable from the good that the English rule has brought the Indians. There is also guilt that is not tragic or is only so to a negligible degree, for example, what National Socialism has done and is still doing to the European Jews. This is, as far as is humanly possible, pure evil; and consequently, it has evoked the horror of the whole world. But that is a more exceptional, a more extreme failure. It is something that lies on the limits of the human and the diabolical. Altogether different is tragic guilt, a guilt that exists most frequently in human life and in human history. Here, there is no pure evil but rather evil that is mingled with good, that lives on the good, that is attended by it. Thus was the relationship of India and England. And for this reason, it could have such a long duration, and for this reason, there are still many Indians today who do not want to give up the evil that characterizes every foreign rule, because they fear losing the good along with it. And now, the other side: no one understands the Indian freedom movement better than the American people. And even today Gandhi is looked upon here as one of the greatest living people at the present time. And this picture will continue, no matter what is now taking place with him or through him. Everyone in America feels that it is something good to desire the freedom of one's own land. But now, tragic fate is arising so that at this the first great opportunity to struggle to gain freedom, an event taking place somewhere else entirely has threatened this freedom most gravely: the Japanese victories in Southeast Asia. Japan does not bring freedom but rather a more wicked, more ancient, more enslaving form of bondage. And the Indian freedom movement, at the moment at which it has a chance to be successful, is becoming a movement that is helping to further a new, more wicked servitude. That is tragedy in the world's history. No one should make it a matter for petty, moral scolding against one or another group. We should understand what is taking place and, from it, gain a new incentive to win the world order in which, to be sure, the tragic is not altogether overcome but still many tragedies, such as that between England and India, are overcome.

The other tragedy in the world's history is that which is now taking place in Russia. I am not thinking, first of all, of the immeasurable suffering that the invasion of Russia has cost the Russian and German people. I am also not thinking about the horrible suffering that the last winter has brought inside Russia. All of that is terrible, is misfortune, but it is still not tragedy. It becomes tragic, first, by being a question of two nations that had and have been dependent on one another, more, perhaps, than any other two great nations. By that, I am not thinking about the possibilities of economic replenishment, which are almost limitless, but rather I am thinking about the common fate that both nations experienced in the last world war: to be conquered. This fate brought revolutionary movements in both lands. To the generation that returned from the war, it brought the desire for a complete reorganization, for the removal of all the more deeply lying social wrongs that were jointly responsible for the First World War. In both lands, enthusiasm for the new world order, a revolutionary energy, was a source of great hope and great devotion. And then their paths parted, and the tragedy began. In Russia, the revolution in its most radical forms was led to victory and was defended against the assault of all forces of opposition. But out of the horror of civil war, a resistance against, and an abhorrence of, the system arose within Germany, just as it did in all European lands, a system that made its way within such rivers of blood: the tragedy proceeded. Then, in resistance to this fear, Germany was driven more and more to the side that was being resisted. The results of the very moderate German revolution were overthrown by the reactionary powers, step by step. And when National Socialism came, with the intention of making a counterrevolution, it found ample support from those who were frightened by the spectacle of the Russian Revolution. And when

National Socialism was in power, it found support from the re-actionary forces of the entire world for the sake of its opposition to Russia. The tragedy had taken a further step forward, then already evident in the Munich negotiations. Then, the dishonest treaty of National Socialism with Russia followed, which hurled all forces that were fighting for a reorganization of the world, in all countries without exception, into a frightful confusion. It appeared, by this time, as if everything that had lived in the hopes of the war generation after the First World War had been devoured by the abyss. Despairing, many turned their backs on history. A wave of cynical doubt passed through the youth. There appeared to be nothing more onto which one could hold, upon which one could hope. In this, you know that I am describing your experiences. But perhaps you do not know to what degree it was going on in all other lands alike. Seen spiritually, this was the high point of the German-Russian tragedy. Seen superficially, it was the moment in which—on Hitler's order—the mutual rending of both nations began. But by this moment, the most evil matter spiritually was already past: the fraud that had driven all forces of reorganization into confusion and despair! And now the tragedy of both nations unfolded. Therefore, in spite of the natural propensity for national self-preservation, there should be no joy among you over the victories that are now being won. Whatever they also mean militarily, one thing they surely mean: they deepen the tragic antagonism of two nations that—with respect to their greatest strengths—belong together, I repeat, more than any two other great nations with so different cultures. A hatred is arising within the Russian people for the destroyer of their new, grandly developing world, a hatred such as the First World War did not bring to it, a hatred that—like a tragic curse—is being preserved, resulting in the ruin of both nations. Perhaps there is no one outside you, the German Opposition, who can remove anything of this curse. If you show that you share in the inclinations for a new world that has held its own in Russia through such awful woes and in multiple imperfect and tyrannical forms, then the Russians will understand you and, through you, the best Germany. The tragedy is powerful, but it is not all powerful.

And with that, I come finally to something that expresses, perhaps more deeply than anything else, the antagonism of the Christian, socialist, and democratic philosophy of life toward National Socialism. National Socialism knows of the tragic in life. It understands it as well as all paganism understands the tragic. It educates for tragic heroism, it educates for death. But National Socialism knows only the tragic, and nothing about that which triumphs over it, as the ancients themselves understood it. And therefore, their education for death and heroism is an education for the extinguishing of all personality and for the mechanization of all humanity. Christianity understands the tragic; it understands it in its ultimate depth as guilt and sin. Democracy and socialism had frequently forgotten it and were forced to learn it anew in the tragedy of our age. But they all have something that stands beyond tragedy, a hope that is more than the hope for the life of a nation or a race. They have a hope for the human race on the other side and on this side. They believe that the strength of agreement even among nations is ultimately greater than the strength of the cleavage out of which the tragic nature of history arises. When the Germans surrendered to National Socialism in great masses, they cast their beliefs in the unity and hope of humanity away from themselves; they voluntarily submitted themselves to the dominion of the tragic, and the tragic won power over them and drove them to the destruction of others and of themselves. The significance of the German Opposition is to see the tragic, with all sharpness, without illusions, and, at the same time, to conquer the tragic within itself by means of hope, for the sake of itself and for the sake of the world.

9.
THE GERMAN
TRAGEDY
AUGUST 1942

MY GERMAN FRIENDS!

When I last spoke to you, the events in India and Russia brought me to an interpretation of the present world situation as world tragedy. Today, I want to apply these thoughts to the situation in Germany and to indicate some points in which the tragic has become so powerful that it may seem as if no further hope remains. There are three groups of people in Germany: some still believe in victory, or at least in a favorable peace, and want to see nothing tragic in Germany's situation; another group sees that the tragic destruction has already begun and is not to be stopped any longer and thinks that nothing further remains for themselves than to wait for the destruction of the whole thing; the third group, and they are those of you to whom I am attempting to speak in this address, are those who see the tragic disaster and yet can look beyond it.

The air raids on the German cities have brought the horror of the war closer to individual Germans, including women and children, than has the news from distant theaters of war, even when the news of the death of a loved one follows on the heels of the war reports. And not only the horror of war but also the tragedy of the present world is brought to the consciousness of all, without exception, in this way. Yet it is not only human lives that are being devoured by the fire that rains from heaven but also the places in which human life and human culture have unfolded for four hundred years. So it was in England, when the German bombs rained down on the old heart of London and destroyed the monuments to a common European past. So it was and is in

France and Russia, where the destruction of cities and villages is proceeding day after day. So it now is in Germany, where creations of the European international family that a hundred wars have left remaining are now being turned irretrievably to dust in the present war of extermination by the members of this family. And we are not yet at the end; we don't know what will remain of the world in which we have lived. Certainly less than we would have ever imagined. When we heard of the downfall of the great, ancient empires, of the destruction of Babylon and Carthage and Jerusalem, we did not think that our cities of millions could ever be struck by a similar fate. They seemed to be too great for that sort of destruction. And when we read of the four horsemen,[22] who, according to the book of Revelation, would ride along over the world—war, hunger, fire, pestilence—we took that for poetry and as a worthy object of a great picture;[23] but we were too far removed from that to take it for reality. Now it has become a reality! The four horsemen of destruction are raging throughout Europe and the entire world, and fire is raining from heaven in ever-fresh streams. The conception of the end will not be realized in human memory until Europe, and particularly Germany, is reduced to a heap of ruins.

It would be wrong to offer moral invective in relation to this enormous event, indicting others and clearing oneself. The event is too large, too superhuman, for that. It goes beyond all our understanding. Just as no individual person can estimate the extent of destruction that is overtaking humanity in every moment of this period, so no human standard can grasp the meaning of this event. One can attribute responsibility to many individual people, to many individual matters. One can say much that is true concerning the causes for this world destruction. But as a whole, it goes beyond our understanding, beyond our imagination. It is tragedy, real tragedy, that we are experiencing, that Europe in particular is experiencing. Whoever has not understood this has understood nothing, no matter the side on which he stands.

I started with the destruction of the German cities; to this I now return in order to show what I mean. In German propaganda, the air raids on Cologne and Lübeck and Bremen[24] and Hamburg and Mainz are presented as an expression of the British destructive will. Every one of you who hears something like that will ask himself the question: and what was it when we sought to destroy

London and Birmingham and Manchester and Coventry? I can assure you that there are only a few Britons and Americans who rejoice over the destruction of [German] churches and old town houses. They suffer because of that and do not want it to be a source of pride. And yet it is true that the same people who suffer because of the destruction, and for whom it is nearly impossible to think about the children who are buried beneath these ruins, that these same people are calling for attacks as urgently as possible. One can experience this double attitude daily. And I am convinced that among the Germans were also many who felt the same conflict within themselves during the annihilation of British children and British cultural monuments. Whoever doesn't feel it is no longer human but only a part of the inhuman machine of total war. But whoever senses it senses the tragedy in which he stands and has access to the present world tragedy.

But we must search for the European and German tragedy within even deeper layers than in the destruction of innocent people and the places of their ancestors and of their great past! Before it could come to this destruction, the spiritual center and the spiritual creativity of Europe had become lost. A world had lost its focal point and its meaning when the period of the world war began, in which it is destroying itself. Much would be gained by successfully raising the people in all affected countries to this perspective. We are attempting to do it here; you must attempt to do it there! We are surprised to learn that many leading people in the democratic countries know that this is not about Germany or England, nor about America or Japan, but about a world catastrophe of immense proportions that represents tragic destruction and—perhaps—a new future. And not only is this so with people of prominence. It is astonishing to hear how ordinary people in the democratic countries are offering resistance to a parochial nationalism or a new imperialism. They sense the tragedy that it was their own wrong policy after the First World War that made the creation of National Socialist rule in Germany and Europe possible. They want to overcome tragedy, and they fear nothing as much as again falling victim to it and, through a false peace, giving rise to a new tragedy. Such people are your allies, even when they are waging war against Hitler's Germany. They are bearers of a better future, because they have understood the present and are not driven by petty, nationalist reproaches and excuses and demands. How is it going with such people inside Germany? Are there any? Are there many who know what this is about? Do they know of one another? Do they know of us? Will they be there, will they emerge from the ruins and build anew with us, when the four demonic horsemen have given vent to their fury? Everyone who hears this question, everyone who is able to see the tragedy of Germany without completely despairing, every one of you to whom I am speaking should give answer inside yourself, in your innermost self. And the answer should not be: perhaps we will still be victorious, perhaps there will still be a good peace, perhaps our cities will not have too many ruins, perhaps we will not suffer too many deaths, perhaps it has not been so bad in the world from which we are coming! All such answers are deceitful. People don't completely believe these answers themselves. But they also can't bear to reject them completely. They don't risk looking tragedy in the eye. But they must do so, you must do so, we must do so, because it is only on the other side of tragedy that genuine, not deceitful, hope appears. It is only through the night of the self-destruction of one world that the path to a new world proceeds.

Permit me to illuminate still another side of the German tragedy that is, perhaps, the most difficult to look in the eye. Since ancient times, people have known that there are instruments of providence that, through the evil they do, clear the path for the good that follows. But at the same time, they knew that these tools were not, as a result, less guilty; they knew that destiny uses them. According to the biblical story, Judas himself was an instrument through which the salvation of the world was realized.[25] But the sorrow over him was not eased as a result. The Christian nations called Attilla the scourge of God over them, but that did not keep them from fighting against him until he had fallen. In the same way, National Socialism is also the scourge of a world that had lost its life-meaning and the instrument of a providence that will bring something new. But that changes nothing in terms of its guilt and in terms of the necessity of fighting until its downfall. When it has accomplished the work of tragic destruction, which is destined for it, then the destroying tragedy will turn against it and drag it into the abyss. Perhaps it is not so difficult to see this. Perhaps you see this more precisely than anyone else. But the difficulty and the double tragedy for Germany is that it surrendered itself to it—half willingly, half unwillingly—and became its instrument and, as a result, was itself the instrument of a destroying and self-destroying destiny. That is the most difficult thing in the German tragedy. And whoever wants to understand what the fire that is raining from heaven on the old German cities means, and what the death of German youth in snow and on desert sand means, and what the hunger and the enslavement and the slowly approaching catastrophe of the German people means, whoever wants to understand that must know about the twofold guilt and the twofold tragedy of the Germans. They allowed themselves to be transformed into the instrument of the spirit and the power through which a world is being destroyed, a world that was ripe for it. But the pain over this power and its instrument, the German people, will continue to last, although destiny is making use of it. And this pain will be fulfilled, step by step. And just beyond this pain stands the hope that also—indeed, that especially—exists there for the German people, and of that I want to speak another time.

10.
BRINGING GERMANY
TO POLITICAL MATURITY

AUGUST 28, 1942

MY GERMAN FRIENDS!

When the role of Germany in the coming world order is spoken about, the friends of Germany ask themselves whether the German people will, at some time or other, come to political maturity. Some have doubts about it and say that the creative powers of the Germans, which only blind hatred can dispute, are directed at everything other than political development. From that they draw the conclusion that Germany must again be turned into the land of poets and thinkers and that other lands, above all the Anglo-Saxon, must take over the political side of the new world order. A politically dependent or, at the very least, largely subordinate Germany would be the best not only for Europe and the rest of the world but also for the Germans themselves. Others do not believe that this is the right path. They are of the opinion, and I think they are in the right, that even thinking and writing are turned topsy-turvy when they are undertaken without the possibility of political development and without the earnestness of political responsibility. A thought that, from the beginning, must forever surrender being carried over into reality is dreaming. A writing that has no relationship to social reality becomes frivolous. And when the intellectual life of a nation falls into dreaming and frivolity, then it loses the power of resistance against political adventurers and criminals and easily becomes a victim of tyranny. Without political responsibility and passion, intellectual life becomes one lacking in seriousness, and a nation without an earnest, politically responsible intellect is a danger to itself and to the rest of the nations. For this reason, it is senseless in every way to be willing to relieve a great nation of its joint political responsibility for itself and for the world. The poets and thinkers who arise in such a nation are dangerous precisely because they play and dream. A hundred years ago, a German poet described the dangers that were contained within the dreaming German philosophy of the classical period, dangers for Germany as well as for Europe.[26] He described the dangers in such a way that it was possible to believe he had experienced firsthand what has taken place in the last ten years. He foresaw the political calamity that would spring forth from a politically irresponsible philosophy, doing so with prophetic clarity with respect to the details. No! Germany must not again become the nation of poets and thinkers while other nations relieve it of its political responsibility. That would mean crippling Germany from the start, even its writing and thinking, and turning it into a source of future perils for the world.

But if we say no to such a solution, then the question arises with all greater force: is the German nation capable of political responsibility? Is a politically mature German nation conceivable? And if so, how can it reach political maturity? Who can lead it to that? I do not doubt that you, the ones who belong to the German Opposition, agree with me when I reject the dangerous illusory ideal of the poet-and-thinker nation. But if you agree with me, can you help me answer the questions that result from our answer? Will you and can you be those who bring the German nation closer to political maturity? Will you and can you assume political responsibility?

One thing is certain: political responsibility falls into no one's lap who has not fought for it. And if this happens, as in the debacle of 1918, then it is immediately lost again.[27] Only those who are now fighting—in order that another, politically mature and responsible Germany arises from the decline of National Socialist Germany—are able to become and remain the political leaders. At present, this battle can take place only in secret. But it must take place, day after day! Mature political thoughts must occupy many among you; ever new people must be initiated into these thoughts. And wherever it is possible, something or other— even if it be the smallest thing to translate into reality—must be attempted as a part of the education of the German nation toward political maturity. There are no paths of education for political maturity other than that of political struggle. It has no significance to give a nation political teachers, their own or completely foreign, as is now being frequently demanded within democratic countries, when there are no groups within this nation that are fighting politically. It is essential and fruitful when movements engaged in the struggle learn from others who have richer experience. But it is meaningless and unfruitful when people who by no means have the intention to take a stand politically are being instructed about political ideas and life-forms. Whether a politically responsible, and with it, an intellectually serious, Germany shall spring forth from the ruins of present-day Europe ultimately depends on the struggle of the German Opposition, and on it alone. Assistance that you are given from the theorists and practitioners of politically more mature nations can be useful if you yourselves are leading the struggle. They can only hurt if you yourselves do not lead it.

Why is this so difficult in Germany? What has held back the political maturation of the German nation for so long? How was it possible that a land so highly developed culturally so easily lent itself to be a tool of a destructive power of fate? The first basis for this was the retreat of the German, particularly the German Protestant, religion from this life into the life to come.[28] One sees that clearly when one lives for long in countries in which that is not so. Neither the Catholicism of the Romance countries nor the Protestantism of the Anglo-Saxon countries has so strongly banished the people from this life into the life to come as was the case in the downfall of Germany, especially Evangelical Germany. The Anglo-Saxon churches and sects, as also in the Catholic church, have always felt responsible for the political and social arrangement of the world. They have, for this reason—especially in the Anglo-Saxon countries—certainly contributed much decisiveness to the political education of the individual person. My friends of the German Evangelical church! You must take upon yourselves this responsibility, if you want the German nation to come to political maturity! You can no longer speak of the kingdom of heaven as an otherworldly power that should not have any power in this world. For with that you hand this world over to satanic powers such as those that have power today in Germany and that are destroying the church along with the nation.

This task is all the more important at the present, when undoubtedly many people are being driven to escape into a pure
world to come by the tragedy of the present world. It was this way
frequently enough in German history. It was understandable yet
nevertheless wrong. It can happen this way again now, if the German religious opposition has not learned what was to be learned
in these ten years: that if the political is isolated from God, the
devil takes it into its hand. I am not speaking to you as many representatives of the American churches speak to their audiences:
that a government with a good system and good policies is itself
the kingdom of God. Certainly, this is not so. But I am saying to
you that the messengers of the kingdom of God have the standard
by which every system and all policies must be measured and that
therefore they are responsible to the highest degree for political
reality, even if they themselves are not politicians. The adversaries of Christianity among the present German rulers are themselves much clearer about these matters than many pastors and
theologians. They understand that, from the standpoint of the
Christian proclamation, their policies are condemned, and for
this reason they persecute the bearers of this proclamation. All
the more should you, the ones who stand for its truth, elaborate
its political significance and contribute to it, in order that the German people may at last reach political maturity, to which it, like
all nations, is entitled.

Another reason for the political immaturity of the German nation is the escape of its spiritual leaders into the inwardness of the
heart from the external realm of political action. When the freedom struggle of the French burghers shook the old order of dom-
ination and servitude, even the German poets and thinkers were
most deeply moved. All the great ones of the German classic period at first welcomed the French Revolution, but soon the fateful reality came to pass that the Germans, instead of taking an
interest in the political freedom struggle, were speaking of inner
spiritual freedom, and they set themselves against political freedom. The freedom that the person has, even if he is born in
chains, became a slogan over against the freedom that severs the
chains. A freedom of thought, which in actuality was a freedom
to dream, replaced the freedom of life. Again, I want to prevent
a misunderstanding: certainly, there is a spiritual, internal freedom, without which external freedom is not of much value and,

indeed, in the long run, is lost. And certainly, there is a freedom even in chains, a human dignity that can be broken by no force. But this freedom is there only as long as the person perceives his chains as chains and is seeking to sever them. Whoever feels that he is no longer in chains has lost even inner freedom. That is why, over the long run, there will be no spiritual freedom without political freedom and why it forms part of the German misfortune that the bearers of the German spirit were not at the same time bearers of the German political will. And for this reason, I am summoning all those who understand themselves to be responsible for the German spirit, in order that they may bear the greatest responsibility of all for the German political realm with precisely that understanding. To a great extent, whether political maturity will ever come to Germany depends on them.

The third reason it has not come to Germany until now is its separation of nation and authority. Already the word *authority* suggests this separation. Its opposite is *subject*. But that is a false, inhuman opposition. There is one nation and its government, which belongs to it and is accountable to it. The political does not stand side by side with the human, just as it does not stand side by side with the religious and the intellectual. It is a part of what it means to be human, the absence of which makes full humanity impossible. That the German nation has separated its human from its political is the reason its humanity was not fully developed and its politics fell into the hands of inhuman powers. We are longing and working in order that the frightful events of the present may turn the German person into a politically mature and, for this reason, fully developed person. We want the separation of the intellectual and the political, of the religious and the political, of the human and the political, this root of the German misfortune, to be conquered in the misfortune of the present—first, within the German political opposition, and then, perhaps someday, within the entire German nation.

11.
THE INTELLIGENTSIA
AND GERMANY'S CONQUEST
SEPTEMBER 4, 1942

MY GERMAN FRIENDS!

Today, I want to speak to a group of people that is, perhaps, small in its supporting circle but great in its consequences and its effects: I mean the bearers of the scholarly work, of art and literature, of music and public discourse. Even if they were a hundred thousand, they would be few in proportion to the millions of German people. But among these millions, there is no one who is not influenced in any way by this group, even if only in the language that he speaks and the technology that he uses. For this reason, the leaders of the intellectual life of a nation are infinitely important for its destiny. This group of intellectually leading Germans is more responsible for the tragedy of Germany and the misfortune that it has brought on the world and itself than the masses of the nation are, and nearly as responsible as that small stratum of landed proprietors and large entrepreneurs who handed over weapons and capital to National Socialism, because they trembled in the face of social reorganization. Why did a great portion of the German scholars, writers, and artists make common cause with the forces of reaction, which held the stirrups for the present regime? Many will say what many of these stirrup holders are saying today: we did not know that the rider whom we helped into the saddle would ride the German nation and many nations with it into the abyss. We were in error, and we have made amends for that. Such an admission is certainly valuable and more promising for the future than the attitude of those who, even today, when the abyss has already become visible, pronounce their attitude at that time to be correct. And yet, the admission of error is not enough. One must understand how the error could come about, what roots it had, and one must exterminate these roots, in order that new errors and new harm may not grow forth from them.

What are the roots from which one can account for the breakdown of the German intellectual leaders, how can they be exterminated, and what mission does an intellectual-bearing stratum have in the reconstruction of Germany? Every thinking German should put this question to himself, above all, those who rank themselves among the bearers of intellectual life.

The questions that I am putting forth are not limited to Germany. They are being asked and discussed everywhere. This week, in a large American city, a convention of scholars took place at which a speaker stressed to the others the need for science to serve in the reconstruction of the world, not in the interest of technology but in the interest of the intellect.[29] Technology, as a scientific leader said of allegedly mechanized America, is ambiguous: it creates tools of construction and destruction to the same perfection. It is neutral toward good and evil. But science is not permitted to remain neutral toward good and evil. It must place itself in the service of the good. Much harm could have been avoided if the intellectual leaders of the different nations would have learned the lesson from the First World War that the mind must serve the good life, and it must not be left to its own devices. It is good to hear such voices, and it would be good if they could also be heard in Germany. But that is such a rare thing, not only now when, generally, voices of truth can no longer be heard but even before, when everyone could say what he thought. Even in that time, many scholars believed that it would taint science if it stepped down into the muck of daily life. And many artists were doing more in terms of that which is beautiful than in terms of true-to-life style. And if the bearers of the intellect arose and made it otherwise, if they used science and art to expose the dark, lower strata of human existence, they were derided and resisted. People found superficial beauty more important than deeply penetrating truth. They had anxiety before the truth—most of all, the bearers of the intellect themselves. People found a battling science, a revolutionary mind beneath their dignity. And so it happened that today they have an enslaved mind, a trashed art, and a science in service to destruction. From the Reich Culture Board, in which the

German mind is imprisoned, only shreds of intellectual creation enter into the consciousness of the German people. The distinguished scholars and authors who abided by the highest standards on behalf of the real life of the person have been made devoid of power by this life. They wanted no intellectual power over life, and now that which is contrary to intellectual life has won power over them. There is no vacant space. The aspects of life that are not shaped by the mind rebel against the mind and destroy it. And this has happened in Germany. The faith in the intellect had been lost in Germany, because the faith in the strength of the intellect to shape life had been lost. And this faith had been lost because the intellect that was found in oneself and in others did not issue from life. I am saying all of this, although I know that there were also others who fought a desperate battle against this empty intellect, in universities, in schools, in the theater, in literature, in art. Everywhere, there were some for whom the intellect meant life, struggle, revolution, mission. But where are they today? In exile, in the concentration camp, in seclusion, in the grave. They were betrayed by their colleagues; they were hated by the so-called intelligentsia; they remained misunderstood by the masses. No one protected them when they were persecuted by the nonintellectual and the anti-intellectual. When solitary, they perished or escaped. And the ones who should have helped them acquiesced, accommodated, permitted their only weapon to be taken: the sharpness of the mind. That is an immense part of the German tragedy.

When I last spoke to you, I sought to answer the question why the German nation has never come to political maturity. One of the bases is the outlook of the intellectual leaders of Germany, their unbelief in the power of the mind and their betrayal of the intellect. They believed in their science; they believed in their art. But they did not believe that both science and art, literature and discourse, have meaning only when they express the life of every individual within the nation and give his ardent desire for a better life articulation and form. In a deep sense, every thought and writing and utterance and form must be revolutionary. It must attempt to give expression to the everlasting discontent with everything that is—a discontent that distinguishes the human being from the beast—it must attempt to change human life, the personal and the social. It must be a bit prophetic, it must condemn and demand, it must give hope. If it does not do that, it is a beautiful sport, but without seriousness. It is a dream but not truth; and what is worse than its being sport and dream is that it creates a diversion from the truth. The unveiling of the truth is not pleasant to those who have power and misuse this power at the expense of others. For this reason, they fear the intellect and seek either to wipe out its bearers or—what is more important in the long run—to buy them and to place them in their service. And thereby, we are in the midst of the tragedy of the German intellect: it exalted when it should have condemned; it veiled when it should have unveiled; it kept silent when it should have spoken; it retreated when it should have fought; it betrayed when it should have tolerated. While the bearers of the intellect themselves were unaware of it, they were bought by the ruling powers as civil servants, as successful authors, as famous men, as minions of wealth. Again I must say: this does not apply to all. But perhaps to more than in other civilized nations. Even among the great ones of German literature and philosophy, there are only a few who did not at some time or other make their peace with the rulers of their time. It forms a part of the German tragedy that one like Goethe lived in a royal palace and, indeed, as he himself said, as a private individual. It forms a part of the German tragedy that Hegel equated reason, this most revolutionary of all forces, with the Prussian state and in this way turned it into a harmless office piece for higher civil servants.[30] It forms a part of the German tragedy that the German historians sought to show how a great past has led to a still greater present, for which it is the duty of every German to rejoice. It also forms a part of the German tragedy that scientists and engineers could identify and control nature, to be sure, but never asked: to what end? For whom? What happens to the human being who is doing all of this? What does it look like to the masses? What does it look like within the souls of the individuals? What do human beings live on, their bodies and their souls? Admission into the Holy of Holies of science was barred to such questions. But precisely in this way science ceased to be holy, let alone the Holy of Holies. It became neutral and fell, when the hour had come, to the power of destruction as welcome tools in its hand.

Can the German intellect be saved from this tragedy, given that it enjoined the entire German nation to abandon hopelessness when the German mind continued in its servitude to the ruling powers? Indeed, there is no reason for the sort of despair [this question implies]. The revolution, which this war signifies, has revolutionized even the true bearers of the German intellect. The captivity of the critical mind under the National Socialist dictatorship has made the bondage that the German mind has always cherished so frightful and so inescapable that even the eyes of the most blind are being opened. Something remarkable has taken place: the bearers of the intellect, who, half without knowledge and will, had sold themselves to the powers of the German middle class, have been sold again by these to the powers of National Socialism. And the new masters, as frequently happens to the slaves, are a thousand times worse than the old. While they felt free or at least half-free before, they now understand that they are in bondage. And that is the hope for the German intellect. Now it must either wither or become revolutionary. Now it is summoned to the struggle for liberation and cannot evade it without surrendering itself.

I have spoken today, in the first place, to the bearers of the intellect, the scholars and writers, the artists and orators. But the intellectuals of every nation not only form the nation but are also formed by it. And for this reason, I call out to the German nation: do not consent any longer to your philosophers and authors conjuring up a world that is not yours and that leaves you in your misery. Demand intelligence from them that is in fact intelligence, that does not glorify a wicked reality but unveils and unmasks the roots of this reality; the intellect that sees a new reality and builds in partnership with you, the mind that says what you feel and thinks what you hope. Allow the old, feeble mind to decay behind the walls of the Reich Culture Board and make room for the new mind that changes reality.

12.
HOW ONE SHOULD VIEW THE ENEMY

SEPTEMBER 12, 1942

MY GERMAN FRIENDS!

Recently, the federal propaganda minister published an article in the periodical *Das Reich* that has provoked much attention among thinking people. The article admonishes the German people because there are still many Germans who not only listen to British radio but even largely give it credence. That shows, writes the propaganda minister, a deplorable deficiency in national hatred for the English. And then he proceeded with the concession that among the English many were admirable, but that in spite of the recognition of their good side, as a German one must hate them, for only then could a war with them be led successfully.

These remarkable, inconsistent propositions give me occasion, today, to reflect on a question with you that is of critical importance for the conduct of the war, for the struggle against National Socialism, and for the postwar organization. I mean the question: how should one view the enemy?

To begin with, permit me to say this: the accusation of the propaganda minister, that the German nation still has not learned to hate pertains to those matters that the world has written that present a positive account of the German people. We who are fighting against National Socialism and for the future of the German nation in a new world are most deeply grateful to all those whom the minister admonishes. They have shown that the principles of National Socialism, out of which hatred necessarily follows, have not yet completely poisoned the soul of the German nation. What Goebbels laments is a preservation of a fragment of the honor of the Germans. And since he hates nothing more than the absence of hatred, he is therefore the best evidence for the fact that the National Socialist endeavor to corrupt the entire German nation has still not succeeded. That is the first important reflection to which Goebbels's unintentional disclosure gives occasion: the most refined and most wicked of all poisoners of the German people must admit that his poison has still not worked as he had wished.

But you will ask, if hatred toward the enemy is poison, what becomes of our hatred toward the National Socialists? Can we fight them if we do not hate them? Is it possible not to hate them when one knows what is being perpetrated by them daily and hourly in the way of horrors? Certainly, we don't hate the British and Russians, so you will continue. We are fighting them because we must. But with the National Socialists it is something else: we are fighting them because we hate them, thoroughly, with our whole heart, until their complete destruction. Nothing is more natural than the fact that you speak in this way, that everyone who is being done boundless harm by the National Socialists, inside Germany and outside Germany, in all lands to the limits of the inhabited earth, feels this way. I can't imagine that in the entire history of humanity a historical power has brought forth such universal, earth-encompassing, all-consuming hatred against itself as that which German National Socialism has: not because it has gained unlimited political power, not because it was victorious in many battles, not because it has overturned much tradition but because it has done all of this in a way that is inhuman and that destroys life and life's meaning. It has given rise to a tidal wave of hatred, not only toward itself but also toward its instrument, the German nation, because National Socialism itself was born in hatred, came to power in hatred, and exercised its power with hatred.

But if that is so, you will ask, don't we have to hate them? In the first place, don't we belong to those who have borne the tidal wave of hatred toward National Socialism? When you speak in this way, do you not sense at that moment that you have earned a commendation from the mouth of the propaganda minister? Do you not sense that at that moment you are being just as the National Socialists want you to be, servants of hatred, just as they themselves are? And for this reason I am telling you in full awareness of what it means, and having the deepest conviction that it is true: you are superior to the National Socialists to the de-

gree to which you keep yourselves free of hatred toward them!
You are identical to them to the degree to which you permit yourselves to hate them.

But, you will ask again, can we fight against them if we don't
hate them? And now you have yourselves become entangled, because now you have articulated the thoughts on the basis of
which Goebbels admonishes the German nation: you have agreed
with him in that you suggest that without hating you cannot fight.
And in the same way, the tidal wave of hatred that has risen up
today against National Socialism and against the German nation
in all the world is a victory of the National Socialist, even when
they themselves are being washed away by this wave. Your sermon of hatred will bring fruits even if the preacher has himself
become a victim of this hatred. The evil that lies within hatred
will beget lasting evil.

Therefore, we should not hate, you will answer, when our
friends or brothers or sons or fathers are being tortured to death in
a concentration camp; we should not hate when we lead a miserable life in anxiety and slavery; the Jews should not hate when
they are subjected to the most cruel process of extermination; the
conquered lands should not hate when their men are being shot
and their children are being killed through hunger; the countries
engaged in combat should not hate when their country is being
devastated under the breaking of all treaties? Is this challenge
even human? Is it not superhuman? It may be that it is Christian.
But does the call to love people such as the National Socialists,
does the call to bless such enemies, have any real meaning? Is it
not the expression of the dream of another world? Was not the one
who required the love of enemies[31] a dreamer, the hatred of whose
enemies naturally brought him to the cross? But if you, the opponents of National Socialism, ask in this way, then you have been
caught again. Because even the National Socialists, your opponents, speak like this. That is surely the reason they have begun
the struggle with Christianity. That is surely the reason they are
taking Christianity so seriously—even if they do so as their enemy. That is the reason they are taking it so much more seriously
than you who are fighting against National Socialism on behalf of
the Christian culture; but at the same time, you join the National
Socialists in their hatred of the enemy and, in that way, surrender
the depth of the Christian culture to your opponents.

Permit me now to leap from the ethical-religious to the political and to say: a victory over National Socialism will be attained only if the victors gain it without hatred. If it is won with hatred, then the conquered have, in reality, been victorious, and a new period of hatred will drag the world further into the abyss!

An example from the previous war will make this clear: in Versailles, justice and hatred struggled with each other. In extensive regions, hatred was victorious, and the answer to it was the hatred of the defeated. But it was not the only answer: the other was the bad conscience of the victor. And this bad conscience of the finest people in England and America was one of the reasons there was hesitation before a position against National Socialism was taken. They did not believe they had the right to proceed against the preacher of hatred after they themselves had been overpowered by hatred. Whoever hates is committing wrong. And when he then repents of his wrong, he frequently does even more wrong: he ceases to battle the hateful. That is a piece of history that has led from one world war to another.

But within this history lies, at the same time, the answer to the question that is asked in the article of the Reich propaganda minister: will there be successful battle without hatred? The answer runs: ultimately, a battle can be successful only without hatred. Every battle with hatred prolongs the battle while it begets new hatred.

What, then, is hatred? It is the will to recompense the other's evil with evil. But to repay evil for evil, one must himself do evil, and then, instead of prevailing over it, one has given the evil new power. There is but one other will than that of retribution, namely, that of salvation! But it forms a part of salvation that the evil is recognized and broken, and that those things it is doing are prevented, overcome, and punished. For this reason, National Socialism must be disclosed in its wickedness, broken in its will, hindered in its conquest, and conquered in its power. And this challenge is an object not only of cool reflection but of highest passion. We do not want to take your passion when we take your hatred. We wouldn't be able to! For nothing great takes place without passion. But hatred is no great passion, and it can create nothing great; it can only destroy.

What, now, is the passion that stands behind our common struggle against National Socialism? It is the passion for salvation! The passion for the good always has the one aspect that it is passion against the evil. If one wishes to call this passion against the evil "hatred," then it is a holy hatred. But this is directed not against people but against powers within the person for the sake of the salvation of the person. Such a holy hatred, such a passion for the salvation of the person, the great messenger of the love of enemy has displayed. It would be the victory of National Socialism if it could justly deny to Christianity passion, holy hatred, holy enmity. But it cannot justly do so. The conception of its charitable institutions and all of its great representatives show exactly the contrary. Christianity hates the evil, but it has the passionate will to save the evil ones.

It is important to all that the battle against National Socialism is being led in this spirit. Only then does it have a chance of being victorious. Otherwise, it has still lost, even if it is outwardly victorious. That applies to the opponents of National Socialism outside Germany in the same way that it does to the opposition inside Germany. That hatred which is not holy hatred against evil but unholy, vengeful hatetred against the evil ones cannot be victorious, even if it is outwardly victorious. When Goebbels demands hatred for the sake of being victorious, we demand renunciation of hatred—so that we are not conquered as conquerors! We refuse to direct the hatred that he has directed against us toward him. We will not conform to it; we will refuse to become National Socialists in order to conquer National Socialism. We know that at precisely that point, we would be conquered by it.

Much concerning these matters is being thought and spoken in the Allied nations. Precisely because people in many circles sense this war to be a battle for everything human and holy, they want to keep it free from hatred, without taking the passion from it. They want to conquer the National Socialists, annihilating their power of evil, calling those responsible among them to account. But people do not want to give room to the hatred, least of all hatred toward the German nation. The leaders of the churches, the laborers, and, above all, the struggling youth think and speak in this way. You should join forces with them in the passion that overcomes hatred, which does not avenge but which will save a shattered world. National Socialism can fear nothing more than such a victory. Only if its force of hatred is conquered is it itself conquered.

13.
WHAT IS
WORTH DEFENDING?

OCTOBER 6, 1942

MY GERMAN FRIENDS!

There are speeches that are events, like battles and coup d'états; one such speech was the address that Germany's Führer delivered at the opening of this year's Winter Charity Drive.[32] It was a speech that differed in tone and content from everything that has been said by the leading authorities in Germany since the war's outset. Every thinking German must have asked himself the question: what does this mean? What is happening? Where are we being led? And not only in Germany but also in all the rest of the countries much reflection has been devoted to it. I feel the need to speak with you today about it and to ask myself and to ask you how the change expressed in Hitler's Winter Charity speech is to be understood and evaluated.

The general feeling in all countries outside Germany is that Germany has resolved to switch from attack to defense, from the offensive to the defensive. The offensive has reached its limit. The resistance of those attacked has intensified from month to month, in the east just as in the west. Further expansion of the front would bring about perils that they wish to avoid. But more important than this is the aversion of the German nation to further conquests, which, even if they were possible, would bring no victory. Out of every word of the Winter Charity speech speaks the desire that says to the German people that their sacrifices shall not serve further offensives. Out of every word, the inner resistance of the German masses to National Socialism's plans for world conquest can be heard coming forth. A survey of the great gains of the German armies, which in comparison with the gains of their opponents are, in reality, astounding, is given. But no forward-looking view is derived from this, only the declaration that that which has been gained should be defended. It becomes self-evident that as with every defensive, there are also assaults. But the major line will be the defense and not the attack. For three years, it was just the opposite. For three years, every speech was a fanfare of attack, every battle—even if there were occasionally defensive battles—a battle of assault, whose strategy was a pure strategy of offensive. Immense promises were made to the German people, immense threats pronounced against the enemies. Many of these threats and promises were kept, many remained unfulfilled. But this time, nothing was promised but a final commitment to the eastern front and nothing threatened but revenge for the bombing attacks on Germany. It is no longer said to you that "tomorrow, the world will belong to you!" Rather, it is said to you that you will be able to keep what you have won in an incalculable defensive war.

And now I want to ask: what should actually be defended, and is it worth the defense? There are things that are worth being defended, and there have been defensive wars that have finally led to victory. But is that which National Socialism is defending also worth being defended by the German people? It is clear what National Socialism wants to defend: the power that it has seized, first in Germany, then in Europe. But is this an object worthy of defense by the German people, a defense that, whether successful or not, will transform Germany into a heap of rubble. It is clear that National Socialism will do everything to preserve its power over Germany: not only because everyone who is in power wants to keep himself in power but also because the end of the power of National Socialism is the end of its existence and that of all its supporters. If ever a group has defended its life, the National Socialists are doing so. The blood of their adversaries, which they have spilled in cowardly cruelty every day since their ascent to power, cries out against them. And they hear this cry whenever they do not artificially close their ears. For this reason, their defense will be a desperate one, and more blood of innocent people will be spilled under the law that every crime requires a new crime in order to conceal itself. But is this defense an affair of the German people? Are not the German people, as the first victims of this tyranny, also the first power against which this tyranny must defend itself? In supporting this defense, are not the German people standing on the side of the aggressor? Every German must pose this question to himself. Every German, all who are wavering, fearful, divided, all who stand partly for the National Socialists, partly against them, must now decide. They all must ask themselves: do we want to go to the rampart behind which the National Socialists are entrenching themselves? Do we want to commit further crimes of oppression together with them, or at least cover them up through silence? Do we want to perish with them in the defensive struggle for their rule? Or, do we want to remain outside the entrenchments and follow those who have led the struggle against them? It will become more and more impossible to remain undecided, to stand against National Socialism and at the same time to support it. Officers and soldiers, civil servants and salaried employees, authors and scholars must decide where they want to place themselves in the defensive struggle to which National Socialism is now constrained. And woe to those who decide wrongly and want to protect themselves from the consequences of the old crimes with new ones. One day this terrible chain will come to its end. And then there will no longer be salvation.

Many Germans will agree and will declare that they would welcome nothing more than the collapse of National Socialism and all of its defenses. But, they will continue, what we are defending is not National Socialism but the German nation. And to defend it, we must join forces with the National Socialists. But what, then, in reality, is being defended? In the first place, conquered lands in the west as well as in the east. Millions of German soldiers are defending hundreds of millions of foreign people who—day and night—think and wish for nothing other than freedom from their defenders. They regard those against whom they are being defended as their liberators and those by whom they are being defended as their enslavers. Is it a [worthy] goal for the German nation to defend its power throughout most of the regions of Europe, the power to have foreign nations plundered, to exploit them and to deprive them of their leaders, to carry them off into slavery in Germany, to destroy their institutions, to allow their masses to starve? Is that a goal worthy of a defensive war, in which hatred toward the German people will rise to an immeasurable point and in which only rubble and impoverished beggars will be left over in all of these lands — just as in Germany itself? If Europe was an undivided whole, if all countries voluntarily took part in this defensive war, to defend it would be a goal worthy of the greatest commitment. But there is no such Europe. The National Socialist conquerors were not able to create a united "world," not even in Europe. The unity that now exists is unity in being downtrodden, not freely formed unity. Is it a goal worthy of an incalculable war of exhaustion that this unity of suppressed, violated, and ruined Europe be maintained? For the National Socialists, it is certainly a goal. Because as it stands today, their rule in Germany depends on their rule in Europe. But is it a goal for the German people? Do the German people want to suffer further so that German officers and civilians in a dozen conquered lands may live as slave owners and slave exporters? Is the slavery and misery of more than a hundred million an object for which the German people should lead a self-destructive defensive war, month after month, year after year, to an incalculable extent? But, one will ask, is not this defense the external line for the defense of Germany? To which we must answer: of Nazi Germany, certainly; of Germany, certainly not! What, then, is the Germany that it would be worthy to defend? Its freedom is certainly the first answer. But this freedom was certainly taken from it when it came under the power of a tyranny. Who is free today in Germany, free from fear, free to speak, free to act? A few at the top; all others are less free than they ever were in German history. This war against Germany is fundamentally a German war of liberation, and it will be this all the more to the degree that the Germans themselves participate in it further on the side of their liberators. Perhaps you will say: it's better to have internal bondage than external bondage! But there can no longer be any external freedom, in the sense of the sovereignty of the individual states after this war. No nation will be free in this sense. All nations of the world will join together in an all-embracing unity! Do you want to defend Germany against this unity, which is, at the same time, the only path to the approaching freedom? Or should the German culture, language, literature, art, religion, education, family — the German house, as it were — be defended? But hasn't all of that been long since absorbed into the one German reality that has remained, that of power, that of warlike, conquering, and now self-defending power? Is the defense of this power for the sake of power, the defense of this all-consuming monster, this destroyer of body and soul, this destroyer of religion and culture, worthy of being defended? Isn't that, in reality, the defense of the National Socialist ruling class and nothing else?

My German friends! After three years of attack, the defensive phase has begun. What are you defending? Do you want to defend your subjection, the subjection of the conquered? Do you want to defend your misfortune, the misfortune of many nations? Do you want to defend your tyrants and the exploiters and oppressors of hundreds of millions? That is the question this big change in the German strategy puts to every German.

14.
POWER
POLITICS
OCTOBER 13, 1942

MY GERMAN FRIENDS!

One thing has clearly emerged from the speeches of the German leaders in the last weeks: Germany is pushed to limits beyond which it cannot expand its power. The last time we spoke about the fact that, at this stage, the big change has taken place from one of attack to one of defense, and we asked ourselves what should properly be defended. Perhaps the answer to this question has been given to you by honest National Socialists: the power that we have won we want to defend! Politics is the struggle for power. Our politics is the struggle for power over a nation. Foreign policy is one nation's struggle for power over other nations; if possible, over continents and the earth itself. No one can doubt that this is the political conviction of National Socialism, indeed, that it is the core—the main part—of all the convictions it possesses. From the belief in power as the highest of all human values has emerged its intention to conquer first Germany and then the world. And since it was a truly fanatical belief, it brought successes to National Socialism that no one in the world would have allowed themselves to dream some years before. It has created one of the greatest concentrations of power of all time; it has completely subjugated the German nation and Europe, with few exceptions. It has threatened all the great powers of the world and has brought upon the earth the greatest of all wars. Everyone impressed by the development of power was and is confused, fascinated, frightened, or inspired by that which has taken place. And many who believed in justice and humanity their entire lives have become wavering in their beliefs. They ask themselves whether the religion of power is not, indeed, the truer religion. Until a year ago, it would have been difficult to answer this doubt. When the German armies pushed forward through the expanses of Russia and there seemed to be no limits for them, one would have vainly attempted to show the power worshipers the dubiousness of their idols. Today it is different: the "so far and no further" has been clearly spoken, and it has been not only spoken by fate but also understood by the priests of power worship; the speeches of the German leaders are the echo of that call of fate! For that reason, it is possible to speak today about power and to demonstrate its limits, not only its external ones, which fate has made apparent, but also the internal limits that apply to every power.

An example can display the inner limits of power, even the power of National Socialism. No one today appears to be more defenseless to German power than the conquered European nations. Without weapons and without economic independence, they are surrendered to the mercy of the German conquerors and to the instruments of their power. They are being robbed, sent into captivity and slave labor; they are being punished, starved out, killed, without being able to defend themselves against it. They present a picture of complete powerlessness, and the German conquerors one of unlimited power. But as soon as one looks more closely, the picture looks entirely different. From Norway to Greece, from Poland to France, a resistance of the powerless is growing, against which every power of the rulers struggles in vain. Out of the powerlessness of the defeated nations is rising up a power whose shadow is even today darkening the light of the German victories that had seemed to glimmer. The German armies were strong enough to break the power of the enemy lands. But neither the German army nor the henchmen of the National Socialist reign of terror are able to break the power of powerlessness and its resistance. Where does this power come from that looks so completely different from the idol that the power worshipers revere? What are the roots of this power, about which there is no discourse in German schools, youth groups, and political training schools? It is the power of suffering for justice. The power idol that National Socialism preaches day after day and whose veneration is ingrained in the souls of German children has an adversary for which it is no match: justice. You know what the National Socialists have done with justice. They have said that whatever is of use to the German nation is just; they have sold justice into the slavery of power. But this seemingly powerless, enslaved justice is the strength that has risen up against them, that is spreading a power into all conquered and unconquered lands, and that has forced the Germans onto the defensive. For every Dutchman, Norwegian, Frenchman, or Serbian shot dead, many new ones are standing there to maintain the resistance against that power which is nothing but power. The British bomb attacks are being welcomed in the occupied lands, except when they kill their own countrymen. Hunger, even starvation, is preferred to being carried off into slavery. They refuse to place themselves on the side of victorious power, although they could have advantages from that. The few in the occupied lands who allow themselves to be bought by power lose, as traitors, every actual power and can exist only with the help of the conquerors. In all this, something is apparent that shows the limits of pure power more clearly than any theory. It is as if a lesson in the history of the world is disproving through practice what the German nation has absorbed in false theories. Power that is not united with justice is only apparently power and is, in reality, the deepest powerlessness; and justice that possesses no outward power is only apparently powerless but is, in reality, an invincible power. Why is this so?

To answer that, we want to consider how it actually came about that National Socialism came to power in Germany and how it could succeed in breaking any resistance, at least outwardly; because there was a moment in German history when many Germans believed that National Socialism represented the higher justice. And even if there was never a majority that thought in a National Socialist way, there were still countless people who longed somewhere in their souls for the victory of National Socialism. They thought that the injustice of the last peace would be transformed into justice. They thought that the injustices of the social order, above all the continuous unemployment, would be overcome. They believed that a German unity would be created on this basis and that the just claims of Germany in the world would be fulfilled. They gave National Socialism power because they believed that it would be the representative of a higher justice. And not only in Germany was this so but also in many of the now-conquered lands. There were influential groups within them who believed with most Germans in the injustice of the last peace and wanted to give the National Socialists a chance; indeed, even in the now-enemy lands, they thought this way for a long time and refused to create difficulties for the new German rulers. Through the beliefs of many that they would bring justice, the National Socialists came to power. Even the worshipers of power had to enlist the aid of justice. They did not want justice; they wanted power and nothing else. But they had to arouse the belief that they wanted justice; otherwise, they would not have achieved their goal, neither in Germany nor in the world. Yes, even today, they are still telling the German people that they have brought them a better justice than they would find in democratic lands. Even today, they are continuing to tell the European nations that they are fighting for a more just order in Europe. Even today, after they have trampled justice underfoot daily—in theory and in practice, in Germany and outside Germany—they require the appeal to justice for the sake of their power. But then; no one believes what they say today anymore. The sacrifices that they have offered to the idol of power—their own and their nation's—are crying out against them and are drowning out all intelligent speech among those who want to strengthen their power with declarations of belief in justice.

It is simply the case that the significance of power is not power but rather life! Power should protect life, by protecting the rights and being that every living thing has. A power that does this is life-creating, because it wants nothing for itself but stands for the just claim of everyone over whom it has power. Such a power is unshakable because it is built on the acknowledgment of all those who experience justice by it. As soon as this acknowledgment disappears, as soon as it is grasped that a power stands for arbitrariness and not for justice, its foundation is undermined. So it is today with the power of National Socialism. It is undermined, but of course, it is still not broken.

For the uncanny thing about power is this: once it is there, it develops tools that can continue to maintain it after its true foundation, justice, has disappeared. And then the time comes when it becomes particularly cruel, tyrannical, and bloody. Its bearers know that the foundations of their power have disintegrated. They sense that no one respects them any longer, that no one believes in the justice with which they want to adorn themselves any longer. But they still have the tools of power in their hands. And because they suspect that their power is coming to an end, because the idol of power is abandoning its worshipers, they are using its tools for ever-increasing oppression and, thus, for ever-greater injustice and, thus, for ever-faster self-destruction. This judgment is now coming to pass on the National Socialist power worshipers; it is coming to pass in the conquered lands; it is coming to pass in Germany itself.

Friends of the German Opposition: that is your hope! See to it that more and more Germans grasp that a power that has destroyed justice is surely no longer power, even when it still has the most enormous tools of oppression in its hand. Tell the Germans that the idol of power has turned against its worshipers today and will destroy everyone who stands with them.

15.
THE PUNISHMENT
OF WAR CRIMINALS

OCTOBER 20, 1942

MY GERMAN FRIENDS!

A question is being much debated at present in the general public of the Allied nations. It relates to the treatment of Germany after the war. And since the internal German propaganda uses this debate to give rise to fear of peace and hatred toward the Allies, I want to speak to you about it today.

It is the question of the so-called war criminals and their punishment. In the last weeks, the governments of the occupied lands in London and Washington have vigorously demanded that after the collapse of Germany, those who have worked as tools of an indescribable reign of terror in the occupied territories, and who are intensifying the terrors week in and week out, should be called to account. The Russian government has demanded the same for those who are active as slave drivers toward the inhabitants of conquered parts of Russia. The British and American governments have agreed to this: the president of the United States was the first to do this some weeks ago, with the qualification that he doesn't want mass retribution. We know that in all countries affected, lists are being drawn up of those who have been guilty of the command and execution of particular atrocities. And it is certain that it will not be the case, as it was in the last war, that the punishment of these criminals and their human tools will be set aside as impracticable. And that brings to mind the previous war and the results that the war-criminals paragraph in the Treaty of Versailles had on the Germans. Among all the difficult terms of the treaty at that time, this paragraph, as well as that related to the war guilt, made the strongest impression. They

wounded German sentiment more than the cessions and the pro-
visions for disarming. Even those who perceived the disarming
as a fortunate thing for Germany, as the liberation of Germany
and Europe from an intolerable burden, were struck at the time
by the moralistic condemnation of these paragraphs. It is easy for
National Socialist propaganda to awaken the memory of these
matters and to use them for the production of hatred and desperate battle goals. What can the German Opposition do to oppose
the use of the statements of the Allied nations about the punishment of war criminals in this manner? There is only one path: to
unite the will of the German people with the will of the Allied nations; to show the German people that the war criminals are actually criminals against everything that human dignity and
human hope signify; and, above all, to show the German people
that the war criminals are, first and foremost, criminals against
the German people.

This is really not difficult to show. Everyone among you
knows an endless list of such crimes against body and soul,
against the property and honor of Germans with whom you were
acquainted or friends or of whose misfortune you have heard in
a roundabout way. Every one of you knows the type of person
who is trained for these crimes and does them in cold blood and
with a clear conscience. And we all know that these are not the
lapses of individuals, which were disapproved of by all responsible people, but that it is a system that is concerned here. The
crimes of this war against the conquered are the continuation of
the crimes against the Germans in the years before the war. The
same system that has created the one has created the other. Because of that, everything in this war is so different from the last
one. The first land that was conquered in this war was Germany.
And countless are the victims of this conquest: hundreds of thousands of refugees; hundreds of thousands of people who have
died in concentration camps or prisons or who have been broken
in body and soul; hundreds of thousands whose existence, even
apart from the war, is destroyed, their consciousness of being human beings taken away, the sparks of hope that make life possible stolen from them. The same kind of people who did this to the
German people have now set upon the conquered lands — not the
fighting soldiers but those who followed them, with and without
uniform. In this group that walked behind the fighting armies are

the war criminals against whom the outrage of the world is directed and against whom the outrage of the German nation, which was their first victim, should be directed much more.[33] I mean those who are responsible for the shooting of innocent people and for the legal and illegal robbery of the property of others. Those who carry off populations—leading men and women into slavery, blotting out places from the earth, allowing masses of people to starve and freeze to death and waste away in concentration camps—are criminals. What they have done to you they are now doing to others.

And because this is so, why should any German hesitate to demand the punishment of these thousandfold criminals and—what is more—to take this on themselves, as soon as it is time? The German people should no longer allow there to be a lot remaining for the Allied nations to do.

When the lists of the criminals are published, it may prove that most of those named are nowhere to be found, not because they have hidden but because the judgment is already executed upon them. You, the German Opposition, should fill as many Germans as at all possible with this conviction. You should tell them that foreign nations will not sit in judgment over the German people but that the German people, in conjunction with the other victims, will sit in judgment over a powerful gang of criminals and their accomplices, that the Germans will begin this judgment and will carry it out as far as possible, even before the others arrive.

But perhaps many will ask, why punishment at all? Is it not enough, in the political struggle as well as in the war, to conquer and render the enemy harmless? Doesn't "punishment of political criminals" sound a lot like revenge; doesn't it recall the contemptuous acts of revenge with which the National Socialists pursued their earlier enemies, after their victory over them; and doesn't punishment of military criminals recall the military acts of revenge and extermination in the wars of earlier periods? Certainly, this question will be asked, and certainly, it will be used by the National Socialist propaganda, which would have a right to do so the least of anyone. Consequently, what can we answer?

Punishment is the form in which the violated legal system asserts itself against the one who has broken the law. Everything that the National Socialist criminals have done is a violation of the most innate law, of the most common instinct for the good and the

humane. Things that were accepted among primitive nations—the
sanctity of contracts; the protection of foreigners; the differentia-
tion between the combatant and noncombatant sectors of a population; the defense of the family; the respect for that which is
human even within the enemy, even among the accused and the
convicted; the maintenance of the law even in the face of the powerful—all of that has been systematically negated and trampled
under foot in National Socialism. Without doubt, there have always been periods of decay in which rulers have despised all divine and human laws. But still, these were only short episodes at
whose end stood downfall. What is being attempted today is the
fundamental and permanent abolition of ordinances, without
which a human group—and, more than ever, humanity as a
whole—cannot live. It is wrong to characterize that as a return to
primitive stages of humanity. That would be an insult to the primitive peoples. It is much more an attempt to create, with every
means of highest intelligence and technological maturity, a world
in which that which is human has disappeared. You all know the
faces of the storm troopers who march through the streets, ossified and dehumanized. They have been robbed of their personalities, their natural feelings, their own will and thought, their
conscience. And now they are behaving like cogs in this horrifying machinery that is incomparable in its destructive capacity and,
like every machine, incapable of creating even the smallest thing.
There is nothing like that in any primitive culture. Here and there
in history, something of the sort has been attempted, but there was
still too much of that which is human in the human being for it to
be able to succeed. Only National Socialism has dehumanized an
entire generation, step by step, with sophisticated methods. It has
cut it off from all natural human relationships, from everything relating to goodness, justice, truthfulness, and love. And in place of
human feelings it has planted fanaticism, hatred, contempt, cold
cruelty, and indifference toward their own life and toward other
people's lives. And with these instruments it has subjugated the
German people and then forced it to subjugate other nations. It has
attempted, with diabolical shrewdness, to draw all Germans into
solidarity with its crimes. Nothing pleases the National Socialists
more than when the entire German nation is pronounced guilty
abroad. But this pleasure is given to them by no one who is in a
responsible position in the Allied nations. Only some fools,

fanatics, and ignoramuses attribute the crimes of National Socialism to the entire German nation—no one else.

And now we understand why the war criminals must be punished: not out of vengeance, not because of the victories of German soldiers, but for the sake of the violated human dignity. It must be apparent from world history that no one can destroy the humanity within themselves and within others without exterminating themselves. It must be obvious that there are eternal laws that no one can violate without falling under their judgment. Not only the inhuman machine of death that National Socialism has created must be broken but also those who have created it, who have dehumanized the people and have diabolically reversed the world order. The punishment of the war criminals, in the first place by the German people and then by all remaining enslaved and wounded nations, is the response of the divine world order attacked by the National Socialists. It is the response of human dignity, which is trampled into the dust by the dehumanized instruments of National Socialism, first in Germany and then in all of Europe; it is the response of the community of human beings and of nations, which is struck in its innermost being by the National Socialists. It is the response of that which is divine in the world to the attempt to distort it into that which is diabolical.

16.
GERMANY'S PAST, PRESENT, AND FUTURE FATE

NOVEMBER 3, 1942

MY GERMAN FRIENDS!

Today, I want to speak of the German fate itself, not only of the present but also of the past. Because the fate of the present is determined by the past, just as the fate of the future is determined by the present.

The question of the German fate is all the more important when much is being spoken about the German character in the lands of the Allied nations. In wide circles, National Socialism is regarded as an expression of the German character. First, some days ago, a statesman in a responsible position delivered a speech in which he reproached the German nation for demonstrating its warlike, aggressive character during a century of continual wars of assault. Others are reproaching the Germans for the fact that their military ruling strata, the *Junkers* and their civil entourage, have been permitted to rule and to incite one war after the other over the centuries. The Germans are being reproached for having developed a submissive character that makes it impossible for them to engage in resistance to their governmental authorities, even when they are being led by them into war and destruction. And it is being said, finally, that this character of the Germans may express itself in German literature and philosophy. Yes, and what is more, Lutheran Christianity may show traits of this mixture of subservience within and militant spirit without. In many speeches and writings today, these thoughts are being conveyed. Through exhaustive investigation, people are attempting to prove this from history. All of this is being used for war propaganda, and plans for the future formation of Europe—and the role of Germany within it—are being built upon it. A representation of the German character has resulted in the world's public opinion, of which the German Opposition must know so that it can see what an immense responsibility for the German future weighs upon it. For if this picture is being sketched in the souls of the nations and is to remain there for generations, then woe to the German nation. Such pictures concerning the character of a nation are more important for the future organization of the world than any military means of power. National Socialism itself has set the most frightful example for that: the caricature that it drew of the Jewish people and that it has imprinted on the German youth has brought about the ruinous fate for the Jews. No decent German, and least of all anyone who belongs to the religious or political opposition, believes this caricature is true. And yet it has had an immense result. Why? Because for centuries, strokes of this picture have been imprinted on the souls of many Christian people, and a picture of the Jewish character developed in the unconscious of great masses about which they themselves were not clear. They would not have recognized it if people had shown it to them, and yet it operated within them and prevented them from offering a stronger resistance to the anti-Semitic hate propaganda.[34]

It is an irony of the world's history that, today, precisely the same thing that took place in Germany with the sketching of the Jewish character is taking place in the world with the sketching of the German character. The danger that is locked inside this is huge. It begins when this caricature of the Germans sinks into the unconscious depths of the souls of other nations and remains lying there, even when the war is long since past and the explosion of hatred that it is awakening is long since forgotten. It will then be successful in creating unscrupulous antagonism toward that which is German for an immeasurable time, using this unconscious aversion to everything German to turn a great, creative nation into an ostracized and despised pariah of humanity. And even well-meaning representatives of a chastening justice will say to the Germans that what they have done not only to the Jews for centuries but also to the Poles and Czechs for generations is being requited in this way. Images of Poles and Czechs have also been imprinted in terrible distortion on the German unconscious. And the result displays itself now in the barbaric treatment that the formerly innocent Germans have bestowed on these nations.

In all this, one of the most frightful tragedies of fate is being prepared; and nothing should remain untried to prevent this tragedy, as long as there is time.

First of all, I can tell you one thing from which you can see that a hope still exists that the greatest evil is being prevented: not all see the German character in the distortion in which it is being drawn by those who want to do with the Germans what the National Socialists have done with the Jews and the Poles. First, some days ago, the archbishop of Canterbury dedicated a large part of a speech to the question of the hatred of Germans and with the strongest words cautioned against that. And that is not a voice in the desert but the voice of the humane and most precious portion of the people of the Allies. Everywhere, there are still great masses whose unconscious is friendly to the German nation precisely because they regard it as the first victim of National Socialism. Another character sketch of the Germans can still be drawn within these souls; but sometime or other it may be too late, and then—I repeat it—woe to the German nation!

Character is fate. The German character is a result of the German fate. But character is also decision and therefore able to determine and to change fate. Will the Germans be in a position under the leadership of you, the present opposition, to free itself through new decisions from the curse of fate that lies over it? That is the question of the German future.

The German nation is situated in the middle of Europe, unprotected on all sides. Since the Reformation Era, it has been the war theater of Europe, first in the religious wars, then in the wars of the absolute rulers, then in the freedom wars. Germans and non-Germans live together in many borderlands. A national federation has been successful among the Germans for only seventy years. All of that was fate and determined the German character, and this character then determined fate anew in both world wars. A fateful cycle, a tragic interaction of fate and character. It must be broken in two, here and now! The fate that National Socialism has brought on the German nation must drive the German Opposition and, in its train, the German masses to a decision in which this tragic cycle is abandoned and a new period of German history is begun. As we are frequently startled by a new characteristic within individual people that is suddenly manifested and alters the entire character sketch, so it should take place with the

German nation. That is our great hope! The possibility for professional German-haters to carry on their craft must be prevented through a decision, an action, a new beginning of the German nation that no one can dispute. The militaristic features must be wiped out through a transformation that, with one stroke, alters character and fate.

And the same applies to German subservience. Even it has its historical roots: while innumerable petty states made a unified state impossible in the southwest, the Prussian state developed in the colonial northeast, which, under the leadership of the *Junker* class, created German unification and naturally imposed its character on the united nation. But even before, the feeling for personal freedom had been taken from the German people through countless minor princes and potentates. In distinction from the western countries, there has been no effective, revolutionary middle class in Germany. The German middle class wanted to be just like the German aristocrat, and the German laborer imitated the German middle class; and the German peasant has never recovered from the crushing consequences of the great Peasants' Revolution [also known as the Peasants' Rebellion]. That was fate, and that has formed their character. And character has then called in fate anew: the unresisting subjugation beneath the Nazi dictatorship. Here as well is a tragic cycle between fate and character. This cycle must also be broken in two if the German nation is to live. It will be almost more difficult to break than that between warlike character and warlike fate. The cycle between subservient character and the fate of becoming subjugated is so greatly bound with the German being that it will be like a rebirth if it is conquered. But that, more than all else, is the task of the German Opposition. They must show what the German character truly is: that it has the power for self-renewal; that the inclinations that one rightfully hates in the Germans do not determine the complete picture.

The fact that there is a German Opposition is, in itself, already a demonstration that the caricature of Germans is untrue, just as the caricature of the Jews is. The more visible the opposition becomes, the greater the revolutionary impact it wins, the faster that caricature will vanish. A German revolution against everything that holds the German nation in subservience and that has incited it from one war into the other would be that which breaks through the doom that lies over the German fate and that distorts the German character and has created the enmity of the world against it. Whatever form this revolution may have, however long it will take before it can become reality, it must come; and inwardly, it must be prepared today! It must not again be a simple collapse like that of 1918, when the character of the German nation was not changed. It would then lead to more evils, and the old curse would soon be revived. Germany needs a revolution that is both its rebirth and its victory over fate.

17.
DARK CLOUDS
ARE GATHERING

DECEMBER 1942

MY GERMAN FRIENDS!

One strike of lightning after the other is flashing from the dark clouds that are gathering over Germany. Are there still many Germans who are closing their eyes and their ears, like children, in order not to see and to hear? Or have they awoken, and are they looking with fearful anticipation at the inevitable? It takes courage to look destiny in the face; and many have still not done so, even when a destructive fate already has them in its claws. It takes superiority to see one's own downfall, to cover up nothing, to disguise nothing, and to meet it calmly and with strength. Only those who are able to see the new life beyond destruction can look destruction in the eye. Only those who can conceive beyond it and cope with it can give consent to their own downfall. I am speaking today to those among the German people who have such strength. I am speaking to you who are strong enough not to close your eyes and ears in the face of the violent storm that will soon burst over Germany from all sides. I am speaking to those who sense what is coming but who still don't want to know it, because they can't bear it. I am speaking to those who go on living from day to day, completely unconscious, and don't suspect that an end has come and that every German must know about this end. Because only if many Germans meet the downfall, which is unavoidably coming, is a new ascent possible for the German people. Only if many say yes to the destruction of that which is now being destroyed can the new develop. And for this reason we are calling out to you: open your eyes, risk hearing the truth, risk saying yes to the fate that is coming!

1942

There can be no doubt that a destroying fate is drawing near from all sides. When the offensive of this year came to a standstill in the mountainous ramparts of the Caucasus and in the wreckage of Stalingrad, long before the Russian winter had set in, a cloud had arisen in the east. None of Hitler's promises and no mass sacrifice of German men could drive it away any longer. Now it is standing on the eastern horizon, still far away from Germany. Already the first violent lightning flashes of the Russian offensive have descended from it and have—as acknowledged by the German military report itself—caused great destruction on the German front. And the cloud bank in the east is growing with every day! Can you close your eyes to that for much longer? Dare to see the truth!

And in the west, clouds are amassing, still far off, on the other side of the English Channel and—invisible and unimaginable for a majority of Germans—on the other side of the ocean. Out of the smoke of American factories and the boundless weapons that are pouring forth from them daily, the clouds are rising from which unending destruction will come over German people and German cities. Here and there, such a flash of lightning has already gone down, and the result has been a destroyed city and thousands of slain, wounded, and homeless people. When the violent storm draws nearer from the west, it will easily be hundreds of thousands and millions. Can you close your eyes and ears to this much longer? Open your eyes, dare to hear the truth!

And in the south, clouds have amassed in the heat of the desert sun and over the deadly waters of the Mediterranean. They have already brought more storms than those in the east and the west: it was a completely destructive flash of lightning that traveled down out of these storm clouds over the unfortunate divisions of Marshal Rommel. He could save only rubble, pursued day and night by the lightning flashes of the clusters of hostile planes; everything surrendered that was won in battles lasting for years. And at the same time, those unexpected flashes of lightning came out of an apparently clear sky, those flashes that plundered the Axis forces in Africa, as a whole and with few exceptions. They foretold the storm that is now brewing from the south against a weak Italy and, with it, against Germany's southern front. Open your eyes, dare to hear the truth!

And there is a fourth place where the storm clouds of fate are gathering against Germany: they are growing out of the mists of hatred that the German conquerors have drawn toward themselves in all conquered lands! Here and there, storm clouds have already been discerned—in the Balkans, in France! The sinking of the French fleet in Toulon was the first heavy flash of lightning that has gone out of this cloud.[35] Not only that, it deprived the German fleet of a powerful addition. That is important but by no means the most important thing. The most important thing is that, through it, France has finally found itself again, and when it found itself again, it found itself on the side that is fighting against National Socialist Germany. All attempts of the "Lavals,"[36] who wanted to rob France of its great revolutionary tradition, have failed. The truce is broken. France's equivocal role has come to an end. The old France is newborn and stands on the side of the democracies. This is perhaps the most disastrous flash of lightning that has struck the National Socialist enemies of the spirit in the battle of the spirit. Open your eyes and see what the ship ruins in the harbor of Toulon are saying to you! They are the moral judgment on the new order of National Socialism! They signify its end. They show that it is something different to conquer lands than it is to win people. What the German armies have conquered the German executioners, who followed closely on their heels, have lost. Out of the mists of hatred that the executioners have generated, sinister clouds are gathering. Out of them, the most disastrous flashes of lightning will descend. Listen to that, German officers and soldiers, German laborers and civil servants! Hang the hangmen who are bringing the hatred of the world upon you and who are worse enemies for you than the hostile armies in the east and west and south.

It is a frightful picture that presents itself to the perceptive German today. I understand why many are unable to see it, why many go numb when they see it. And still I must call out to you: dare to say yes to the fate that is approaching you! Because even if it is a downfall, it is a better fate than that under which you are now standing. It will be justice even if it is tribulation, while today is injustice even if it is power.

I haven't spoken yet of the worst matter: of a crime that Germans are committing daily; of a crime against humankind such as occurs only once in millenia; of a crime that means blood guilt for generations for those who are doing it and for those who are tolerating it. The place where it has been taking place, for months and with ever growing cruelty, is Poland. The victims are hundreds of thousands of innocent people who have lived among you, whose neighbors and friends you were, with whose children your children played. And other hundreds of thousands are being sacrificed whom you don't know, who have never done you an injustice, who have led a life in poverty and, frequently, in great purity and piety. And today they are being hauled away to mass death by German hangmen, by those who are the trash and the disgrace of the German people, and you are standing by! Can you stand by any longer, German officers, when you still have a sword to use and an honor to lose? Do you know that in France, when these unfortunate ones were supposed to be handed over to the German hangmen, all the churches became united for the first time in centuries in order to prevent staining the French name with this manhunt? Do you know that the parents whose children were exempt from going along to Poland were handing them over to strangers on the sides of the streets in order to save them from the death that was otherwise certain? Picture, in your souls, these mothers, and calculate the guilt that you are incurring when you are eyewitnesses to it! Do you know that the cattle cars that roll through the German cities with this burden of wretchedness are bolted up for days; that no bread and water is let in, no dying or dead are let out; and that at the end of such a journey, frequently over half of the deportees are lying dead on the ice-cold floor of the car? And you want to continue to be spectators of that, German clergy, you who are praying for German victory? And do you know that in Poland itself, women and children, old men and the sick are being driven together and being shot down with machine guns? That German physicians are found in the camps who inoculate their victims with air bubbles in order to kill them in the most certain and inexpensive way? A shriek went throughout the entire world in these weeks when reports about that came together from all sides! The world is truly growing accustomed to depravity, and yet it listened and cried out when all of this turned from a rumor into an established fact. I can tell you that the hearts of many who sympathized with the truly repressed Germany became numb and hard in these days.

I have spoken of the dark clouds that are gathering from the east and west and south over Germany, and of the misty clouds of hatred that are associated with them. But worse than all of that is the heavy cloud of blood guilt that has been brought upon the German people by the National Socialists and that will lie over them even when the first guilty parties have long since perished. Their downfall has begun, and no one can stop it any longer. But their guilt will burden the nation that has become its instrument for a long time.

18.
WHERE HOPE LIES
THIS ADVENT SEASON
DECEMBER 8, 1942

MY GERMAN FRIENDS!

We are in the Advent season, the season of waiting and expectation! In years gone by, hope filled the hearts of children and thoughts of love the hearts of adults in these weeks before Christmas. Even if people felt distant from childlike beliefs in the Christmas story, they couldn't remove its charms, and they looked forward, with the children, to days of light and joy and human warmth. How is it this year? What do you look for in this Advent season? What is your hope, your expectation? It is a dark Advent season this year, darker than any that the German nation has experienced in this war. On all fronts, the clouds are amassing out of which the storm of impending years will burst forth. Everyone who knows something of the events of the war in Russia, in Africa, in Asia, on the sea and in the air cannot doubt for a moment that the turning point has been reached! The next months and years will slowly grind down the power of the Nazi armies, and no sacrifice that is being forced on the German nation can change anything about it. But the Advent season surely announces the coming light and not the growing darkness, the coming salvation and not the coming destruction! What does such an announcement have to say to the German nation today? Can you feel today what you once felt in the weeks of Advent? Do you have anything to which you can look? People cannot live if they have nothing for which to hope. So we want to reflect with one another on the question: to what can Germans look today? For what can they hope?

There is one group among the Germans that has nothing for which to hope and has nothing to which they can look other than death! They are those who, by inhumanity and cruelty, deprived millions of others of every hope. They are the executioners and torturers of National Socialism, who turned death into the object of desire for countless people in Germany and the conquered lands because there was nothing more in life on which they could look. For these murderers of fortune and life, Advent, that is, "the coming," is nothing but the coming of judgment! Relentlessly, inescapably, it is closing in on you who are guilty with respect to the misery of the innocent and the shattering of life's fortune for millions! You, the National Socialist executioners and torturers, can look only to the verdict that is already being pronounced upon you and whose sentence is death! It is pronounced upon you in the hearts of those whose fortune in life you have destroyed. It is pronounced in the will of those who bear the sword of justice against you. It is pronounced in the world order that you have violated and whose vengeance you cannot escape. That is the judgment message of the Advent season. And whoever continues to hear it—and has not yet participated in the blood guilt of National Socialism—should renounce National Socialism even today! Many of you are standing on the boundaries. You don't want to have anything to do with the crimes of National Socialism, but you also don't have the courage to say no. And so you are being implicated and are coming close to the danger of falling to the same judgment as the true perpetrators. Renounce your loyalty to them!

What should you look on in this Advent season; where does a hope lie out of which you can live? That is the question we have asked ourselves. And the first answer was: there are many in Germany who have nothing to which they can look other than judgment and death. Moreover, Advent gives hope even to the wrongdoer: to be sure, not for this life, in which a chastening judgment befalls them, but for eternity, in which there is forgiveness and salvation even for the most grievous sinner! Nevertheless, such a message won't be understood by those who rule the German nation today. They don't want to know anything about that which lies beyond death and which can even give hope to the criminal. They understand only death, and they will be struck by it with irrevocable justice. Many among them already understand that today, and their anxiety before judgment's arrival is driving them to ever new crimes and ever deeper despair.

What should you look upon? What is your hope? There is still another answer to this question, other than that of the hopelessness that must be given to the National Socialist executioners! There is still something that the German nation can look to, still a hope out of which it can live. Surely, the Advent season of this year is the arrival not only of judgment but also of salvation. Even as dark as everything is that you see in the present, in the future shines a light on which you can look in the spirit of the Advent season. There is still a hope available to the German nation!

Certainly not the hope with which many looked on the rise of National Socialism, misled by passions, interests, folly, and self-deception! These hopes were buried, by many people earlier, by many later; only a few are ignorant enough to maintain them today. The rebirth that National Socialism promised the German nation was a rebirth into evil and destruction. It was never an Advent hope and can never become one.

The hope for every vision that was founded on German victory is also shattered: a homogeneous Europe, led by Germany as part of a complete world unity. If there was ever such a possibility, the German nation has forfeited it in this war. When it gave itself into the hands of the National Socialists, it ceased to fulfill its mission in Europe and the world; it isolated itself from the rest of humanity and, out of its isolation, gave rise to a war of conquest that brought it the enmity of the greatest part of the world and the implacable hatred of all the conquered nations. The initial military victories are no longer a basis for hope. They have not united but divided. They have not created but destroyed, first the rest of Europe and now, slowly but surely, Germany itself. The light on which you can look isn't found here. Here there is only darkness.

The hope that remains for the German nation lies beyond the collapse of its false hopes. Just as it is in the life of the individual, so it is in the life of nations. Nothing is more difficult and more painful than such catastrophes of hope. But at the same time, nothing is more purifying! And the hope of Advent is given only to those who have gone through such purification. I believe that National Socialism was the outbreak and the concentration of nearly all that was diseased within the German soul. Long have these poisons accumulated within it. In the great crisis of the 1930s, they won the upper hand and shook the German nation in frightful, feverish convulsions. It was an illness that could have led to death. But it is my conviction that the deepest power of the National Socialist poisons is broken. The German nation began to eliminate them, even if with the assistance of serious intervention from outside. It would have been good for Germany and for the world if these interventions had not been necessary, if the soul of the German nation would have eliminated the National Socialist poison by itself. It was too weak for that, but now the purification has begun. And that is the light on which you can look in all the darkness of the present: a purified nation!

But, you will ask, is that still possible? Won't intervention from outside completely destroy us? After everything we have gone through since the First World War, do we have the strength for rebirth? It is easy to answer the first question: no one in a responsible position among the adversaries of Germany wants to take hope from Germany. They want to prevent a similar, all-destroying sickness such as National Socialism from breaking out once again. They want a healthy Germany, which has found itself again and therefore can find the world again and therefore can be found again by the world. The faster you expel the poison that is still shaking your body, the faster intervention from outside will come to an end, and the more certainly a new Germany will grow out of the ruins of National Socialist Germany. It is that to which you should look. That is the German Advent hope, the only one that has remained for you as a nation.

And I do not doubt that Germany has the inner strength for this rebirth. It is sometimes good to look into one's own past in order to draw courage from it for the future. No nation in Europe has a greater past than the German nation. Scarcely any nation had encountered so frightful a misery as the German nation did after the Thirty Years War. And still it rose from the dead. It has shown that it has powers of rebirth. It has them even today. Although made defenseless by the National Socialist poison, the soul of the German nation is stirring in impenetrable depths and is regaining the powers from which it once lived. Even in this year of darkness, there is a German Advent. There is a light in the future on which you can look. It is a hope available to the German nation!

19.
THE FOURTH ·
WAR CHRISTMAS
DECEMBER 15, 1942

MY GERMAN FRIENDS!

How are you celebrating the fourth war Christmas of the Second World War? Most of you will still remember the fourth and final war Christmas of the First World War. Many will think back on restless nights in the rain, the cold, and the fire on one of the fronts in the west and the east. Many will think back on poorly lit Christmas Days, with hunger and with worry about home. And everyone who can still think back will remember how, from one Christmas to another, the lights became darker, the heart colder, the despair deeper. Isn't there a similarity in this war? On the first war Christmas, certainty of victory and an expectation of good things. On the second war Christmas, triumph and disappointment that there was still no end in sight. On the third war Christmas, the shadows of the Russian winter and of the one hundred thousand–fold dead, the joy of victory dampened and anxiety deepened. And on this, the fourth war Christmas, the sense that there is no victory to anticipate and no end to foresee, or perhaps the fear that a terrifying end is imminent. Why does it have to come to that again? Why was the "never again," which we all extolled with all the world at the end of the last war, in vain? Where did this agonizing repetition of the same fate as that of the previous war come from? Why are the shadows of death and grief again in nearly every German house? Why is there again want and privation? Why is there again anxiety and despair? Why is there all of this once again?

Christmas Day can give an answer to this hollow, piercing "why," a simple and yet all-encompassing answer: because people have renounced the message of Christmas! The German misery of the fourth war Christmas is the misery of a nation whose leaders have attempted to extinguish the light of Christmas. It was the folly of the German leaders that plunged the nation into the First World War. It is the crime of the German leaders that plunged the nation into the Second World War. Folly and arrogance dragged the ailing nation into the First World War from one war Christmas to another. Crime and delusion dragged the ailing nation into the Second World War, now already to the fourth war Christmas.

The crime of National Socialism is a crime against the child in the manger; it is a crime against that which is most fragile and most profound in humanity, the love that gives itself for another. Certainly, there has never been a time when love alone ruled; that is impossible in this world. There has always been violence and injustice and falsehood. The human has always contended with the inhuman. But only rarely, since the first Christmas, have people consciously struggled against the message of Christmas. Only National Socialism has consciously and decisively placed itself on the side of those who persecuted the child in the manger, that is, the messenger of love. Only the National Socialists have advocated hatred and ridiculed love. Only they have consciously placed injustice on the throne and disdained justice. Only they have extolled falsehood, in print and in speech, and held the truth up to ridicule. Sometime read Hitler's *Mein Kampf,* if possible in the first edition, in the light of the Christmas story! Then you will grasp why the German people have to live through the misery of a fourth war winter for the second time. The German nation is experiencing endless suffering once again because it has turned itself into the instrument of those who persecute the child in the manger. It has surrendered itself to force, not the force that is necessary to defend justice but rather the force that tramples all justice underfoot. And now, more and more, it is becoming a victim of the force that it has unleashed and that is turning against it. No one can transgress the child of Christmas unpunished. He is the image of the Divine in humanity. And whoever wants to destroy the Divine in humanity ultimately destroys themselves.

Now, in this Christmas season, when you look back on the years of Nazi rule, isn't much becoming clear that remained unclear before? Perhaps you have frequently not understood why the churches have led such a passionate defensive struggle against

National Socialism. I know that many among you reproached Pastor Niemöller and his friends for unnecessary stridency and for interference in politics. "Haven't the National Socialists dealt with the churches in a way that is completely lenient? They have permitted them to exist, despite all the restrictions. The Christian message can still be proclaimed every Sunday. There is still a Bible and a hymnbook in most homes. Why," many Christian people have asked, "do they have to carry their opposition to that extreme? Why not make a compromise? Has the martyrdom of Niemöller been truly necessary?" So you may have continued to ask recently. Today, in the light of the fourth war Christmas, you can no longer ask that. Today, it is clear why those men have struggled and suffered: for the sake of the salvation of the German people from the spirit that has led them to ruin. Not only have they attempted to save the church, they have attempted to save the nation from the dominion of the enemies of Christmas. Niemöller and all who have struggled with him are seeking to preserve the Christian Christmas for the German people. Today, when the trouble that the National Socialists have brought on the German people is becoming so visible, everyone must understand why and for what the churches have fought and are still fighting.

You have heard, perhaps only by hearsay, that the struggle over the Christmas message is raging in the whole of Europe. All churches in the occupied lands, especially in Norway and Holland but also in France and the eastern countries, are fighting against the spirit of National Socialism. Of course, there are traitors to the Christian proclamation, just as there have been in Germany, but the great majority of Christians everywhere have kept free of that. They have grasped — in the German as well as in the foreign churches — that there is no communion of those who bow before the child in the manger and those who call the blood of the Nordic race holy. All of you who have celebrated Christmas in your youth, who are preparing Christmas for your children, who still have a feeling for the warmth and depth of the Christmas message, you must decide in this fourth war Christmas: do you want to continue on the path on which you deny and persecute the child of Christmas? Do you want to continue on the path that is leading Germany and you to ruin? Or do you want to turn back and find the child in the manger once more and celebrate a genuine Christmas with your children and loved ones?

You can't have it both ways. Whoever follows National Socialism must persecute the child in the manger. Whoever obeys the Führer who has become a *Führer* (leader) unto death must turn aside from the star that points to Bethlehem. Whoever respects power above all else must despise the powerlessness of the child in the manger.[37] Whoever preaches hatred must disparage the love that gives of itself, must disparage Christmas. You cannot celebrate Christmas and believe in National Socialism. You cannot serve Christ and the Antichrist!

If the fourth war Christmas, with all its infinite suffering, has shown the German people the decision, one way or the other, between Christmas and National Socialism, then it has done something great; then it has laid the basis for German rebirth.

Christmas is the festival of children, because it is the festival of the child of Christmas. Nowhere is the calamity that National Socialism has brought on Germans so visible as in the children. It has murdered the souls of the children, just as Herod—the persecutor of the Christ child—murdered their bodies.[38] The churches, in their struggle against the National Socialists, have fought above all for the souls of the children. Many brave teachers in Germany and in the subjugated lands have struggled along with the churches for the salvation of the children from the National Socialist poison. In their lessons, everywhere in the German countryside, loyal caretakers of the souls of children are trying to weaken the poison that they have to administer to the children. They are attempting, within the limits of what is possible under a tyranny, to keep awake the forces of opposition among the youth. The Christmas message has not yet completely faded or been distorted into its opposite. There are still teachers and students who know not only war heroes but also the child in the manger, who was set apart for the purpose of showing a new heroism on the cross, that of sacrificial love.

German parents! What do you want to say to your children when they ask you for the Christmas message? Can you tell them, and explain to them, the Christmas story? Can you do it without falsehood? You can't do so if you're unable to tell them that the words here are something different from what they hear daily and hourly. German parents! In this fourth war Christmas, show your children that there is still another path than that which leads to blood and tears and misery. Tell them that today, in all the world, people are making their way in spirit to the child of Christmas, in spite of war and hatred and mutual murder. Tell your children that in all hostile lands, children are worshiping the child of Christmas, who is equally near to all and equally loves all people. Overcome the spirit of hatred that is being sown daily in your hearts and those of your children with the spirit of love, the spirit of Christmas.

All Christians, all true human beings in all nations, want your community, my German friends. They want to celebrate Christmas with you in the spirit that is more powerful than all discord. They seek you and your children. They want to snatch you from the claws of those who revile love and shatter community and persecute the child of Christmas. Cut yourselves loose from them and celebrate the fourth war Christmas as the festival of love that can save you and your children and your nation after the sermon of hatred and violence has driven you into the night of this fourth war winter.

20.
A Guiding Light in the Darkness of the New Year
December 1942

MY GERMAN FRIENDS!

The end of the year is approaching. In several days, 1942 will have become history: one of the most important, most decisive years of the world's history. By coming generations, 1942 will be remembered as the year of the great turning point! Until the middle of this year, the united powers of fascism were engaged in victorious aggression. Since that time, they have come to a standstill or have been routed everywhere. The Allied nations have acquired the power to take the offensive, and it doesn't look as if they will lose it again. Even as strong as the fortress of Europe may be, even as powerful as the German defense still is, it is the defense of a besieged fortress, and the question is only: how long can it still be held? The question is no longer: can the fascist powers be victorious? This question was clearly and definitively answered by the year 1942: an Axis victory lies outside the realm of possibility!

But with this great turning point that the past year has brought, other changes have also taken place. The end of the old year directs the eyes toward the new year and awakens the question: what is it we are heading for, and what is it that we should do in light of that which is approaching? How deep will the darkness of the new year be, and where is the light that can guide us in it? One thing is certain: it will be a dark, infinitely hard year. Not only will it be hard in the sense of those who demand ever new sacrifices of you, but the new year will be hard in the sense that the meaninglessness of all your sacrifice will become evident. The new year will bring you the assurance that the war is hopeless and that all sacrifices you bore for the sake of victory were fruitless. And although you will comprehend the hopelessness more and more, you will nevertheless have to surrender the last thing for . . . what? Yes, for what? A question without answer!

But what if you could give a different turn to everything? What if you Germans who hear these words would fight for something that is not hopeless, something for which it would pay to fight and to sacrifice? Could your view on the new year not become a view on a new society, on a new humanity, on a new life of nations and of individuals? I believe this war, like every great turning point of time, has not only the pain but also the bliss of birth within it! Something new will come to be in many nations, not only a new year but a new period of history. Even in Germany the new will come to be; not the new that National Socialism promised and that was a return to the most ancient of all things. Not the new of National Socialism, which is a revival of pre-Christian, even prehuman, instincts. Not the new that acts as if it is superhuman and is, in reality, subhuman. What National Socialism brought was a revival of the most ancient powers, of prehistoric, long since subdued urges and thoughts. It was enmity toward the spirit, toward pure humanity, toward the dignity of the individual person. This enmity is ancient, as old as the nature from which the spirit has liberated itself. When, in the year 1933, National Socialism gained sovereign authority over Germany, humanity and spirit lost one of their greatest battles. The powers of the most ancient past triumphed when Hitler gained power! Nature had conquered the spirit, the subhuman had conquered the human, when the National Socialism of fools and criminals obtained the weapons to persecute the spiritual and the human. In all of this, there was no future; all of this was the elevation of that in the human which should have always remained in the past. National Socialism is breathing down the necks of people and nations like a monster of primitive times. The acts of terror into which it forces its bearers are like a bloody legend of antiquity. People with humane feelings don't believe something like this can happen today. Yet the reports about the one hundred thousand–fold murder of innocents by every monster of antiquity are irrefutable. Consequently, they are terrified in the depth of their soul. We had all believed that what is inhuman in people could still appear only in rare exceptions. We didn't anticipate that it could become present in millions of people. But now, the prehuman past of our species has become present. Now, it wants to rob us of our future.

There will be no future for the German nation until the prehuman monster—National Socialism—is slain. There will be no future for Europe until the "ancient dragon" of which legend tells is conquered: the dragon that is a picture of the prehuman past that rises up and devours the human culture. Woe to the person, woe to the nation that entrusts itself to this dragon, as the German nation has done for a decade!

That is the look into the past for which we must be prepared in this new year. Only then can we look into a future other than that which National Socialism wanted to give us. And that's what we wanted, that's what we must do in order to live.

I see seeds of rebirth among the ruins of the past. I see humanity's arising once again beneath the covering of the inhumanity of our time. Not only will the new year bear a number other than the old, it will also have another character. It will become a year of expectation for the future.

Everywhere that is evident: what only a few people did in past war years—to think about what should come after the war—is now being done by many individuals and groups, volunteers and representatives, states and churches. A public opinion is developing that can be decisive for the formation of peace. And in this public opinion and the proposals out of which it is fed are contained seeds of hope for the future—not only for the future of the Allied nations but also for the future of Germany. It is a lie of National Socialist propaganda when the future is portrayed to the German nation as mere darkness. It is mere darkness, to be sure, for those who are responsible for the murder of innocents, the executioners and torturers who have violated the German name. But for the German nation, it is not only darkness but also light. Ever wider circles of the Allies are becoming united about three matters. The first to be done after the war is to save the European nations from hunger, widespread illness, and mutual destruction. Already, tremendous preparations are being made through which European chaos can be prevented and the foundations of a new Europe laid. The question asked by so many Germans held captive by Hitler, the question "What shall take his place?" is already being answered in its main features for the years after the war. You need not see an abyss before you when you look on the coming year and the collapse of the German armies. The victorious nations will not come in order to take the very last thing you have, as the National Socialists have done in the occupied lands. Rather, they will bring you something so that you will be able to live and begin anew. That is the first light in the darkness that lies before us.

The second is the will of the Allies to create an order of nations in which freedom and security are united. It is not the National Socialist order of Europe that they take for the model, where there is security, to be sure, but at the same time slavery. That is easy, but it is beneath human dignity. Nations don't want to pay for security with the loss of freedom. They want an order of the world that is more secure than that which plunged the world into two wars, but they don't want an order of the world in which there are ruling nations and subjugated nations. That is the hope that Germany has, the only one that is left to it. If the Allies were to apply the principles of National Socialism to the German nation, there would be no German future. But it is precisely against this that they are fighting. They want to take even Germany into the order of freedom and security that they want to create. They understand that the new order is impossible without the assimilation of Germany into it. That is the second light in the darkness that lies before us.

And the third is the struggle for social reorganization after the war. You can hardly construct yourself a picture of how strong the struggle concerning these questions is in America and, above all, in England. You won't be permitted to understand anything about that by thinking that only National Socialism can give social security. But as with the external, so it is with the internal: security with slavery is easy to give. But security united with freedom—that is the great question. And all progressive intellects of the world are striving after it. Government commissions are making proposals that, even a few years ago, would have been unthinkable. The social reality will look different after this war than it did before it. And that is the third light in the darkness that lies before us.

German people, in the new year don't look backward, look forward! Much darkness lies before you; the fate of the world has changed in the past year. It has turned against National Socialist Germany but not against the true Germany. Lights are perceptible in the darkness of the future, three lights: salvation from the abyss of collapse; a new community of nations; a more just social order for all that provides security without loss of freedom internally and externally. Those are the lights that shine forth out of the future.

1943

For Tillich, 1943 was the beginning of the end of the war. The destruction of the German armies in Stalingrad and North Africa, the reduction of the U-boat threat, and the stopping of the Japanese advance in the Pacific reinforced the promise of an eventual Allied victory.

Tillich hoped the victory would translate into social security for the European masses and into some form of a European federation that could ensure democratic evolution for Germany. He had suggested these ideas in The Protestant 1941 and 1942. In 1943, they were the subject of three addresses Tillich presented to the Federal Council of Churches Commission on a Just and Durable Peace, chaired by John Foster Dulles. Tillich's dynamic philosophy of live and ever-shifting configurations of power, expressed in religious-socialist terms, were critical of the Dulles vision of an American-imposed structure of peace. Both Dulles's and Tillich's hopes, however, were thwarted by the inability of the United States and the Soviet Union to cooperate after the defeat of Germany.

Tillich's radio addresses emphasized the nature of German collective guilt for tolerating or encouraging the Nazis. Other peoples had guilt as well. But Germans had allowed Hitler to capture the country and plunge Europe into war; they had accepted the Nazi racial policies, death trains, and murders of Jews and many others. The ultimate destruction of Germany, Tillich believed, was atonement for the evil into which the Nazis had led that nation. He pled for Germans to find ways to resist Hitler and to join in their own liberation.

Tillich heard the condemnation of the Fascists and Germans in the shouts of liberated Italians, who gave the Allied troops bread *and flowers. He wanted the German people, the first conquered, to do the same—to separate themselves from their Nazi overlords, to resist them, and to assist in Germany's defeat in the war.*

Despite short-lived German military gains in counteroffensives on the eastern front, Tillich insisted to his listeners that German hope for victory was gone. He welcomed the Allied plan to subject German authorities to the processes of justice in the countries where the crimes had been committed. He saw in it a promise of rough justice, not just revenge. The following addresses from 1943 strike themes of Allied victory as liberation, German guilt and destruction as punishment, the need for war-crime trials, and hopes for a restored Europe.

During this time, Allied bombing leveled German cities, burying and burning civilians and destroying the works of a thousand years of civilization. Plans for the invasion of France in 1944 were laid, and England and the United States began joint development of the atomic bomb, agreeing to defeat Hitler first and then Japan.

Behind the lines, German losses in war were matched by increasing atrocities in areas under their rule. The Jewish Holocaust continued. Partisans in the occupied territories and resisters at home were either hounded by the Gestapo or targets of special antipartisan operations. German students Hans and Sophie Scholl were arrested and executed for their resistance activities in February. German theologian Dietrich Bonhoeffer and his brother-in-law Hans von Dohnanyi were captured in April. In May, two ruthless operations were launched by the Germans against Yugoslav partisans, with the improbable goal of destroying Communist partisan leader Josip Tito's organization.

The Germans repeatedly committed "village atrocities" as retribution for local support of partisans: Lidice (near Prague), Khatyn (near Minsk), Kuklesi (in Greece), and Michniow and Karpiowka (both in Poland) were some of the places removed from the map, their citizens murdered by the occupying forces for furthering the cause of liberation. No longer confident in Germany's ultimate victory, Heinrich Himmler ordered the destruction of any evidence of the Holocaust. But the genocide continued. Tillich reminded his German listeners of the policies of atrocity and begged them not to support this evil.

21.
WHO
IS GUILTY?
JANUARY 1943

MY GERMAN FRIENDS!

As we looked back, at the end of the old year, on the historical events that we have experienced firsthand, consciously and
perhaps with a share of responsibility, a serious and difficult
question arose: I mean the question of guilt with regard to the
frightful occurrences that have come upon our generation. Who
was guilty regarding the First World War? Who was guilty regarding the overthrow of the empire, regarding the floundering
of the German republic, regarding the emergence of the National
Socialist worldview? Who was guilty regarding its victory and
the duration of its rule? Who is guilty regarding the Second
World War, regarding the bloody ferocity with which it is being
led and the worldwide dimension it has acquired? All of these
questions of guilt hang together. Today, no one can come close
to answering them. Certainly, no one can answer them completely. And yet it is of infinite importance for the war and for the
conclusion of peace that the question of guilt find a proper answer. The question of guilt must be answered so that the causes
of the misery of our time can be removed, whether they be institutions or people. The question of guilt must be answered because the ethical world order demands that the forces of
destruction themselves be destroyed.

In Germany, people frequently have the feeling that the question
of guilt is a pretext to give the victors a good conscience for smash-
ing the conquered to pieces. And now look at German propaganda:
they are repeatedly assuring that it is others who are guilty for
everything—first the German republic, then the Bolsheviks, then

the democracies, always the Jews, sometimes the capitalists, sometimes the communists, sometimes the churches, and sometimes the intellectuals. But always, somebody is guilty. There is no speech of the Führer and no propaganda speech in Germany in which some group or individual is not given responsibility for something or other! No one works more with accusations of guilt than German propaganda. The National Socialist speakers who scorn and tread underfoot all moral laws constantly use the ethical sense that lives in every person. When they speak of guilt, they testify—against their will—in favor of the power of ethical consciousness. Thus, since German leaders themselves put the question of guilt, it is ludicrous that they want to forbid the same by others. The question of guilt must be put; it has been put by the Nazis, and it will be put by the Allies.

The question of guilt encompasses many questions, questions that go back as far as the First World War and further, to the roots of our modern culture. But now, one question stands in the foreground: the question concerning guilt in the present war. Today, I want to speak with you about it. One can speak in different ways about war guilt. One can do it like boys after a quarrel, where each one reproaches the other, blaming the other one for starting it. Even nations behave in this way. Sometimes it is even possible to establish who has started it, for example, which boy first insulted the other or which army first crossed the borders. That is sometimes important to know. It is important to know that Germany first crossed the borders of Poland, Norway, Holland, Belgium, Serbia, and Russia. It is important to know that Japan first crossed the borders of China, Indochina, and the East Indies. It is important to know that Italy first crossed the borders of Ethiopia, Greece, and France. It is important to know all of that, because in that way, it is outwardly clear to the natural sentiments of all people that Germany, Japan, and Italy are the aggressors. No one who has witnessed the invasions of Germany into neutral countries and into Poland and Russia—by treaty half-friendly to Germany—can doubt who bears the responsibility for this war. And the same applies to the Japanese assault on China, on the Dutch colonies, on America. If the question were asked, "Who started it?" then the answer to the guilt question would be easy. In all cases, the Axis powers first crossed the borders. In all cases, they bear the primary responsibility for the bloodiest of all wars! No German propagandist can deny that.

And still German propaganda maintains that others are guilty. How is that possible, since it is surely apparent to all that they are the aggressors? And how is it possible that many Germans, Italians, and Japanese believe in the guilt of others? We want to examine, one after the other, the reasons for the Allied guilt that are stated by the Axis propaganda. Then we will find that not only the outward responsibility but also the actual guilt lies with the Axis powers.

The first reason is generally no reason but rather a system of lies. When the Italians wanted to invade Ethiopia, they created a few incidents and declared themselves threatened by unarmed natives. When the Japanese wanted to invade China, they created an incident that was somewhat greater and speak even today about the "Chinese incident" instead of the war with China. When the National Socialists wanted to invade Poland, they assembled a system of lies about Polish attacks on German border inhabitants; when they wanted to occupy Norway, Holland, and Belgium, they told of preparations for attack by these exemplary neutral and completely unprepared countries. The only interesting thing in all of these lies—which everyone saw through as lies—is the question: to what end? Why not simply attack instead of doing so as if the assault were defensive? Why this expenditure of falsehood? It is the obeisance of the National Socialists to a moral world order, which they cannot acknowledge but to which they must show consideration. It is the concession that there is guilt and, moreover, that they themselves are guilty.

Another reason the propaganda of the Axis powers uses to shift the war guilt from itself is that England and France delivered the declaration of war against Germany and that Germany's peace overtures to these powers were rejected by them. It could be answered, thereupon, that, indeed, Germany and Italy declared war on America, Italy declared war on France, and Japan declared war on America and England. But it is more important that the German attempts to keep peace with England and France took place after the entry into Poland, and that Poland had received the guarantee from England that an attack on Poland would be regarded as an attack on England. When Germany attacked Poland, it understood, thereby, that it was attacking England. And England's declaration of war was an answer to this assault. The guilt of Germany in this war cannot be shifted in this way either.

German propaganda understands that and, for that reason, is using other, more deeply striking thoughts to shift the guilt from Germany. They speak of a battle of those who "have" against those who "have not." They portray the war as a revolution of the proletariat against the capitalist nations. That is certainly difficult to prove when one thinks about Russia, the Balkans, China, and even France and Norway. Germany was, by far, economically ahead of all these countries; and the standard of living of the German masses was, in most cases, better even than in England and many parts of America. And when the great economic crisis came, it struck the rest of the countries, and even America, just as sharply as it did Germany. The National Socialists conquered Germany at the moment in which the high point of the economic crisis was crossed and a natural process of recovery had begun. They interrupted this process, because it was contrary to their interests, and compelled first the German nation and then the entire world to employ the fruits of the greatest portion of all human labor for machines of destruction. They brought the same misery upon those who have as they did upon those who "have not," in order to win power over all. No one can absolve the National Socialists from this guilt.

And so, they are attempting to shift the war guilt from themselves with a final reason. They say that they represent progress and that all other nations—Russia and America and the British Commonwealth—are reactionary. They say that war exists because the powers of reaction want to repress the progressive. But what progress has National Socialism brought? Was it an advance in equality and security? But why, then, the war against Russia, where all of that is much more thoroughly accomplished? Or was it an advance in freedom and human nature? But why, then, the war with America, where this has been the foundation of life for a century and a half? Or was it an advance into a new international order? But why, then, the destruction of the League of Nations and all international law? Not will-to-progress but will-to-power has driven the National Socialists into war. Not against a new world but against the subjection of the world have the nations of the world united.

There is no path onto which National Socialism can shift the war guilt from itself. It alone is guilty. It will enter into history with this guilt. For the sake of this guilt, history will judge it.

22.
MOURNING
FOR STALINGRAD
JANUARY 1943

MY GERMAN FRIENDS!

There is mourning throughout Germany. Not only in a majority of German homes; that was so long ago. Nearly every German family grieves over one who is dead, held captive, or injured. But now, Germany as a whole has begun to grieve. The three days of mourning for the defeat at Stalingrad were the beginning of a mourning that will no longer cease, until a new Germany is born out of the wreckage of that which is crumbling. How should you, my German friends, view these days of mourning? How have you observed the three days of mourning that were ordered? How will you view the days of mourning that will follow, one after the other, in ever quicker succession, all the same, whether or not they are officially commanded as days of mourning? I wish I could speak to you person to person about what this last, most difficult period of the world war means for you! The three days of funeral marches and lowered flags and diminished confidence were the entry into the final period of the war. With what feelings are you entering into them?

To be sure, many among you will have asked yourselves: why this emphasis on the defeats in Russia? Why is mourning commanded when the final victory should be secure for us? Why the description of the terror of the Russian war and the dangers for Germany, when Russia was recently pronounced to be conquered? All of these questions must come to every one of you and fill you with uneasiness. What will be done with us; what do the black pictures mean; what do the days of mourning mean?

I will attempt to give an answer to these, your restless questions—not in order to calm you but in order, first, to disturb you even more deeply, and then, perhaps, to show the path to a genuine calm.

In the days of mourning for Stalingrad, the frightening question that lived in the secrets of most of you was brought into the open: what has taken place? This question is not only asked publicly but has also been answered publicly: evil has taken place, such evil that a three-day mourning period of the entire nation was brought about. Now everyone understands it, now everyone can say it—and by doing so it has lost its sting. It no longer secretly gnaws, it no longer has the charm of hidden knowledge, and it no longer produces the anxiety of doubt. Instead of tearing the nation apart, for a moment it brought the nation closer together through common grief. All of that was shrewd! But was it more than that? Can the public acknowledgment of defeat, can common grief dispel the restlessness that lives in every German heart? Certainly not! Because the restlessness that torments all of you truly springs not only from the question "What has taken place?" and from the painful answer to it! The restlessness within all of you springs just as much from the question: What will come to be? This question has also been put in public and has been answered in public. The answer was: difficulty will come. Difficulty on the battlefields, difficulty at home, suffering unequaled will be demanded of you, of the armies, and of the nation. Everyone senses that it is so, that it is an inescapable fact that it must come about in this way. And everyone is most profoundly disturbed about it. In secret, you understood that long ago. Now it has been publicly articulated. The situation is dark and is being painted in dark colors. But precisely because this is being openly articulated and brought to light, it loses something of its darkness and is easier to bear than the gnawing anxiety of doubt. That was also shrewd. But was it more than that? Can it dispel the restlessness that dwells within your hearts? Certainly not!

You know that no method, no matter how wise it may be thought to be, can cure your restlessness! Because your restlessness is the foreboding of that which must come and will come. And for this reason, days of mourning and black pictures can give you relief for a moment but are ineffective in the long run. For the black in which it is painted is the truth, and the grief that is demanded is justified. Even the days of mourning, even the black paintings, were intended as falsehood. But they are the truth. And for that reason, they can soothe for a moment but not for the duration.

For what have you grieved in the days of mourning for Stalingrad? Have you grieved for dead, injured, captured Germans? But you would have had to grieve for them since the attack on Russia. Have you grieved for the great number of victims? But there were more victims in the failed assaults on Moscow last winter. Have you grieved for a military defeat? But such there are in every war, and they are not taken as cause for days of mourning. In truth, you've grieved for something completely different: namely, for Germany's catastrophe. Germany's catastrophe is not a military defeat, just as numerous military defeats hardly meant catastrophe for England or Russia. They did not take them as catastrophes. They observed no days of mourning, but they are fighting on and turning the defeat first into determined resistance and then into victory. Germany's catastrophe is as little the military defeat at Stalingrad as the military defeat at Dunkirk meant catastrophe for England and the military defeat at Minsk meant catastrophe for Russia. Germany's catastrophe is that the defeat at Stalingrad was the expression of the coming defeat of Germany in general. Everyone sensed that. Even the National Socialist leaders sensed that. And for this reason they set the days of mourning, which were, in reality, mourning over the German fate. Those among you who have grasped this have had the proper mourning. The others haven't understood and have only numbly sensed that for which they were mourning.

With the days of mourning for Stalingrad, the German nation has begun the days of mourning that will not end until the rebirth of Germany. But precisely for this reason, grief is not the end. And precisely for this reason, there is a joy that overcomes grief and a hope that is able to sustain above the restlessness.

You are mourning over Germany! So you say, but is that actually so? Is that actually necessary? Certainly, Nazi Germany must perish. And on the smoke-stained walls of Stalingrad's ruins the inscription appeared in fiery letters: "Weighed, weighed, and found wanting."[39] That applies to Nazi Germany! But does it apply also to Germany? No! Germany is not being weighed and found wanting, but rather the class that first conquered Germany and then Europe and is now being pushed to its limits! The grief for the dead of Stalingrad, the victims of a sacrilegious prestige policy, is at the same time grief for Germany; nothing is more justified than that. All the same, it should not be only grief for Germany. It should also embody joy for Germany, that now Germany will be liberated from those who have thrust it into its misfortune and its disgrace. The mourning that the German nation has to go through all of this inexpressible misery is justified. But even more justified is the joy that now, for the first time, the possibility of a German rebirth has become evident. Germany had permitted itself to be turned into the instrument of tyranny, from which it could no longer free itself, after which it was fastened into chains by it. Other, more powerful victims of this tyranny are on the point of freeing themselves and the German nation. That is the hope that lies in the German darkness of these days. You could not free yourselves. Now you are being freed. The sacrifices that this requires are not being spared! No one can take from you the grief over the fact that you have become an instrument of the National Socialist powers of destruction. Whoever is possessed by evil spirits suffers when higher powers free them. He is sad that evil spirits have seized possession of him. But at the same time, he is happy because the hour of deliverance has come.

This is the way you should feel, my German friends! The days of mourning should be dedicated to mourning the fact that the German nation had fallen into the hands of powers that have led it into shame and misery. The days of mourning should be days of mourning over the triumph of National Socialism in Germany. But at its foundation, there should be a joy and a calmness that comes from the fact that, now, the beginning of the end of these powers has come. You should have the calmness of one who knows he has gone through the fire and has become someone else and has nothing more to fear. A Germany that has gone through the fire and is delivered from its evil spirits has nothing to fear.

23.
The Tenth Anniversary of Hitler's Regime

February 1943

MY GERMAN FRIENDS!

The tenth anniversary of the Hitler regime has arrived. Yesterday it was celebrated. But it was not a day of jubilation as it was ten years ago, when the torchlight processions before the palace of the reichs-chancellor announced the beginning of a new period of German history. It was a new period. But was it a period that justified the rejoicing with which it was begun? Today, after ten years, the entire German nation understands that not rejoicing but mourning was brought about when Hitler was appointed reichs-chancellor. Today, after ten years, every German understands that no second decade, not even a half decade more, is ordained to National Socialism. The tenth anniversary of the Hitler regime is the dreariest day in these ten years for the regime and all who have supported it. It is a day of retrospect, but not a day of prospect. Because in the future lies darkness, and nothing but darkness for all who are responsible for the last ten years of German history.

What have these ten years brought to the German nation? Destruction unequaled in the entire German history! Never, not even in the horrors of the Thirty Years War, has so much of that which is most precious among Germany's good qualities been destroyed as in the decade of Nazi rule. I could speak for a long time about the economic destruction that the rearmament and the war brought. For ten years, the entire German nation labored for only one goal: to forge weapons of war. For ten years, Germany has been transformed solely into a manufacturer of weapons. All labor and all raw materials have been used for this one aim: to create instruments of death. Only the bare necessities of life were produced. The standard of living declined from year to year, and it will decline even further, because weapons manufacturers cannot produce bread; and the factories that are functioning for the purpose of producing the daily needs of life are being ruined more and more each year by mismanagement. And no one can compensate for them. Because weapons, more weapons, has been the only demand for ten years.

I could also speak extensively about political destruction. From the first year of Nazi rule, all political forces that were troublesome to the dictatorship were wiped out or suppressed. At any period of German history, there were diverse powers whose balance constituted the greatness and richness of Germany.

Certainly, division is a peril. But just as great is the peril of a unity that means the destruction of all diversity. When there is no critique, no longer a counterweight, when dictatorship devours everything into itself and tolerates no life beside itself, then it destroys itself and the nation. Arbitrariness and tyranny replace wisdom and balanced justice. Dictators grow into insane pretension, and the masses are robbed of the capacity to think and to will politically. Everything that the German nation gained in past decades and centuries in terms of political experience and education is wiped out. And along with the political consciousness, the sense of possessing rights has been destroyed. Through countless breaches of the law, the National Socialists came to power. All guarantees of the law have been stolen from the German person. It isn't the one who's wrong who's culpable but rather the one whom the dictatorship wishes to annihilate. There is no refuge from the multiple arms of the Gestapo, from the caprice of the Nazi powers, from the wickedness of informers. Step by step, German law has been transformed into a weapon against the rights of Germans. What centuries in the great development of the law created has been destroyed in ten years.

Further, I can speak of the destruction of human prosperity and life in the last ten years. It began with the extermination of minorities and the plundering of their possessions, and it is ending with the victims of the Second World War, in which the German nation is bleeding to death. Just now, decrees have become known that force even sixteen-year-olds into war service. Moloch, the god to whom the sons of the nation are brought as sacrifices, is opening wide his jaws, and millions of German youngsters and men are vanishing into his fiery belly.[40] The war machine was constructed in six years, a war machine intended for the destruction of the life and fortune of countless German people. And now—since the war's onset—it is going through the land, murdering everything that comes into its path, not only the men on the battlefield but also the women and children in the cities. No one can calculate how many human values National Socialism has destroyed in the ten years of its rule, while it destroyed the people who were its bearers. The German nation has become infinitely poorer in creative people since 1933. Many of the greatest ones are abroad. Many were murdered in the first years. So many of the youth have been crushed in their creative development. Many, countless, are decaying on the battlefields. It will last many a decade before the human destruction is again repaired that the one decade of Nazi rule has brought on the German nation.

I could speak of the destruction of the ethical world in the ten years of Nazi rule. After Hitler lifted up the falsehood regarding the path toward rule by the masses in his book, the truth and truthfulness have been persecuted on all paths. In these days, the German nation is looking back on ten years in which the truth was persecuted and truthfulness destroyed. Every falsehood passes as true when it serves the aims of power, and no truth is permitted when it is contrary to the goals of the ruler. The truth is persecuted in political life. Everyone who ventures to articulate it imperils his life. Only in the deepest secrecy can it even be heard and said. The truth is persecuted in daily life, at the market, among friends, within the family. Only rarely can neighbor entrust the truth to neighbor. Only rarely among friends can there be a free discussion concerning the truth. Only rarely can parents say what is in their hearts in front of their children. And the truth is persecuted in the studies of scholars and in the classrooms of the university. It is persecuted in the studios of artists, on the stages of theaters, in the books of authors. The treasures of the German culture and the creative powers of the German intellect are being subjugated to a deadly prior censorship, and every power of dangerous truth is being wiped out. And the truth is being persecuted in the schools. Only under constant danger and constant disguise can teachers plant seeds of the truth in the hearts of children and can children ask for the truth. The truth has been persecuted for ten years in the German land, and truthfulness has been punished for ten years among the German people! But along with the truth, even [a sense of] humanity has been destroyed among an entire generation! Perhaps this is the greatest evil in the picture of the ten years on which you are looking back: that the sense of people's dignity is being exterminated in countless Germans. Two thousand years of German education out of barbarity into humanity have been taken back. The chivalry of the Middle Ages toward the enemy is forgotten, but the cruelty of the Middle Ages has arisen again and has brutalized the hearts and trampled all nobility underfoot. The humanity of the classical age of Germans is being made contemptuous, but the warlike instincts of the German past have become intensified beyond all boundaries. The other is the enemy; this feeling has been hammered into German youth. Now the "other" has truly become the enemy. The possibility of a human community has sunk beneath the German horizon. "German Being or Human Being" has been imprinted for ten years onto the Germans. And thus, many Germans have ceased being human.

Those are the results of ten years of Hitler rule over the German nation: destruction everywhere! What is being destroyed beyond the German borders, of that we cannot speak today. What is being destroyed inside Germany will require a century of restoration. It is an evil picture that has appeared before our eyes on the tenth anniversary of the Nazi regime. It is the picture of an immense, self-inflicted catastrophe upon a great, noble nation. It is the picture of the immense destruction of that which is the most unique and that which is the best, that which a nation acquired over a period of two thousand years. It is a picture over which the German people will grieve for generations. It is the picture of the lowest ethical and human point in its entire history. It will be seen as its darkest period.

24.
THE GERMANIC
LEGACY
MARCH 2, 1943

MY GERMAN FRIENDS!

Lately, we have often spoken about the German future. The great change in the war from the offensive to the defensive first gave cause for this, and then the retrospective view on ten years of Nazi rule. I want to continue the discussion about the German future and reflect with you on what forces can shape the German future. At the same time, I want to disregard everything that will take place on the outside, from the side of the victors and beneath the pressure of the whole world situation. Today, it is more diffi-cult than ever to say anything about this, although never has so much been said and written about postwar organization since the beginning of the war. But all of that is not ultimately decisive for the future of the German nation. What is decisive is what forces within the German nation itself will come forward. What is deci-sive is the extent to which there is still within Germany a pri-mordial will to live. And what is decisive for the German future is the strength with which the German nation finds its way back to its authentic inheritance.

It is necessary for the Germans to find their way back to their past. National Socialism was a historical breakaway[41] without equal. Seldom in the history of the world has there been such a total renunciation of everything that was precious, great, and holy in a nation. Seldom in history has a new species of person been so intentionally and so successfully created that no longer had a connection with the past. The younger National Socialist, bear-ing its imprint, has nothing in common with anything at all that existed in the German past. He is German only to the extent that he is born of German parents on German soil and uses a garbled German dialect. Otherwise, there is nothing German in him. He is a product of the Machine Age, in which all authentic traditions were annihilated. The young National Socialist is himself nothing but a part of a machine that has sacrificed his mind, soul, freedom, and humanity. Never has there been such an un-German type of person on German soil as those whom National Socialism has created. Never was Germany less German than today, when worship and sacrifice are being offered to it on bloody altars. There can be no German future if Germany does not find its way back to itself, if it does not expel the distorted, un-German, inhumane content of National Socialism, just as a body that has regained health expels harmful foreign substances.

After the war, Germany will be politically powerless, economically weak, intellectually wrecked, spiritually wretched. That is the destiny which National Socialism has brought on the German nation and by which it is now already unavoidably gripped. The future of Germany cannot be rescued by eluding the misfortune that the National Socialists have drawn near. For that, it is long since too late. Whoever is building the future of Germany on shrewd methods and political tricks—for the sake of avoiding catastrophe—is building on nothing. Only those among you who clearly see how inescapable the external disaster is can become master builders of the new. They will begin to build even now, but on a basis and at a depth where external misfortune has no power. They will create the human building stones and the spiritual forms from which the edifice of the German future must be built. I want to speak with you, today and in the future, about how these building stones and building forms of the German future must look.

But beforehand, I must ask another question: are there still enough people among you whose will for Germany to live won't be broken by past and future catastrophes? Is there still a strong will to live and a will for the future in the German nation? This question will become more urgent the more visible the dimension of destruction becomes! The German will to live will be more at risk the greater the burden of suffering, a burden that everyone must bear to an increasing degree. The very things that the Nazis have brought—the false revival, the insanely exaggerated expectation for the future, the false fanaticism for Germany—will force the opposite. From exaggerated hope will come exaggerated despair. That is the danger that everyone must see who believes in a German future! Can it be overcome? Is the will to live stronger than the deadly fatigue that will set in on countless people? See to it, you who hear these words, that it doesn't become powerful within you and within those who think and fight along with you. If that were to happen, there would no longer be a German future. The Germans would be like the fellahin, those tribes that fell from the high Egyptian culture, in whom all creative power died out! Shall that be the German future?

There are three foundations on which the German culture was built in the past: the Christian, the human, and the Germanic. Each of these great forces of German history is like a river that has taken up many tributaries into itself, which have then mixed with one another and have produced something unique: two thousand years of German history. National Socialism wanted to cut the German people off from these springs. It wanted to destroy the foundations of the German culture: the authentically Germanic in the same way as the universally human and the otherworldly Christian. The great legacy of the past was reviled and crushed underfoot. The spirit of the sons was set against the spirit of the fathers, not in the way in which every generation must seek its own path but rather in the sense of completely turning away. But it is an old truth that every human group must perish when it can no longer renew the springs out of which it has risen. A German culture cut off from the springs of the German culture is a phantom. It is condemned to quick destruction! Already, we are in the midst of the decay of the culture that National Socialism has artificially created and that it wanted to impose not only on the German nation but on the whole of Christian Germanic Europe.

Permit me to begin with something that will perhaps surprise you: the turning away of National Socialism from the Germanic legacy and the need to return to this legacy. Germanic is more than German. It embraces nations of different languages and histories. But they have common features that have nothing to do with blood and soil but have sprung from the earliest experiences and have expressed themselves in early cultures and thought forms. These common features are neither better nor worse than those of other national groups. But they belong to the Germanic legacy, they are the best of this legacy; and the Nazis would have never been able to overrun Germany if the Germanic legacy had not already been partially squandered. I am thinking of three qualities: chivalry, the need for freedom, and spiritual depth. When we cite these three things and look at the picture of some typical National Socialists, we know what has been lost. Chivalry toward weak people, which belonged to the highest virtues of Teutonic knighthood, has been completely reversed into its opposite by National Socialism. From the outset, they sided with the stronger battalions, pursuing and wiping out the weak. What is done to helpless prisoners, women, children, defenseless Jews on the part of National Socialists smacks in the face of any, however limited, chivalry. It is the desire for human degradation, abuse, and elimination of the enemy that the National Socialists extolled to the German people as German and that they have imprinted on the German youth. Chivalry is strength coupled with nobility. National Socialism is brutality coupled with lust for revenge and a deep inner weakness. No one in the whole of German history has less right to call themselves German than those who have consciously replaced Germanic chivalry with brutality.

Another inheritance that has been squandered and replaced by its opposite is the need for freedom. Whoever knows the Germanic peasants of all periods knows that an indomitable will-to-freedom is characteristic of them. All ruling classes that have passed on over these peasants have not been able to suppress their desire for independence. It was no coincidence when the great philosopher Hegel—in his observations about world history—said that the Germanic tribes have the duty to put into practice the idea of freedom in the world.[42] And what have the National Socialists made out of this task? They have forced an entire nation into a state or party mechanism, in which every remnant of freedom is annihilated. Never in history has there been such a machine of oppression as the National Socialist system. In Asiatic despotism, under the principalities of the Middle Ages, and under the Russian czars, there was infinitely more personal freedom than the individual German has today and had even before the war. There is no longer freedom when children are taught to spy on their parents and neighbors make it so that every free word among themselves is impossible. No one in the whole of German history has had less right to call themselves German than those who have converted freedom into total slavery. No one contradicts every Germanic tradition more than those for whom the individual person is only a part of a horrifying, all-entwining machine.

And the third inheritance of the ancient Germans is the spiritual depth that is visible in the creations of the German past and that represents the greatness and danger of everything German. A glance at the corruption of the German language by National Socialism, at the shallowness of its semi-intellectual products, at the inferiority of its symbols and ideals shows what kind of breaking away from the past is taking place there. Nothing is more un-German than the forms of expression of those who are the priests of German idol worship.

You who form the core of the German future, return to the Germanic legacy of the German past: chivalry, freedom, depth!

25.
THE CHRISTIAN LEGACY

MARCH 8, 1943

MY GERMAN FRIENDS!

The last time, I spoke of the fact that there is only one path for German rebirth: the return to the strengths out of which the German nation has lived and has become great. There are three currents that have gushed forth in the life of the German path: the Germanic, the Christian, and the universal human. We spoke the last time of the Germanic element and found that it was chivalry, freedom, and depth that the German nation received from its Germanic heritage. And we made ourselves aware of how this Germanic heritage has been squandered by the National Socialists, how chivalry has been turned into vindictiveness, freedom into bondage, depth into the prattle of propaganda. We have seen how National Socialism has betrayed and shattered everything that was authentically Germanic with its worship of the Germanic race. And we have realized that a German reconstruction is possible only if the Germanic legacy of chivalry, freedom, and depth is again acquired.

Today, I want to speak of the second current that has poured forth into German history: Christianity. At the moment when the Germanic tribes stepped into world history, they became Christian. And since those days of mass migration, the history of Christianity has become an important part of German history. In the Middle Ages, the German kaisers fought with the Roman pontiffs for the position of highest protector of Christendom. In the Reformation, it was a German monk out of whose struggles of conscience a new period of church history burst forth. In the new age, it was German poets and philosophers who strove for the union of Christian ideas with universal human forms of life. The attempt of National Socialism to detach the German nation from Christianity is the attempt to sever it from its entire history. The Germanic spirit can find no fulfillment without the Christian; and Christianity needs the Germanic essence for its world-historical mission. There are also other great Christian nations: Romance, Slavic, and—more and more—even Asian ones. But if German, Nordic, and Anglo-Saxon Christianity were nonexistent in the world, then Christianity would cease to be a world-historical power. And if one were to imagine Christianity as nonexistent from the history of Anglo-Saxon, Nordic, and German tribes, then the deepest and most creative things growing out of these nations would decay. Whoever is an enemy of Christianity is also an enemy of Germanic culture. When the ancient Germans accepted Christianity, they didn't submit themselves to a strange power but, rather, they found their most characteristic reality, that which gave them fulfillment and meaning. The ancient Germans did not find something unfamiliar but rather their deepest and their best when they became Christian. All movements of the German past testify to this.

And they all are being reviled and besmirched by the National Socialists. To dispose of Christianity, one must sacrifice the entire German past. Because without Christianity, that past is unimaginable for one moment. National Socialism is sacrificing the German past because it hates Christianity and because its spirit is repugnant to everything that two thousand years of Christian culture have brought to the German nation. And National Socialism has to hate Christianity: Christianity is the embodiment of all that is hostile to Nazism, and National Socialism is the embodiment of all that is hostile to Christianity. They are like fire and water. And the attempt of the "German Christians" to unite the two has led only to the water putting out the fire. Under the German Christians, the nationalist tide has completely extinguished the still-blazing sparks of Christian fire! It is a fortunate sign that the "German Christian" movement has continued without success; it shows that there are still forces in Germany that are not consumed by the surging waters of anti-Christian nationalism and race worship. Among those who have rejected the so-called German Christianity are many who were themselves hardly conscious of their Christian spirit but who sensed that the

National Socialist battle against Christianity threatened to destroy what was holy even to them.

When I speak of the return of the German nation to Christianity, I don't mean the return to dogma and ecclesiastical forms. As important as both are for many people—and perhaps will be for more people in the future than in the last century—the German nation as such cannot effect such a change. This is already impossible, because there are different churches with different dogmas and because great masses of the people no longer have access to an ecclesiastical and dogmatic Christianity. It is not a question of that but rather of the Christian world and life perspective, which is powerfully present even where people are no longer interested in ecclesiastical Christianity. Otherwise, why did the National Socialists declare war on Christianity? Because they clearly saw that Christianity was a spiritual power even where people didn't profess it! The National Socialists sensed that the Old Testament belief in justice and the New Testament belief in truth and love lived in the hearts of the masses who did not know much of Christianity.[43] And for that reason, they sought to sever the German nation from Christianity. They knew very well that the influence of Christianity on the German nation could not be measured in numbers of churchgoers. These numbers were small when the Nazis came to power. They have grown since the attack of the Nazis on the churches began. Nothing has helped ecclesiastical Christianity more than the enmity of National Socialism. And nevertheless, that is not the decisive thing. That these outwardly weak churches were able, from century to century, to train the German nation in the Christian spirit is the crucial fact. And when, in the previous century, the masses wandered away from ecclesiastical Christianity, they did it for the sake of the great ideas that they themselves had learned from Christianity: justice, truth, love. First, National Socialism started the battle against them and—for ten years—trained the German youth for injustice, falsehood, and hatred. The return of the German nation to Christianity means, therefore, the return of German youth to justice, truth, and love!

Justice is the discourse of the great prophets of the Old Testament. They proclaimed the God of justice for all nations and all classes. They threatened that their own nation would perish if it should forget justice. They were the deadly enemy of the religious nationalism of the Jewish rulers and were persecuted by them, as everyone today is being persecuted who fights against the religious nationalism of the German rulers. The National Socialists are fighting against the Old Testament because they are fighting against the spirit of justice that speaks there against Jewish nationalism, just as it does against every other nationalism. Every nation that condemns justice is itself condemned. A generation of young people that no longer knows what justice means is, by that very fact, destined to take the path of death. And we see how, with desperate defiance, it is taking this path. The path of injustice is the path of death. Only when the German nation finds its way back to the justice that the great prophets have proclaimed does it have a future.

And the return of Christianity is the return to truth. In the anti-Christian Bible of many Germans, in Hitler's *Mein Kampf,* a doctrine of falsehood has been worked out that contradicts everything that Christianity has said about truth, in the Old as in the New Testament. The praise of untruth is one of the most dreadful poisons that has flowed into the souls of young Germans. People for whom every lie is permitted—if it takes place in service of their cause—people who no longer inquire if something is true—when it is said by the Führer—people who cannot distinguish truth and power must be caught in the net of the falsehood they are serving. The German leaders have already become entangled in the net of their lies. Slowly, the German nation and the German youth are awakening and seeing, with horror, that their eyes were blinded. The truth is triumphing, and the German nation can live only if it finds its way back to the truth, as dreadful as the truth may look.

And the highest thing that Christianity has brought is the message of the New Testament, the message of sacrificing love. You know that it has been replaced by the National Socialists with the message of hatred, but a manufactured hatred. The hatred that the hate-message and the hate-acts of National Socialism have manufactured is so immeasurable that everyone who loves the German nation and its great past trembles for its future. Hatred can be overcome only through love. And this is the path that the best people in the German nation must find: the path to love, to the message of Christianity. Only then will there be a German future.

26.
THE HUMAN LEGACY

MARCH 16, 1943

MY GERMAN FRIENDS!

Previously, we had presented ourselves with the question: from what forces is a German rebirth after the coming catastrophe possible? And we had answered that this is possible only from the forces that have sustained German history until now: the Germanic and the Christian and the universal human. We have seen how Nazism squandered and corrupted the Germanic and Christian inheritance of the German nation. Today, we want to speak of the universal human legacy and to ask what National Socialism has made of it; and we want to consider what you, the ones who are responsible for the German rebirth, can make of it.

The universal human inheritance—*Humanität,* as it was called by the great German poets—came to the Germans as early as the Christian one did. And it came into the most intimate relationship with it. When Germany became Christian, at the same time it opened itself to universal human principles and ideals. Early on, the Christian and universal human currents united themselves. Then they poured forth together into the Germanic current, and the great centuries of German history began. In all of these centuries, Germany was more than a narrow, national state. It didn't stand for itself but for world-encompassing Christendom. It gave to other nations what it had, and it took from other nations what they had. No limited nationalism disturbed the exchange of creative thoughts. Germany was a crossing point of east and west, of south and north. The powerful Hohenzollern, Frederick II, was one of the first who saw the universally human in different nations. Ever since, it has formed a part of the German inheritance to stand for that which is human, for humanity. This inheritance was established as true centuries ago. In the Reformation, Germany gave its best not for itself but for the world: it discovered the inner freedom of the conscience that belongs to every person and that no church and no state can take from him. What has National Socialism done with this inheritance? It has trampled it underfoot!

And then came the time of the great German poets and musicians and philosophers: of Goethe and Beethoven and Kant![44] They had one thing in common: the belief in that which is human in the person, the belief in humanity. Every word of the German classics breathes this spirit, which sees the human within the person, which recognizes the dignity of the individual person and is borne by the belief in that which is human. "Every human affliction punishes pure humanity," says Goethe's Iphigenie. Beethoven composed *Fidelio,* in which the universal human triumphs over tyranny and the dungeons open up before the voice of humanity. When will the dungeons of National Socialism open up before the same voice? Schiller, through the words of Don Carlos, raised the reformative demand of freedom of conscience—a voice that is banished from the stage today. Kant spoke of the universality of moral law, which lays equal claims on everyone, just as the starry sky becomes visible to every person in every land and brings the grandeur of human existence to consciousness for him. He knew nothing of a German starry sky with a German reason and a German moral law; he would be condemned to silence today. And Herder's book about the *Spirit of Hebraic Poetry* or Lessing's *Nathan the Wise*—that great play about humanity against religious and national fanaticism—wouldn't be printed by any publisher today. National Socialism has reviled the human idea and has attempted to wipe it out. It has driven out the spirit of a hundred years of the highest German culture. It has disfigured and destroyed that which is human in the human being. How has it come to this? Prophetic Germans since the middle of the nineteenth century have observed, with restlessness and horror, the barbarity brewing in the German sky: one of them has said people will descend from the human to the bestial over nationality. With the coming of National Socialism, what is being prophesied here has begun: the age of bestiality, the age when human dignity is stamped out, the age when that which is human ends.

There are three things that are relevant to humanism, to the human being as human: reason, human dignity, and humanity. These were the three stars that hung in the sky of the great German century and that have now disappeared behind the gray clouds and the murky fog of National Socialist barbarity.

Reason as a human characteristic does not mean that all human beings think and act sensibly. No one has ever asserted that. No democracy, however fully executed, has believed such nonsense. Reason in the human being means that the human being — and indeed, every human being — has the predisposition to think and to act sensibly. No person, neither sex, and no race is excluded from this. Every person is capable of understanding the difference between true and false, between just and unjust, between good and evil, between believing and lack of belief. The significance of education today is to develop these talents and to turn all people into true human beings, into characters who follow reason, who listen to their consciences, who struggle for truth, who have a sense of the holy in life. The intellectual leaders of Germany struggled for such an education since the earliest times and particularly in the classical period of the German spirit. National Socialism has done everything to destroy the belief in reason. In place of reason it has set the will-to-power. The education for reason is replaced by the education for subordination beneath an all-embracing machine, which is itself guided not by reason. but by will-to-power. The human machine of the storm troopers is the greatest antithesis to the developed human being of the German classics. It is a dehumanized person, an object that others have at their disposal; it needs its reason not in order to develop it but in order to renounce it. National Socialism is the betrayal of humanity because it is the betrayal of reason. German rebirth is possible only when the reason of those who have preserved their own reason — in this time of German insanity — return to power.

Because the human being has reason, it has dignity; its human dignity is based on its rationality. When National Socialism had destroyed reason in Germany, it was an easy thing for it to trample human dignity underfoot. There are few places in the entire history of humanity in which more sin is being committed against human dignity than in the German concentration camps. But the grave thing, and, for the German future, the disastrous thing, is that the degradation the National Socialists have committed on their victims is based not on chance or hatred or malice but on conscious denial of the human dignity in every person. The distinctions of friend and enemy, of higher and lower race, and of strong and weak masked the common characteristics present in all people for many Germans who were not malicious by nature. They could no longer see that every person—even the enemy, even the weak, even the foreigner—has the same personal dignity that they themselves have. They degraded themselves when they degraded others! It will cost much blood and many tears before the sense will again awaken in the German youth that everyone who has a human face possesses a dignity that we must acknowledge, if we do not want to lose our own dignity. How many powerful words there are in German literature and philosophy that give evidence of the dignity of the person, even within the most ill-bred specimens! When will the hearts of Germans again open up to hear these words? One thing is certain: only when it comes to that will there be a German rebirth! Only Germans who know about the human dignity possessed by every person can become bearers of a new Germany. The German youth must be taken back to this inheritance; otherwise, it will be destroyed forever.

And the third thing that makes the person human is this: that he is a member of the human race. I will speak another time about what "human race" will mean after this war, what it will mean for Germany. Today, only one sentence: Germany must be born again into the human race. Otherwise, there will be no German rebirth.

27.
GERMANY'S REBIRTH
INTO THE HUMAN RACE

MARCH 23, 1943

MY GERMAN FRIENDS!

Germany must be born again into the human race. We said this the last time, when we spoke of the forces by which the German past was fed. These were the streams that made German history: the Germanic, the Christian, the universal human. National Socialism has cut the German nation off from all three. But most of all from the third, the universal human—from reason, from human dignity, and from the human race. We spoke the last time of reason and human dignity in the German future. Today, we want to speak of the return of the German nation to the human race.

Germany must return to the human race, because it has always belonged to the human race, because it can't exist without the human race, and because the human race is maimed without Germany.

Germany always belonged to the human race before the Nazis cut it off. There was always a lively relationship between Germany, Europe, and the rest of the world before the Nazis ended it and withdrew to themselves, in order to pounce then upon the rest of the world. Many threads went back and forth connecting all European nations and—through them—connecting all the nations of the world. And Germany was one of the intersections of the strands in this human fabric. Germany gave and took. It was one part, and it sensed itself to be one part, of a larger whole. German knights of the Middle Ages felt themselves to be a part of the great Christian knighthood that was native to all Christian nations, which had the same ideals and the same rules of chivalrous behavior. German monks felt themselves to be representatives of the all-embracing Christian culture, for which they worked according to the same rules as the monks of all other Christian nations. And merchants of the German Hanseatic cities, in exchange with the merchants of all other cities of Europe, created the splendor that delights us still today when we go through their cities. In those great centuries, Germany belonged to the human race, and the human race belonged to Germany. What a miserable effect the arrogant, foolish, narrow-minded nationalism of the Nazis is having on this!

That Germany belonged to the human race and that, for this reason, the human race was open to Germany can be shown in all subsequent centuries of German history. Germany took and gave. It did not refuse to take what others had, and for this reason, it could give to them what it had. Germany gave the human race a new form of Christianity, and in return, it received from the human race new forms of human social relationships. Germany, in absolute community with all European nations, created modern science and engineering. This took place within an inextricable interlocking of giving and taking, where everyone gave and everyone took. Nothing is more foolish than the attempt of the National Socialists to give credit to one nation in this partnership. Nothing is more dreadful than the attempt of the National Socialists to tear away from the German people the memory of its communal association with the human race. Already, many within the younger generation no longer know that Germany belonged to the human race, and many within the older generation have forgotten it. You, the ones who still know—and who, for that reason, are responsible for the German future—awaken, once again, the awareness that Germany belongs to the human race and the human race to Germany.

Without the return of Germany to the human race there will be no German future, because Germany cannot exist without the human race. No nation can exist without the human race, today less than ever. The human race has moved so closely together that a part that wants to isolate itself either is subjugated or must subjugate all others. National Socialist Germany has isolated itself, in order to make the attempt to subject everyone else to itself, and it is now breaking to pieces in this attempt, slowly but surely. Only through a lifting of the isolation, only through a return to the human race can Germany be saved.

Everything that is creative in the German people demands a return to the human race. And the stronger a group endeavors to return to the human race, the more important its role in the German future will be. Every creative politician who is hidden from the ruling authorities, waiting for his time, knows that there can no longer be a German policy that is not the policy of the human race. A policy of humankind: that is the opposite of the policy of conquest, and it is the opposite of a policy of isolation. It is a policy that conforms to a reality larger than itself, as a supporting member of that which is greater. However this will look in the future, whether it will be a European federation or a world federation or an alliance of different federations, it will then be about the politics of the human race. And for all nations—but particularly for Germany, the country of Middle Europe—everything will depend on the fact that the national remains subordinated to the human race as a whole. Otherwise, nation and humanity will be lost.

The creative thinker and scholar who lives in Germany today is cut off from the circulation of the intellectual lifeblood that feeds everything because it takes from everything and gives to everything. He yearns to be out of this isolation, because it means that his creative powers are withering, that he is lagging behind developments, and that he is becoming solitary and infertile. There is science made by Germans, but there is no national German science. There is philosophy created by the French, but there is no national French philosophy. All great thinkers have thought on a human scale. Every scientific progression is a progression of the human race as a whole. When German scholars began to pursue German social science, they ceased to pursue social science and instead began giving patriotic speeches. When German thinkers began to pursue German philosophy, they ceased to pursue philosophy and became mouthpieces of the Propaganda Ministry. No one denies that different languages and cultures exert an influence even on science and philosophy. That is natural and enriching. But it signifies the ruin of the scientific life of a nation when it wishes to be national instead of human. And it signifies the decay of the thought of a nation when it is said to be nationally, instead of universally, valid. Everything that has remained of the German spirit in these years of its destruction desires to return to the human race, to the great community of thought and inquiry.

1943

The German laborer wants to return to the human race. For a century, the German working class was a pioneer for the idea of humankind. The great progressions in the social situation of the masses of German workers were won in alliance with the working classes of other lands. It was the pride of German workers that they were at home with cross-national thinking and feeling, although the individual worker had little opportunity to experience foreign nations. Nothing of the lower middle-class narrowness, of the stuffiness of the national, of stupid nationalist arrogance, which one so often found in Germany, was found in the labor movement. And now, German laborers are joined together by force in the labor front. Even before the war, all cross-national bonds were torn! The German labor movement could give humankind nothing more and could receive nothing more from it. All cross sections were abolished throughout humankind. The German workers were dependent on themselves and were surrendered to new and old tyrants. The labor movement is pushing back to humankind. Like no other movement, it has the forces through which Germany can be given back to humanity. And it needs, like no other movement, the human race, because the struggle for social transformation is a struggle that can be led successfully only on a worldwide scale.

That the German economy is gravitating back to the human race is natural. As long as there is an exchange of goods, the economy must attempt to break national boundaries, not only to its advantage but to the advantage of the entire nation. Every German knows the privation that the sealing off of Germany from the exchange of goods with the rest of humanity has brought. It was first a voluntary sealing off, in favor of rearmament. Then it became a forced sealing off by the war. Other nations have also been guilty of partially sealing themselves off, but none like the Germany of the Nazis. The earth and its goods belong to the human race. And no modern nation can produce everything for itself. Sealing one's nation off or opening one's nation up to the human race: the one means poverty, the other means wealth.

It is also natural that religion in Germany is pushing back to the human race! Only the most primitive tribal religion desires to have nothing to do with humankind! That the National Socialists have created a new tribal religion with the German nation as its idol is the most perfect expression of their isolation from the human race. Christianity exists as a human religion, or it becomes a languishing sect. The struggle of the German churches against National Socialism has temporarily saved them from this fate. But in the long run, it must proceed in the German churches just as it did with those splinters of Christian life in heathen surroundings, which slowly lost their creative power and ossified. The German churches would also slowly ossify if they were not to return to the human race, which is waiting for them. For not only does Germany need the human race but the human race needs Germany. More on that another time!

28.
"Tyrannical Power Has Limits"

MY GERMAN FRIENDS!

The news reports of the last weeks out of the occupied regions and out of Germany have something in common that is worth reflecting on. They all confirm the beautiful statement of Schiller: "Tyrannical power has limits!" We hear of a letter that the Belgian bishops have written to the German governor, and in this they passionately protest against the banishing of Belgian men and women into slave labor. We hear that the Norwegians have blown up an important munitions factory and that the resistance of the Norwegian churches has forced the Quislingers[45] to retreat to a great extent. We hear of the slowing down of work that is driven by German and foreign workers, together, in the arms factories. We hear that in all occupied regions a lively underground press exists, which publishes ten thousand copies in spite of all the persecution by the Gestapo. You yourselves have heard that the Serb resistance is unbroken, although one village after the other is being razed to the earth. You have perhaps heard something about the systematic acts of sabotage against the German military machine. They began in France and spread rapidly into the occupied regions of the whole of Europe. New shootings only created new resistance. You know of the heroic struggle of the Russian partisans, who are a terror for German bases and military supplies. All attempts to wipe them out are unsuccessful. Here, the limits of tyrannical power are visible everywhere, and these limits are also visible inside Germany. In the north, there are concentration camps for German officers and soldiers who, in the resistance—for example, of the Norwegians—have broken down

[137]

psychologically and who prefer to die rather than be made further instruments of tyranny and oppression. German students have been shot dead because they have spread pamphlets against the destroyers of Germany, the National Socialists.[46] Important military bridges have been attacked in Germany itself. News reports out of neutral and enemy countries are trickling through in spite of all censorship and every threat of death for listening to foreign stations.

Never in world history has there been a machine of oppression that amounted, in size and effectiveness, to the National Socialist one. Eventually, the tyranny seemed to have developed instruments from which there was no escape. It seemed as if tyrannical power had become unlimited. It seemed as if the progression of human civilization and all the inventions of the human intellect were destined to serve one purpose: to establish a world tyranny. From the Gestapo to the block warden, from radio propaganda to the surveillance of parents by their children, from the bomber to the tank, a system appeared to be created without gaps. No place for resistance was permitted. No spot for the preparation of revolutionary movements seemed to be hidden enough. Spiritually and physically, everything was seized by the servants of tyranny. Never has the world seen anything like that. In all earlier periods of oppression, there were spots to which one could flee and places in which one could conceal oneself.

And yet the instruments of tyranny were inadequate. Everyone knows today that in spite of these monstrous instruments, this tyranny is condemned to destruction. The limits of tyrannical power have become apparent. The greatest system of oppression that humankind has created is creaking at its joints. It is destroying itself according to the law under which it exists. Tyranny is not—like authentic rule—borne by the will of those who are subject to it. For that reason, tyranny must constantly break the resistance of those who threaten its rule. They must become more and more ruthless in their methods; because along with the methods of oppression, the methods of resistance are becoming stronger. Thus, a growing terror is emerging, more and more refined, brutal, cruel—and unsuccessful. The tyranny of tyrants must become more intense and inexorable in order to be able to hold out, until a point comes when it will go on no more. When it sees everyone as suspicious, when those who were instruments of tyranny yesterday have become its victims today, and when those who today believe themselves to be safe become persecuted tomorrow, then the tyranny breaks down within itself. This point is not yet reached. It would have been long since reached if the tyrants had not found the escape of outward battle. Since the start of the war, they possessed—in the law of war and the fear of national decline—fiercer instruments of their rule than ever before. Thus it was for the first years of the war. But then, the same law had an effect without as it did within: the attack on the freedom of foreign nations brought threats from other nations who were then also attacked, until the entire world set itself against the German tyrants and their accomplices. When Russia was attacked, because there could be no halt for the conquering tyranny, the law of the limits of every tyranny came into force; to the Russian resistance it became apparent that the conqueror is a part of the whole, which destroys itself when it desires to rise above the whole. It is astonishing to see with what certainty the German tyrants did everything that they had to do according to the law of tyranny! It is astonishing to see with what blindness they carried out the law of their self-destruction. What is now still taking place is the continuing and dreadful revelation of this law.

Tyrannical power has limits because it develops forces of self-destruction, and it has limits because humanity is created for freedom. Where does that tenacious resistance of the Norwegians and the Dutch, of the Czechs and the Serbs, of the French saboteurs and the Russian guerrillas come from? Think about German history! There was a time when Germany was subject to the French conqueror, and Germans fought against the Napoleonic tyranny as saboteurs and guerrillas, with actions and writings. There was a time when German freedom fighters were shot dead for the same things for which the freedom fighters of the conquered nations are now being shot dead by the Germans. The German freedom fighters, and with them the Spanish and Russian guerrillas who fought against the Napoleonic tyranny, have been glorified in all German schools and praised in all German speeches as models. And now the European nations are following this example; but they are following it against the tyrants of today, the Germans. My German friends, have you never asked why the same thing should be seen as heroic when you are doing it against others and criminal when others are doing it against you?

They, the subjugated nations, will continue to fight until they have achieved their freedom. Many will die before the goal is reached. But everyone who dies in this battle dies for humankind, for every person, even for the German people. Because the German person also wants freedom, although he has been degraded to being first a slave and then a slave owner. I would imagine that in the depth of your soul, something rejoices when you hear of the heroic deeds of the European freedom fighters. Didn't we passionately sympathize in our youth when we read of the freedom heroes of foreign nations and tribes? Didn't we live with them as if we were they? Certainly, you cannot hear of the freedom struggle of the Europeans and Russians without the painful feeling that the battle is indeed directed against your nation, because your nation has become the instrument of one of the most frightful of all tyrannies! You sense the complete tragedy that National Socialism has brought on the German nation, because you realize that the best in your inner self resonates with the freedom heroes of your enemies.

Recently, we have spoken often of the German future. I would like the German nation to learn something for the entire future from this revolution of freedom against German tyranny: that humanity is created for freedom and that brutal power must destroy itself. Certainly, Germany became the first victim of National Socialism. But certainly, not entirely without its own guilt. It lacked the respect for human freedom; it lacked the will to devote itself to the struggle against the frightful dictatorship of National Socialism. There was too much worship of power, too much subjugation, too much idolatry of authority. The revolution of freedom has begun: go with it, my German friends! Stop being instruments of tyranny! Free yourselves, then you will be free, even when the armies of oppression are routed. The revolution of freedom has begun. Take part in it, you, the first victims of tyranny!

29.
THE PASSION STORY
OF NAZISM

PALM SUNDAY 1943

MY GERMAN FRIENDS!

Only a few days separate us from Good Friday and Easter, the highest of Christian festivals. Holy Week begins, and thoughts of the Passion stir the hearts of the whole of Christendom, the whole of humanity. A period of suffering without equal in size and depth has settled over the world. From the first Good Friday under Nazi rule, when countless German victims were being tortured and murdered in camps and prisons, onward through the Good Friday when the Italian armies subjugated the small Albanian nation with brutal force, until this Good Friday: what a path of suffering for people and nations! In the passion story there is a wonderful place: Jesus is carrying his cross while he is being dragged to the Place of the Skull. Behind him are the weeping women. He turns around and says, "Don't weep for me, weep for yourselves and for your children!"[47] The ruins of Jerusalem proved him right. I know many who thought and said, in the Passiontide of 1933 and the ensuing years of suffering: German people who look on our persecution with grief and indignation, don't weep for us, weep for yourselves for the sake of the curse that will come upon you! When the Jews were being dragged along to extermination in proportions that were growing year after year, Jesus was also being dragged away at the same time; he was again bearing his cross, he was again forsaken and mourned over! And then he spoke again, this time to the German people: "Don't weep for me, weep for yourselves and for your children!" I know that many Germans have heard this imperceptible voice. I know of many who knew from the first day of Nazi atrocities that this would mean the destruction of their cities, the starvation of their children, and the slaughter of their men. All the years of Nazi rule are a passion story, not on account of the suffering that they brought but rather on account of the struggle that was being led in them against everything for which the passion story and the crucified One stands. He has truly been crucified again in Germany. Anything like the prayer for the enemies who brought him to the cross is contrary to everything that National Socialism has felt and thought. It is that which National Socialism wanted to annihilate when it preached hatred and took revenge. Forgiving love, which overcomes all oppositions, was what it despised most of all! The cross was what it fought against with the deepest passion.

In the endless train of those who are being led by National Socialism to the Place of the Skull, the man of Nazareth invisibly proceeds and calls out with every step to the Germans, through whose midst this train is passing: "Weep not for me, weep for Germany, weep for yourselves and for your children."

My German friends! Haven't you yourselves perceived this voice within you? On the day of the deepest German disgrace, when the synagogues were being burned and Jewish men were being hunted down like wild game and deported,[48] wasn't there something within you that wept and grieved for their sakes? And at the same time, the other feeling: don't we have to grieve even more for ourselves? "They were suffering innocently! But we, we Germans in whose midst all of this is taking place, are guilty; and when the curse on us has come to pass, we will not only suffer but suffer as the guilty party." Countless people in the German nation have been conscious of that. They have grieved at an even deeper level for themselves than for the persecuted. They were right to do so. Because now they are suffering the same thing that those persecuted by the Nazis have suffered. And they are suffering it as accessories to this persecution and, for that reason, are grieving more than them!

The ruins of Jerusalem were the confirmation of Jesus' statement: weep for yourselves and for your children! The ruins of the German cities are the confirmation of the inner voice in all sensitive Germans that says: we must grieve more for ourselves than for the victims of National Socialism.

The German grief can lead to despair, and it can lead to rebirth. No one can take this grief away from the Germans. Every day of the war brings more of it! And no one can take the sense of guilt for this grief away from the Germans. On the contrary: the more the truth makes its way through the mist of Nazi propaganda, the stronger the sense of guilt will be. The more the German masses hear of what has taken place in the concentration camps and Gestapo prisons, in the evacuation of the Jews to the east, in the occupied lands, the more the bitter feeling will be associated with the suffering of the approaching defeat and with having given themselves into the hands of a corrupt power! "I've surrendered myself to you!" says Gretchen in *Faust* when she sets her eyes on the Evil One![49] "I've surrendered myself to you," the German nation will say when it sets its eyes on the unveiled, diabolical grimace of National Socialism! And then it will be grateful that it is not rescued by this power! But the grief of having been in the hands of this power and of being brought to the abyss by it cannot be taken from Germany.

But the grief need not become despair. No person and no nation needs to despair. Neither suffering nor death nor guilt is grounds for despair. Indeed, this is the great thing in the picture of the Passion: that here, an incident of suffering and death makes its appearance, an appearance in which the abyss of despair is nearly reached and then overcome. The German people must take the path of the Passion. Already, long ago, it began to take it, and it will be taken to its end. But even at the end, in the deepest distress that can befall a nation, stands not despair but a new beginning.

The best forces in the German nation must now prepare themselves to overcome despair. It is more threatening than all other enemies together. Because it is the end beyond which there is no further beginning. Let us turn, for a moment, to the passion story. Two groups are visible there for whom despair could be close at hand. The first group is composed of the disciples and followers of Jesus, whose hopes collapse altogether when the one whom they had regarded as the savior of their nation and the entire world died on the cross. And yet they did not despair. Immense disappointment did not finish them. They began anew and laid the foundation for the church in all the nations of the world. And the other group was the Jews who had rejected Jesus on nationalist grounds and, a few decades thereafter, experienced their downfall as an independent nation. They also did not despair but rather held fast to their calling. The grief over themselves and their children, their city and their nation, did not drive them to self-abandonment.

The National Socialists will do everything to drive the German nation to acts of desperate self-destruction. You who are full of grief over Germany and who know that it cannot be otherwise: be on your guard that you are not caught in this trap! The National Socialists know that they cannot escape their fate. As a group, they are right to be desperate, because there is no way out for National Socialism. And so they want to drive you to things that mean their downfall but also yours. The National Socialists will do everything to draw the German nation into their despair and their downfall. Above all, they will make you accessories, even much more than up to now. They will commit atrocities against the subjugated enemies that are more evil than all previous ones. They will commit murder in the interior of Germany, more wickedly than ever before. They will drive you along to suicidal resistance! They will attempt to plant a bitterness within your souls that is born out of despair and that will make any new beginning impossible. It is the greatest triumph of the dark powers when they drive their victims to despair. Suffering is still not the triumph of evil; the German nation is in the midst of suffering. But only the suffering that leads to despair completely delivers us over to the evil powers. Guilt is still not the triumph of evil; the German nation has saddled itself with guilt, being turned into an instrument of National Socialism. But only the sense of guilt that leads to despair crushes us completely. The National Socialists have insinuated that they want to plunge Germany into this guilt, into this despair, before they perish with it. Be on your guard against this ultimate destruction, the irreversible end of Germany!

"Weep for yourselves and your children," the passion story calls out to us and to the German people. But it also calls out another thing to us: don't give up hope! Easter morning is not far! German rebirth has begun!

30.
THE TOLLING
OF EASTER BELLS

EASTER SUNDAY 1943

MY GERMAN FRIENDS!

Good Friday is over, the day that—of all Christian feast days—best expresses your mood. Easter Sunday has come, the feast of rebirth into life. It has also come for you who are standing on Good Friday and will, perhaps, stand there for a long time! Goethe's *Faust* describes how the bells of Easter morning keep Dr. Faust alive at the moment when he has placed the goblet of poison to his lips. I believe that many Germans have lifted the poisonous goblet of despair to their mouths and want to plunge themselves into death and self-annihilation. And the moment may come when it is no longer individuals, not even many individuals within the German nation, but rather the nation as a whole that will reach for the poisonous goblet of despair. If it should come to that, then the Easter bells may resound in the depth of the German soul, just as they resounded in the gloomy room of Dr. Faust.

Faust had all knowledge until he saw that he was further from the truth than ever. That drove him to despair. The German nation had all power until it saw that it was further from a good life than ever. His knowledge shatters, and Faust reaches for the goblet of poison. The German nation's power is shattering, and it is reaching for self-destruction! Faust is saved by the message of new life! The German nation can be saved by the message of its rebirth. This is what the voice of the Easter bells is calling out to every German today: rebirth!

No one knows how it looks in the hearts of most Germans. Perhaps even the Germans themselves don't know. Certainly, all kinds of things are fighting for the upper hand within them. There will still be many who exist as if it were before Good Friday, who want to know nothing of the path of suffering that the German nation has to take. There will still be many who believe in victory or in a favorable peace or in a compromise that is not too unfavorable. There will still be many who hope to avoid the Good Friday of the German nation. And a fragment of this hope will still be in many who are not so confident, who have grasped that there is scarcely another stop on the path downward. They cannot conceive that the catastrophe is unavoidable. And nevertheless, they have a premonition of it and cannot free themselves from the nightmare of this premonition. They know and yet do not know. And because they still don't completely know that the Good Friday of the German people is unavoidable, they can't completely understand what the Easter bells are saying to them and to the German nation. Perhaps most Germans belong to this group. They have a premonition of the path that leads to Good Friday, but they don't want to admit it. It is the most difficult thing for a person to admit the inevitable to himself, and perhaps it is even more difficult for a nation than for an individual. Perhaps the will to live is even more powerful in a nation and leads even more easily to self-deception than in the individual person. But some time or other, the inevitable is here, and with it despair.

And there may be others in the German nation, in these spring and Easter days, who know what is in store, who are no longer fooling themselves, who see Good Friday, and who see the cross to which National Socialism has nailed the German nation. They see Good Friday, but they don't see Easter. They are in despair and are slurping up the poison of despair. Many of the finest and strongest people in Germany belong to this group. Many of the youth belong to it, who sold their souls to National Socialism and are now being dragged along by it into the abyss. In their despair, they are destroying whatever is within their power, becoming more savage and more cruel than ever before, and dying from the death that they brought. I wish I could speak to them and open their ears to the voice of the Easter bells and yank the poisonous goblet from their hands, just as the Easter bells did for Dr. Faust. Others will despair and turn their backs on everything that has to do with Germany and its future. They will withdraw into the solitude of their thoughts. They will seek a refuge for their own private existence, while the catastrophe closes in on the nation. Or they will say in idle pain: let us die with Germany. They also have placed the poisonous goblet of despair to their lips—not as violently as the others, more slowly and more sorrowfully, but just as hopelessly! The Easter bells must take from them, as well, the poison of sorrow from which no further life can emerge.

And then there are in Germany the sort who not only have a premonition but know that the Good Friday of the German people is unavoidable and who, nevertheless, do not fall into despair but rather see out beyond the time of misfortune. To them, the Easter bells say: rebirth! The rebirth of nature, the rebirth of hearts, the rebirth of the German nation.

Wherever there is rebirth, there must have previously been death. But not everywhere where there was death must there be rebirth. Many a seed dies that bears no fruit. Many a nation has died of whose rebirth we know nothing. Many a tribulation has been suffered that has created no strength. The rebirth of a nation isn't something that happens automatically. Only when many individuals rise out of the night of destruction can something new take place in a nation. Easter speaks of an eternal law of life, of a great possibility to which every life can conform, of the summons "Die and arise!" But it is up to us whether we apply this law to ourselves, whether we allow this possibility to become effective, whether we subject ourselves to the calling "Die and arise." Many of the fighting, suffering, nearly dying nations of this war have understood the great law of life, of Good Friday and Easter. East and west of Germany, nations are being reborn, although it is still outwardly Good Friday for them. We know so little about the inner selves of the people in these nations, just as we know so little about the inner selves of the people in Germany. But we see various signs which suggest that something new is coming into existence in them, that rebirth is taking place. They have grasped that a nation which lives only to itself, and which scorns the community of nations, perishes in its isolation. They have grasped that a nation in which one class exploits the others is opening its doors to the conqueror and dies in class hostility. They have grasped that a nation which acknowledges no ultimate religious values but seeks only the penultimate—power and money— squanders its inner strengths and disintegrates. They have knowledge of all of that in the nations on which the catastrophe has fallen. They were on the brink of despair, but they haven't drunk from the poisonous goblet of despair. They believed in rebirth, and that has given them the certainty of a future.

How is it going in the German nation? There are also forces within it that know what is at stake. Today, they are still condemned to silence, as seeds—dark and invisible—have their source in the earth. But they are there, and out of the now-dark earth of German existence, seeds everywhere will push to the light and develop. Even in Germany there is Easter, resurrection from the night of National Socialism. Just as in all lands over which the solar eclipse of National Socialist tyranny has lain, so there are also in Germany indications of a new rising of the sun, of a new Easter morn. Already the earth is shaking, and its tremors are beginning to roll away the stone[50] that the National Socialist henchmen have placed before the grave of the true Germany. In vain, they attempt to hold it fast—and, with it, Germany—in its present sepulchral darkness. They won't be able to do it much longer, and Germany will rise again from the dead.

Those aren't false words of triumph. They don't mean that anything is being dispensed with on the German nation's path of suffering, that it will not become too unpleasant, that the old will more or less return. That wouldn't be rebirth. Even a reborn Germany will continue to bear traces of that which is now happening to it. Ultimately, much in it must remain dead. Otherwise, the new won't be possible. The spirit out of which National Socialism emerged belongs to decay and not to new life. For that reason, separate yourselves from it, all of you who want to become the bearers of rebirth. Allow nothing of the National Socialist decay to penetrate into you; it could become deadly for the resurrected Germany! Don't attempt to avoid the cross where all false, foul, and evil things are being set aright! Don't betray the Germany of the future out of sympathy for the present, decaying Germany! Allow what has to decompose to do so, and prepare yourselves for the new that will come to be, beyond death and despair. Prepare for the Easter of the German people.

31.
BLINDNESS
PRECEDES RUIN
APRIL 27, 1943

MY GERMAN FRIENDS!

For some days, the shooting of American pilots in Japan has been talked about in America and the other lands of the Allied nations with increasing agitation. Certainly, you have already heard about it. Some months ago, a bold group of American pilots made a bombing raid on the Japanese capital.[51] On that occasion, one plane had to land. The crew was captured, condemned in a show trial, and shot dead. When the news—which was confirmed by the Japanese government—became known, an enormous wrath gripped the Americans, a wrath that is still growing today. There is only one voice today in America, and this voice says: repeat the attack, as soon as possible, and with ten times the strength. No responsible person says: do the same thing to Japanese prisoners of war! The Americans refuse to be forced to the same level of barbarity on which the Japanese stand. But if, in this way, the Japanese war leaders wanted the Americans to be deterred from further air attacks, they've achieved precisely the contrary. As soon as it is militarily possible, American pilots will be over Tokyo and will look forward to death by shooting with the same composure as they would death in battle with Japanese pilots. How was it possible that the Japanese leaders miscalculated in this way, in a way conceived to deter a nation such as America with the barbarity of a former age? Perhaps they did not want this at all. Perhaps they didn't have the Americans but rather their own nation in mind when they ordered this horrifying violation of international law and of all principles of human civilization.

And with that, we come to something that concerns you, my German friends, just as much as the Japanese: that which people call blindness. You know the old saying that when the gods want to ruin someone, they blind him beforehand. So it was with the shooting of the American pilots in Japan. It is a thousand-year-old blindness that lies over the Japanese nation, which has led it to great successes and in which it will finally be destroyed. For the gods—or, rather, the evil forces in the soul of humankind and nations—act in such a way that they first give successes in order to make humanity secure. When they have become secure, they become further and further driven. In the blindness caused by their success, they can no longer see the abyss toward which they are hastening and into which they are ultimately falling. How was it in Japan? An island, attacked by no one for hundreds of years, secure within itself, warlike, and ready to attack wherever there was an opportunity. Out of this situation, national self-idolatry was born, which is stronger in Japan than anywhere else. Japan is a holy land. The Japanese are the chosen nation, which is supposed to rule Asia and the Pacific and perhaps America and Europe with them. The Japanese emperor is god on earth, in the direction of whose palace the Japanese bow each day. These thoughts are not a cleverly devised theory. They are in the blood of every Japanese person, they play a dominant role in his daily life, and they play a dominant role in his attitude to all other nations of the earth. They don't see others. They see only themselves. Even the most intelligent politicians among them are blinded by the beliefs in their superiority, in the holiness of their land, and in their destiny to rule great parts of the world. Out of this blindness they became barbarians and aroused the hatred of the civilized world against themselves, more than through the malicious breach of the peace and the attack on the American fleet. That was also against international law. But it was at least action in battle and not the brutal murder of defenseless prisoners. The belief in their own sacredness has turned them into barbarians. The belief in the invulnerability of their land turned the air raids on it into a monstrous occurrence, which threatened the entire war atmosphere in Japan. And for this reason, the American pilots had to die. They are victims of a blinded nationalism, which is no longer able to see the consequences of its self-idolatry and its contempt for others. When the foreign bombs fell down on them, the danger was that they would lose their most holy beliefs. Only the swift death of those who were responsible for it could, in the opinion of the Japanese leaders, avert this danger. In their blindness, they didn't see that with this action, they increased this danger tenfold.

Japan is Germany's ally. This was never very honorable to Germany. But now it has become shameful. Japan will be able to clear its name in the memory of the human race when it stamps out its warrior caste and gives up its self-idolatry. The Allied nations are resolved to accomplish this goal, with or without the help of the Japanese nation. And nothing has confirmed this decision like the official murder of American pilots. Like a flash of lightning, this has made clear to the entire civilized world what is to be expected from a nation that has fallen into a condition of destructive blindness, through a thousand-year-long period of self-idolatry.

The German nation ought to see itself in this mirror. The present rulers of Germany take second place to the Japanese warlords in nothing when it comes to barbarity. Admittedly, they have shot no prisoners of war. It wasn't possible for the National Socialists to destroy, so broadly, the sense of honor of the German army by giving themselves up to such a service of execution.[52] But the shooting of innocent hostages, the extermination of an entire village for acts with which they had nothing to do, the mass murder of Jewish old people and children and women, the hell of the concentration camps: all of that surpasses the Japanese crimes against international law.

The basis for all of this is the same as in Japan: national self-idolatry and the blindness associated with it, which destroys others first and then itself. The nationalism that the Nazis have brought to life, the beliefs in the holiness of the German soil and the superiority of the German race, have had the same results as the corresponding belief in Japan: barbarity and arrogance, the inability to see oneself correctly and to see that justice is done to others. Just as completely as in Japan, it brought the initial result: wide circles of the German nation were possessed, as if by a narcotic. People worshiped the Führer and, in the Führer, themselves. People did without everything that the German past—with respect to humanity and Christianity—had planted in the German nation. People lost all standards, broke all internal and external boundaries, and seemed to be confirmed in their beliefs through unparalleled successes. The intoxication of victory, the intoxication of self-idolatry, blinded leaders and blinded followers. Divine and human laws were trampled underfoot, treaties broken, rights taken away, people enslaved and destroyed. All of this occurred, but those who did it didn't see themselves. They had no mirror in which the horrifying countenance of the evil spirit that drove them appeared. This is what blindness means. The Germans had no more of a mirror than the Japanese. Everyone who wanted to hold up a mirror to them was silenced: in the churches, at the universities, in the newspapers, in books. These National Socialists made it impossible for the German nation to see itself and its actions in the mirror. They broke every mirror. They blinded the nation, and in the end, they blinded themselves.

And so they did not see that they were running into the abyss: the Führer didn't and the nation didn't. They didn't see that the treaty-breaking attack on Russia was an act of blind arrogance that contained within itself their own downfall. They didn't see that the declaration of war on America made the defeat of Germany unavoidable. Above all, they didn't see that the inhumanity and barbarity of their association with everyone who was handed over to them mustered the feelings of the whole world against them. Every new crime against the Jewish people created new enemies for them among all decent people. Every new shooting of innocent victims in the conquered lands stole sympathy from them and aroused the wrath of the indifferent. But blinded self-idolatry drove them further and further on their path. And today, scarcely anyone else in the world doesn't demand the extermination of this new barbarity and all of its bearers.

My German friends! If these words that I've been addressing to you for more than a year have a meaning, it is this: to give you a mirror in which you can look at yourselves, your leaders, and the world around you. The National Socialists attempt to smash every mirror. They want the German nation to remain in its blindness—into which they've driven it through a slow poisoning—as long as possible. They know that when the German nation sees again, it will be over for them. When the German nation sees the hideous face of National Socialism in the mirror of the rest of the world, it will turn around and destroy the bearers of this hideous face and the blindness of the German spirit. Infinite disaster, the death of millions, could be prevented if this should happen soon. You who hear these words, pass on the mirror that you've received! Show as many Germans as you can where they stand. Show them how the world sees them. Show them what Germans—in destructive blindness—have brought about in the world!

It is a dreadful saying that the gods blind those whom they want to ruin. They have blinded the German nation, and now they have begun to ruin it. But who are these gods? They are the evil instincts that are in every nation, with whose help the Nazis came to power and which they have used for further and further blindness. Once the power of these instincts is broken, the eyes of the German nation will open. Our own wish is that this may happen soon. It will be a dreadful moment when the German nation sees itself in the mirror, but it will be a moment of salvation. God opens the eyes of those whom he wants to save, however terrible this awakening may be. The path to the salvation of the German nation is that on which it regains its sight.

32.
FATE
AND GUILT
MAY 18, 1943

MY GERMAN FRIENDS!

When I spoke to you the last time, the German collapse in Africa had already occurred. One hundred thousand German soldiers, nearly a dozen generals, and countless weapons were conquered by the Allied nations.[53] The southern flank of Europe is exposed. Defenseless, the Italian ports wait for the crushing attacks from the air. The Italian population is fleeing from the coastal region inland and from the south to the north. Indeed, in the north of Germany, one German city after the other is being turned into an expanse of ruins. And if they are not completely destroyed by the first attack, then follows a second and third and fourth and so on, until the war industry is made useless and life has become hell for the inhabitants. And there is no letting up, day and night. Will it come to us today? Will I be buried beneath rubble tomorrow? So everyone instinctively asks themselves! And their shaken nerves wait for the warning signal or the interruption of the radio program. Disaster is in the air! Where will it descend?

What does all of this mean? It means that it is not yet the end, but it signifies the beginning of that which is leading, sooner or later, to the end. It means that fate has begun to reveal itself.

In the first years of the war, when the German armies marched from one victory to another, fate seemed to turn a kind, even a shining face toward the Germans. Many believed that this was the true and actual face of destiny. They overlooked the dark trains, the heavy sacrifices, the crimes of the Nazi tyrants, the suffering of the subjugated inside and outside Germany. They were fascinated by the smile of fate and forgot their own secret fear that there may yet be something different behind this smile. They forgot that already once in this generation, Germany had triumphed itself to death. They forgot that an initial smile of fate had already once changed into frightful seriousness and into a picture of horror. Admittedly, there were always some within Germany who saw through the friendly mask of fate and recognized the frightful inclinations that were concealed behind the smile. But they were few, and they had to keep silent. Today, only a few still believe in the smile of fate. Nearly all see its frightfully serious face. Fate has begun to show its true countenance to the German nation, and no one can overlook it any longer.

Or are there still fools among you who think that a third offensive in Russia can turn fate, after the first and second have failed in spite of all initial successes? Even if the German armies went again as far as the Volga or as far as the Urals, which they have twice attempted to do in vain, what would that change about the attacks from the south and the west? Is there a German so childish as to hope that the destruction of German cities will suddenly stop? Just as, up to now, the forces of destruction have grown day after day, night after night, so they will grow even further. There is no escape. With unrelenting certainty, as calculable as a machine, fate is approaching Germany. No one can stop it! What the National Socialists say about the final victory they believe as little as anybody else. Perhaps many among them still believe in a long resistance. But if they believe in it, then they also know what a long resistance means: destruction and death to an inconceivable degree and, ultimately, collapse! The longer fate is postponed, the more frightfully it will be disclosed; and it can't be turned away.

Every German should grasp that today. Every German should have the courage to face his serious fate, just as he has looked at smiling destiny. Every German today should know, and bear it upon his heart, that he stands beneath a fate that can no longer be turned away by any bravery and any willingness to sacrifice. Become conscious of fate, in order that you can bear the fate that is inescapable.

What can people do in the face of an inescapably dark fate? Here, there is only one truly human path: namely, to consent to fate and, in this way, to take the sting out of it! That is what has to be said to the Germans by everyone who means well by them. Every sermon, every serious speech, every personal conversation about the future should ask and answer this question: how shall we meet the fate that has now been revealed and that is unavoidably approaching us? And the answer should always be: we must take it upon us, we must say yes to it and, by this, show that we are greater than our fate. From time immemorial, people have reflected on the darkness of the fate of individuals, families, and nations. All great tragedies, from the Greeks up to the present, deal with this darkest question of human life. And frequently, fate is described in the same way as the German fate has now developed: first smiling, then threatening, then destroying; first blinding people and generations and then ruining them!

And there was always the one answer that was given to the question of fate: whoever is strong enough to take it upon himself has defeated it! He hasn't defeated it externally: even then, the disaster takes its course! But he has defeated it inwardly. He is higher than, not lower than, his fate. He can create something new, in which the old fate is overcome. And that is what the German nation must do today: not looking away from fate nor closing their eyes to it but looking it in the eye. And not running away from it but standing up to it. Then its ultimate power is taken from it. Even the fate that is coming upon Germany will be deprived of its power when the German nation has taken it upon itself.

The authors of the ancient tragedies knew why this is so. They knew why the one who bears fate conquers it. And they made it clear to everyone who can see and hear: fate is never only chance; it is always also guilt. Our character makes our fate. The German character has made the German fate. The German fate is also chance and guilt at the same time. The German guilt is that the German nation has been turned into the instrument of a power that has diabolical traits: National Socialism. And this guilt is deeply rooted in the German character. It is the Germans' false sense of allegiance that has shattered every resistance to the National Socialist tyranny in the German nation. It is anxiety at the prospect of resistance to evil, when that evil comes from above and has the power and authority of the state behind it. It is the wavering between self-abasement and self-conceit that one finds everywhere in Germany. It is the worship of external power, which has been fostered for so long in Germany and which has become an idolatry more and more. All of that forms a part of the German character, side by side with much that is great and remarkable. Among the traits of the German character German guilt is rooted, and with it, German fate. Without the false sense of allegiance, the National Socialists wouldn't have succeeded in erecting their absolute dictatorship. It is now ten years since that ignominious meeting of the Reichstag, when the majority of German parties voted for the Enabling Act, which gave the German nation into the hands of its tyrants and butchers. Without German self-conceit, the attack on Russia and the declaration of war on America wouldn't have occurred. In a less self-disdaining and, for that reason, less arrogant nation, there would have been people who would have held back a megalomaniac from the path to destruction. Without the idolatry of power and the belief in the omnipotence of the military organization, no responsible German would have believed that it was possible to oppress Europe by brutal force of arms. All of this is German character, German guilt, and, now, German fate. There is no other way to meet it than to see the guilt, to take the consequences upon oneself, and to change its character. All three are equally difficult. Many will still attempt to put the blame on others: the Jews, the Russians, the Anglo-Saxons. But who still seriously believes that? Many will still hope that they can elude the consequences of guilt. But didn't they know—long ago, in the depths of their heart—that this will be impossible? Many will still declare German character to be the best in the world and reject every change in the German character. But don't they already recognize—even if reluctantly—that there must be something wrong in a nation that has brought down on itself such a fate, twice in one generation?

Look toward your fate, and take it upon yourselves. Then it can lose its sting! Then something new can come into existence out of the crushing reality that is inescapably approaching!

33.
TWO KINDS OF DEFEATISM

MAY 25, 1943

MY GERMAN FRIENDS!

After the defeats of the German armies in Stalingrad and Tunis, after the destructive air attacks of the Allies on Germany, after the decrease in the sinkings by U-boats, the feeling has become strong among you that everything is surely in vain. People call this defeatism; and the dictators are attempting to do everything to combat this frame of mind. They are seeking to prevent the truth from being known by Germans. They reinterpret unfavorable events until they seem favorable. They give a distorted picture of the situation of the Allied nations. They exaggerate small differences and conceal the fundamental unity, namely, the unlimited determination to destroy National Socialism. They seek to silence everyone in Germany who knows information about the real situation. They punish everyone who gives expression to feelings of futility. They rage against defeatism in Germany and Italy. But the more they rage, the more they admit that the nations of the Axis sense what is imminent.

For the feeling of the futility of further resistance, they use the word *defeatism,* that is, belief in defeat. They intentionally use a hateful word to cast suspicion on the true instinct of the nation. They reproach those who know the truth for their knowledge. It is as if the captain on a ship that is sinking would conceal from the passengers that the ship is lost and would forbid the lifeboats to be lowered. He knows that he can no longer save himself and prefers that everyone be sunk with him. The dictators are now doing exactly the same thing with their nations. They know that the ship into which they've lured their nations is sinking. They know that with every day in which they conceal it, more Germans and more Italians are being sacrificed. But they want the German and Italian people to sink with them. They don't want to lower the lifeboats, because doing so would no longer help them. And for this reason, they are silencing everyone who knows what they know and who asks: why continue to go on, why drive to destruction, why not save your nations? These questions are becoming more and more urgent. The outlook on the condition of the ship—and that nothing can save it—is more and more clear. And the measures of the dictators to shut the mouths of those who know and to confuse those who feel are becoming harsher and harsher. To know that the ship is sinking is called defeatism. To see that the water is already penetrating everywhere into the hold of the ship is called despair. Closing one's eyes before that which is, this is called bravery.

My German friends! Don't be misled by the word *defeatism*! Take on the responsibility of being branded as defeatists for the sake of the truth. When you do so, you will be those who will bring salvation out beyond defeat. But those who today call you defeatists will sink into sure defeat.

There are two kinds of defeatism. The one sees the end after every defeat and, for this reason, hastens the coming of the end. No one approves of this defeatism. It is the attitude of the Quislings, the traitors in all countries, those who act as pessimists and are sad when things go better than they thought. Every nation and every group must defend itself against those kinds of defeatists. But there is yet another kind of person who sees defeat and disaster. They see what is actually coming. Within them is a deep fear. They don't want to see what is nevertheless forced upon them with a certainty that can't be overturned. They prefer to keep silent, and yet it forces them to speak. They see defeat, and yet they are not defeatists. They are, if anything, prophets. Jeremiah was such a prophet. He took upon himself the difficult work of foretelling the destruction of Jerusalem. He was hated and unpopular with the Jews, just as he would be today with the Nazis. In that respect, the ancient Jews and today's National Socialists are completely alike—that they put up with no one who sees and announces defeat. At that time, they were called prophets of disaster. Today, they are called defeatists. The ones who see defeat today are the successors of the great prophets, and they will be in the right, in the same way as those prophets. Those who shouted, "Salvation, salvation," in ancient Israel didn't speak the truth, but rather those who saw the destruction to come. Not the nationalist propaganda of victory prophets but rather the message of justice of the prophets of disaster has survived the millenia. The "Salvation, salvation" callers in Jewish antiquity descended into the disaster that came over them and are forgotten forever. All times remember the prophets of defeat.

There is one characteristic that distinguishes the prophet from the defeatist chatterer. The pessimist sees black because his soul is dark or even because he thinks he can do business with his pessimism. The prophet announces disaster because he grasps that the disaster is judgment. Jeremiah based his visions of destruction not on the fact that he saw the superior power of the empires but rather on the fact that he recognized the injustice of his people.[54] Injustice destroys a nation: that was the point of view from which the prophets announced the inescapable judgment. Their defeatism was their knowledge about divine justice. In this knowledge, the best people in Germany should unite and say what they know, just as the prophet did, even when it can occur only one to one. Whoever among you has the power to see what is coming should also have the power to say it, wherever an ear is open to it. A group of knowledgeable people has to stand up in Germany, first continuing to keep themselves in hiding, later emerging and creating the future. Then it will prove to be the case that today's prophets of disaster will be the true proclaimers of salvation tomorrow. So it was in ancient Israel; so it must be in present-day Germany. Those who today proclaim judgment and take upon themselves the humiliation of being hunted down as defeatists will tomorrow proclaim and bring salvation.

Germany must be defeated for the sake of the injustice that is occurring within it and through it. Defeat is not necessary because the empires are stronger than Germany. Certainly, they are stronger, but they are so because German injustice has united them. They are stronger because what National Socialism has done, inside and outside, has given them a good conscience. They will be victorious because they have become instruments against the injustice that has triumphed in National Socialism. And they are also stronger because the German soldiers and laborers are being weakened by inner doubt. The German soldier who sees the injustice in the conquered lands, the German laborer who sees the injustice in his collaboration with enslaved foreigners, the German civil servant who sees the injustice in the treatment of all, of foreigners and of his national comrades—none of these can fight with truly good consciences. They have the sense that they are working and fighting—and dying—for a cause founded on injustice. But can one die for injustice? Certainly not. And so it comes about that labor and battle are being done with less passion, that the will to stand to the last is weakened. No one is as powerful as the one who fights for justice with good conscience! Even the strongest person becomes weak when he no longer believes that justice is on his side. Weren't the surprising defeats of the German troops at Stalingrad and in Tunis perhaps based on the fact that, suddenly, at some crucial moment, the question became living in many: what is this for? What is certain death for? Is it worth dying for the sake of injustice? Is it worth sacrificing a hundred thousand in order that a small group of tyrants can remain in power? A soldier who puts such questions can no longer fight to the death. And doesn't every German soldier have to ask this question? Isn't he himself a victim of the injustice that is ruining his nation? Didn't he lose his human rights, his security in the face of arbitrariness, his identity before the law, and his value as a person when the present tyranny was erected? Shall he go to his death, now, for it? That which has made the opponents of the Germans strong has made the Germans themselves weak: the injustice of the leaders and seducers of Germany. No system of life that is built on injustice can last for long, least of all one that has elevated injustice to the highest principle, such as National Socialism. For this reason, you who see the unavoidable defeat are successors of the prophets who spoke the message of judgment against a corrupt political system.

If we ourselves were to imagine for a moment that the structures of National Socialism were erected to be lasting—that the concentration camps, the robbing of individuals and nations, the degradation of people, and the hatred and falsehood were to remain in power forever—we would have to despair over the moral order of the world. For this reason, as difficult as being conscious of defeat is for every German, he must have the strength to say yes to it, because the defeat of Germany is the defeat of one of the most horrifying systems of injustice that has ever been. When

National Socialism seized Germany, there was only one salvation for Germany: the disaster of war and defeat.

For the defeat of injustice is ultimately salvation and not disaster! When the blind supporters of Hitler conquered Germany with the cry "Heil Hitler," they were calling "salvation" (*Heil*) that which was "disaster" (*Unheil*) and which was revealing itself daily as destruction. My German friends, when you see the disaster today that is inevitably drawing near and you are called prophets of disaster, then you are, in truth, proclaimers of salvation. For no salvation is possible until the dominion of injustice is broken. You shall never be defeatists in that you give your last word to disaster. The approaching defeat of Germany is not the last word. It is the liberation from that which would make any future impossible. It is the judgment that must precede a new beginning. There is no escaping this judgment; there is no coming to an agreement with the system of injustice. There is only one path to the salvation of Germany, namely, through the disaster that you see in its inevitability and to which you must say yes, as seers of disaster—no, as seers of salvation.

34.
THE DEFEAT
OF NAZI BELIEF

JUNE 1, 1943

MY GERMAN FRIENDS!

National Socialism has understood how to set all Christian churches against it. It began with the German churches. The great church struggle of the first years of Nazi rule is still in the memory of all people in and outside Germany. Niemöller's cell in the concentration camp is a constant reminder not to forget that struggle, a reminder that is still heard today everywhere in the world. After the German churches, the churches of the conquered lands were forced onto the defensive by the Nazis and their collaborators, the Quislings. It is particularly the Norwegian church that has offered, and is still offering, resistance. The churches in Sweden, Denmark, and Holland sided with them. The spiritual power of this resistance is becoming greater and greater, and the force of the impact of the attack weaker and weaker. In reality, the churches have already won victory. The anti-Christian attack is repelled. The worldview of National Socialism has yet to become two decades old, and National Socialism itself won't become any older. One can speak of all of these things as facts, although the National Socialists still rule an entire continent and all Christian churches in it are abandoned to them, defenseless. The struggle of the spirits is decided: against paganism, in favor of Christianity. Just as it was in the great final battle of the Roman Empire against the externally powerless church, so it was in the last ten years of the battle of the National Socialist tribal religion against the Christian spirit. Modern paganism has lost, just as ancient paganism did. The Christian principle has once again displayed its invincibility.

This inner, spiritual battle, which has been led by the churches without any weapons, nevertheless has a deep connection with the external battle in which the weapons of all attacked nations are destroying the war machine of the Nazis, step by step. I want to speak with you today concerning this connection of Nazi belief—and its defeat—with Nazi power—and its defeat.

Why, in fact, has National Socialism led the battle against Christianity? Certainly not for the reasons for which many academics have attacked religion in past decades: because of its miracles and mysteries, because of its dogma and customs. All of that would have been completely unimportant to the National Socialists. This they would have willingly permitted from the churches, if they hadn't suspected a real enemy in Christianity. The Nazis grasped, better than many Christians, what Christianity is about. They grasped that the crucial things in Christianity are not teachings and forms of public worship but rather a particular attitude toward life. And for the sake of this attitude toward life, the Nazis started the battle against Christianity. Because the Christian attitude toward life is the complete contradiction of the Nazi attitude. People must decide in favor of one. And the Nazis have tried everything to prevent a decision in favor of Christianity, above all among the younger generation. For this reason, they have persecuted the churches.

There are two attitudes toward life that have wrestled with one another in the Nazis' battles with the churches. The attitude toward life as National Socialism represents it is older than Christianity. It comes from the time when every tribe considered itself to be the greatest in the world. God belonged to the nation and the nation to god. They were indissolubly united with each other. When the nation fell, the god also fell. When the nation became powerful, the god also became powerful. And just as every individual lived off of the nation to which he belonged, so he had to give it everything. The law of the nation had to be his law. The truth of the nation had to be his truth. The justice of the nation had to be his justice. But there wasn't only one tribe and nation. And so a battle of tribes came about, nation fighting against nation and god against god, in mutual destruction. That was the world that Christianity, and before it, the great prophets, found. They sought to take humanity beyond this world of fighting gods to something higher, to the one God and the one people of God, beyond all tribes and nations. They proclaimed the one divine law, the one truth, and the one justice for all. They proclaimed the God who looked not on tribe and nation and race but rather on the face of every person and on the justice in every nation. That was the message of the prophets and apostles. With that, they brought something new into the world, something great, insurmountable, against which all attacks in nearly three thousand years were unsuccessful. These attacks couldn't be successful. And the attack of National Socialist paganism also could not be successful. Because the human heart says yes to the Christian message and not to the idolatry of nation; yes to justice for all and to the unity of the human race. With the power of this certainty, the Christian churches have fended off the attack of ancient paganism. And what the churches have done in the spiritual battle has been confirmed on the battlefields.

The will-to-power of one nation, and the idol that it has created, was broken when it ran against the united wills of the rest of the world. Every battle in the east and south is a part of the great battle in which the dragon of pagan idolatry is being killed. Someday you must see your defeats in this light. They are, as it were, the realization of the one great defeat that National Socialism has already suffered: its defeat in the struggle against Christianity. One cannot run up against the one God, the God of the world, in the name of a national god. Whoever attempts this is crushed. When the empires of the past did so, they were destroyed. When the heroes of primeval times did so, they brought death and destruction upon themselves. When ancient Israel did so, it was surrendered to foreign powers by the God who was its God. When the church of the Middle Ages did so, it was smashed into pieces. And when the German nation did so in the twentieth century, it was twice repulsed and stripped of its power. In the whole of history, we see that each reality—even the most powerful nation, even if it was a chosen nation, even if it was the church itself—is broken down when it rises up against the one God. There is no individual person and no individual group of people, no tribe and no nation, who is appointed for world rule. The only ones who have the promise to possess the earth are the "meek,"[55] that is, the ones renouncing power.

What is now occurring in every hour on the battlefields is evidence of the truth with which Christianity has overcome the pagan world. When the Christian churches became lethargic and feeble, when they withdrew into the corners of pious feelings and old traditions, the space became free for the return of pagan national religion, which calls itself National Socialism. It believed that Christianity would end and that pagan national gods could celebrate a cheerful resurrection — first and foremost, the German god. And they even found Christians who were prepared to welcome these gods that had arisen again. But finally, they struck against the rock of the Christian proclamation and broke into pieces, and the risen gods were sent with disgrace back into their thousand-year-old graves. And as the German god reeled back into the grave in which it belonged, his followers and all who had to fight for him as slaves were thrown back, step by step. The world, which, like the churches, was surprised and overrun for a moment by the German god, came to itself. It united itself, and the high priest of the German god, the German Führer, made it easy for the world to unite itself. With insane arrogance, with a wild overestimation of himself and his god, he attacked nearly all powers of the world and forced them to unite. This is the deep blindness of every idolatry, by which all ancient powers have been destroyed: that it confuses the idol with God himself, that it equates its own limited power with the highest power and, in this way, destroys itself.

Allow me to say once again: what is now occurring on the battlefields, on the land, in the water, in the air, is the same as what occurred in people's hearts when they resisted the temptation to national idolatry. It is the breakdown of the new paganism, of the belief in the national god and his justice. It is the return of the German nation into the community of nations that accepts the Christian principle. The important thing is not whether they are good or bad Christians; true Christians are in the minority in all nations. The important thing is not even that these nations have converted to Christianity. Rather, the important thing is that they accept the Christian principle of the unity of humankind. The important thing is that they stand for the unity of justice and the dignity of every person. So much is being perpetrated against these principles in all countries; it is crucial that they are accepted and not, as in National Socialism, rejected. When it turned itself into the instrument of the new pagan national god, Germany was expelled from the community of nations, a community that placed itself under the Christian principle. Germany is returning to the community of Christian nations to the extent to which the spiritual and political power of this national god is being broken. Every defeat in the battle with the churches, every defeat in the battle for the souls of the youth, every defeat in the battle with the rest of humanity is a step on the path of Germany's return home to Christianity and to the human race.

35.
NAZISM AND THE IDEALS
OF THE FRENCH REVOLUTION

JULY 5, 1943

MY GERMAN FRIENDS!

On the fourteenth of July, the victory of the great revolution that changed the face of France, Europe, yes, the entire world, was once celebrated in the old France.[56] Today, under German occupation and under the rule of the reactionaries in Vichy, the fourteenth of July can be celebrated only silently. But whether or not a more public celebration is possible, the day of revolution will be celebrated with more fervor than ever before in the hearts of most of the French. The day of freedom will have more meaning in this year of the French nation's bondage than at any other time since the revolution. In bondage, they will again experience what freedom is worth and that it is worth dying for. A revolutionary France is waiting to be able to take part in the battle against its foreign and domestic oppressors. The ideals of the fourteenth of July, of the day of the storming of the fortress of tyranny, are not yet dead in the French nation. They were in danger of withering away in the period between the wars. The French nation had become weary after the First World War and its dreadful losses. And this weakening was used by small groups of reactionary politicians, military officers, and high-ranking civil servants to cheat France out of the ideals of the fourteenth of July and the great revolution. They weakened the French resistance at home and in the field. They preferred the rule of the National Socialists to the rule of their own people. They would rather have a Nazi Europe than a democratic Europe. For this group of French reactionaries, the fourteenth of July is an embarrassing day. They would most prefer to wipe out the memory of the great revolution and return to the times of royal despotism, with or without a king—in any case, with new despots. But the French nation has not forgotten. It has again and again overpowered the attacks on its freedom, the internal as well as the external ones; and now it will again lead the battle and will gain freedom, just as it gained it on July 14, 1789.

What does all this have to do with Germany? It has this to do with Germany: that the National Socialists, hand in hand with the French reactionaries, want to turn back world history to before the time of the French Revolution. For this reason, they were welcomed by the Lavals and Petains.[57] For this reason, Paris and—in the end—all of France was abandoned to the Germans without much struggle. For this reason, the French rulers parted with the Western democracies. It was an alliance of French reactionaries with the Nazis that brought the downfall of France, just as the alliance of the Nazis with British reactionaries would have brought the downfall of Britain if the British nation had not forced the battle for freedom in time. Europe has experienced an uprising of all reactionaries against the ideals of the French Revolution. And the shock troops in this battle against the spirit of the fourteenth of July were the German National Socialists.

How do matters stand with the ideals of the great revolution, which are said to be dead by the Nazis and which they wanted to replace with their own ideals? Is it true that the whole of European history since the storming of the Bastille, the fortress of the French tyrants, was an error? So it is being preached daily to you and your children. New fortresses have been set up. Today, they are called concentration camps. All who place themselves in the path of the new tyrants are being sent there unjustly and without sentence, just as all who placed themselves in the path of the old monarchical tyrants vanished into the dark chambers of the Bastille unjustly and without sentence. The French nation defended itself against this when it burned down the Bastille and freed the prisoners; and the German nation should turn itself against this by burning down the concentration camps and releasing the captives. It would be something great if at some time the German nation would do what the French nation did a century and a half ago and free itself from its own tyrants. If the German nation would someday do this, with complete devotion and without that compromise that has spoiled all previous German revolutions, then it would be ripe for freedom throughout the future. An authentic German revolution against tyranny and for freedom could change the entire fate of Germany; it could bring Europe a new future. Germans and French could fight together for the ideals that are being trampled underfoot today in both lands. In the spirit of these ideals, the European curse—the enmity between Germany and France—could be overcome. The alliance of German and French freedom fighters could become the bridge from west to east. It could bring the tragic self-destruction of Europe to an end.

What are the ideals of the French Revolution, against which National Socialism preaches hatred and contempt? Have they become obsolete? Were they an error, and must world history be reconsidered? I don't believe it. I believe that the ideals of equality and freedom, in whose names the fortresses of French tyranny broke to pieces, are today shining more brightly than at any time since the days when they were first grasped and won. Today, whoever has no right to defense and is dragged into prison or to their death has learned what it means that everyone is equal before the law. Today, whoever is deprived of all civil and political freedoms grasps again why there have been martyrs of freedom for centuries. Today, whoever is being betrayed, without protection, to the arbitrary use of power by a ruling clique, kept under surveillance by informers, agents, and secret police, can subsequently experience what it meant when this total system of despotism was crushed and, as a free person, one was accountable to the law alone. Today, we can again experience what the fighters of the eighteenth century experienced in Europe and in America. This experience of freedom is the real enemy of all tyrants and all of their beneficiaries. For this reason, they want to go back before the French Revolution. For this reason, they want to allow the people to forget what one of their most valuable memories is: the victory over the seemingly impregnable power of ancient tyranny.

I do not say this to challenge you to return to the French Revolution and to bring it back into Germany. Nothing in history can be brought back. Even the ideals of freedom and equality before the law must be understood anew and realized anew. On French public buildings are written not only the words *freedom and equality* but also the word *fraternity*. Of the three, it is that word which most points to the future; and even more, it is that ideal, without whose fulfillment neither of the others is lasting. How was it possible that in the land of the revolution for freedom and equality, freedom and equality were betrayed by powerful groups, betrayed so completely that they allowed their worst enemy in, simply because he also was an enemy of freedom and equality and had the power to suppress them? It was possible because the third of the ideals, fraternity, was not realized in any sense! We are no longer speaking today of fraternity but of social security for all, or of freedom from privation, want, and fear. So the declaration of the war aims of the Allied nations—the Atlantic Charter[58]—calls it. Here lies the difference between our ideals and those of the French Revolution: today, we know that freedom and equality before the law are lost if they are not borne by freedom from want and equal opportunity for everyone. This was not understood in the nineteenth century. And for that reason, in this century the belief in freedom and equality was undermined, step by step, and collapsed beneath the catastrophes of the twentieth century.

The National Socialists say that the ideals of the French Revolution are finished. But they are finished only if the third ideal, the task of our time—social security—is not realized. Don't be deceived, my German friends! With a half-truth, the Nazis have captured many worthwhile people. They have pointed to the lack of freedom and the inequalities of the social order that emerged from the French Revolution. Today, no one can close their eyes to that anymore, and in reality, no one is doing so. And then they've said: therefore, we must go back before the French Revolution and everything that has grown out of it. And this was the Nazis' deception! In this way, they wanted to secure their despotism against every attack of free people. They wanted to go back instead of going forward. They wanted to cause freedom to be forgotten instead of protecting freedom through social justice and security. We cannot simply return to the French Revolution; even the French are unable to do this. But even less can we go back before the French Revolution, as the Nazis and all selfish reactionaries want to do. We must go forward in the spirit of the universally human ideals that gave the French Revolution its irresistible force. We must go forward to a new form of freedom and equality, a form in which freedom includes social security and equality includes social justice. It is your task to realize this, my German friends. In this spirit, you must fight against Germany's old and new tyrants. In this spirit, you must look back with your French brothers on the victory that they won over the tyrants of their day. In this spirit, you must look forward to the day in which you, together with them, free yourselves from the tyrants of your time.

36.
THE DEFEATED
CHEER THE VICTORS

JULY 19, 1943

MY GERMAN FRIENDS!

It is being reported out of Sicily that the inhabitants have greeted the victorious soldiers of the Allies with joy and have given them bread and fruit. It is being further reported that the Sicilians gave open expression to their hatred toward Fascists and Germans. Such reports are being kept hidden from you, but here they surprise no one. We knew a long time ago what the mood was in Italy. Every neutral party that traveled to Italy since the beginning of the war gave the same report. The Italian nation wants to have nothing to do with the war. It was driven into the war by the Fascists, and the Fascists are long since captives of the Nazis. They are observed by the Gestapo in their every step. Without German soldiers, they could not last in their own nation. What they have to do is decided in Berlin and not in Rome. And what the Italian nation has to do is first decided on by the National Socialists and then by the Fascists. They had determined that Italy should make the cowardly attack on the defenseless Ethiopians, and the Italian nation had to take on this humiliation. Nazis and Fascists led the war against the Spanish nation and its lawful government on the side of the rebels, and the Italian nation had to say yes to the misfortune of the Spanish nation. Fascists and Nazis drove the Italian people into the inglorious war against small, defenseless Albania. They drove them into the pitiful attack on Greece, which, without German help, would never have been successfully conducted. Nazis and Fascists forced the Italian people to stab already defeated France in the back and, thereby, forced them into the Second World War. They transported

Italian soldiers out of the warmth of their home villages and cities and into the freezing countryside of Russia. In this long series of humiliating and meaningless wars, the Italian people were the first victim. Not one of these attacks on weaker parties was borne by the enthusiasm of Italians. Not one of these wars was a national war. They were wars of ambitious rulers who have turned a nation into a tool. They were wars of the Fascist conquerors, not of the Italian people.

And so the remarkable thing is taking place, that the defeated are cheering on the victors, because the victors, the British and Americans and French, are coming not as victors over the Italian people but rather as victors over the oppressors of the Italian people. Something like that has not often occurred in the world's history. Usually, when hostile soldiers conquered a city, they were received with gloomy, depressed silence or outbreaks of open hatred. Only some traitors were pleased that their work was successful. Now the entire nation is pleased and is relinquishing its own government and its allies. The Italian people are declaring that they hate the Fascists and the Germans and are giving the soldiers marching in bread and fruit!

My German friends! There is something in this picture that is wrong. The Italians declare that they hate the Fascists and the Germans. They should declare that they hate the Fascists and the Nazis. And the German nation should join them. When will it come to that? When will the Italians and all German allies grasp that they have become victims of the same power that the German nation is lying beneath as well—international fascism? You must stop thinking that this is a war of nations. You must not compare it with the First World War or with the German-French or Russian-Japanese wars. There is something different going on in the present struggle of nations: it is about different goals from national ones. From the standpoint of expanding its national power, the Italian nation has had enormous losses. All of its African possessions are gone. With each of its losses in terms of power politics, the Italian nation is winning from the standpoint of human life and human dignity. It is winning back its freedom, although foreign soldiers are standing on its soil. And the Italians sense that. They are freer under the tanks and airplanes of the Allied nations than they were under the Axis and the bundles of rods of the Fascists. They are freer beneath the open rule of the Allied armies than beneath the secret rule of the German Gestapo. They sense that two forms of human life are struggling with each other: the one that is borne by Fascists and National Socialists and the other that is borne by Western democracies. The Sicilian peasants and tradesmen who gave the soldiers of the Allies bread and fruit do not know much about England and America, about democracy and human rights. But they know very precisely what it means to live under Fascist tyranny and under National Socialist control. From free people they turned into slaves of a party, into the instruments of a dictatorship. They were incorporated into the large machine of the Fascist state. They had their right to free speech taken. They were denied impartial justice. They have been plunged into one war after the other, the significance and basis of which they did not know. They have been economically ruined and politically incapacitated. That they know. And because they know that, they welcome their national enemies as human and political liberators.

What has begun in Sicily, in the extreme south of Europe, will continue step by step to the north and east and west of Europe. Everywhere, the victorious soldiers of the Allied nations will be welcomed by the people, not only by those of the subjugated nations but also by those of the fascist conquerors. In all of Italy—in Naples and Rome, in Florence and Milan—the destroyers of fascism will enter as saviors of the Italian people. And when the people have no bread and no fruit to give them, they will express their thanks to them in other ways. So it is, and so it will be, in Italy. And in Germany? There is still no part of the German land occupied. We still do not know how the German people will accept its liberators from the Nazi yoke. But one thing we have already heard: the inhabitants of the bombed cities have no feelings of hatred toward the British pilots who are destroying their homes and killing their relatives and laying ruin to their places of work. They are suffering, and yet they do not hate the visible cause of their suffering, the enemy pilots. What they hate is the deeper, true cause of their distress, the inner enemy, whose victims they have become: the National Socialists! Of these people it is expected that they will behave in exactly the same way as the Sicilian population: they will welcome their enemies as their liberators. The movement that has begun in Sicily will not be blocked even by the Alps. It will spread to Munich and Dresden and Frankfurt and, finally, to Berlin and Hamburg. They will wait for the enemies as they do for liberators. They will join the great movement against European fascism. They will breathe a sigh of relief in the German villages and cities, despite the destruction, because the air of freedom will again blow through the German lands.

So it will be! But if that is so, why wait? Why draw the hatred of nations toward Germany instead of toward the Nazis? The Sicilians declare that they hate Fascists and Germans. Why Germans? Why not Nazis? If the Italians hate their Fascist tyrants, why don't you hate your Nazi tyrants? But what am I asking! You hate them, yes. You have experienced worse things beneath their rule than the Italians beneath the Fascists. You feel the Nazis to be the enemies of your freedom even more than the Italians do their Fascists. You long for liberation from them, like all conquered nations. So show the nations that this is the case. Show them that they must hate not the Germans but rather the Nazis. Show all the oppressed in Italy and France, in Serbia and Norway, that the German nation stands on their side, suffering with them and yearning with them for liberation! Take from them the basis for hating the Germans, and unite with them in hatred toward the Nazis!

It is infinitely important that this takes place soon, that it takes place now! The Sicilians see the German soldiers who take away food from them and have the last word in their land; those are the Germans for them, but they do not see the German people. And so they hate the Germans. The French see the occupying army, which, at their expense, is better fed than they and whose officers are their great masters. Those are the Germans for them, but they do not see the German people. And so they hate the Germans. The Poles and Russians see the Gestapo agents, at whose command their national comrades are being shot dead. Those are the Germans for them, but they do not see the German people. And so they hate the Germans. German people, show yourselves to be against the Gestapo and the generals and all the other instruments of National Socialism. People are seeking after the Germans behind the hideous face of the Nazis. Show yourselves, you true Germans, so that the confusion between you and your oppressors stops! Just as the Sicilians hate you without knowing you, so you are hated by Frenchmen and Italians who do not know you, by

Poles and Russians and Serbs who know nothing of you, and by Norwegians and Greeks who have forgotten or have never heard that once you were also conquered by the Nazis. Show them all that you are there, that you want to oppress no one, that you've suffered even longer and harder beneath the same conquerors as they. Show the nations of the world that the enemies of the Nazis are your friends, that you welcome those who are liberating you from the Nazi yoke. And more than that: help yourselves to your liberation, more than before. Everything depends on this: that you do it soon, that you do it powerfully and, to a great extent, visibly. The entire future of Germany depends on the fact that the Nazis, and not the Germans, are hated. And that can happen only if you separate yourselves from them, not with words when it is too late but with deeds as long as there is time.

37.
COLLECTIVE
GUILT

AUGUST 9, 1943

MY GERMAN FRIENDS!

One of the proudest German cities is a heap of ruins. Ten thousand are buried in the ruins. A hundred thousand are without homes, dependent on the hospitality of strangers or the help of the state, in grief over the loss of everything that made life dear to them: people, property, work, the city of their fathers or their choice, in whose brilliance they shared. The ancient story of the rain of fire that fell on Sodom and Gomorrah[59] has become truth in one city, which was famous throughout the entire world and which was proud of its spiritual and moral culture. Many people of Hamburg will ask: why has this struck so dreadfully, directly at us, when we were surely the least ready to open our doors to the destroyers of Germany? What is our particular guilt; why are we, of all people, chosen among the seventy million Germans? And perhaps the refugees from the other destroyed cities will follow and ask: why us of all people? And perhaps, then, those will join in whose husbands or sons or fathers have died on the battlefields and will ask: why me, why me of all people? And perhaps the masses of the German nation will hear this question and will likewise ask: why our nation? Why have we become the victims and tools of the National Socialists, in order to become the victims, now, of the rain of fire and of want and of death on the battlefields and of inevitable defeat? Why us, why us in particular, for yet the second time in a generation? So will the entire German nation ask when the trains of misery from Hamburg and Cologne and Essen and Russia and Italy pour out over the land. That is a question that is as old as humanity. At all times, people

[178]

whom a heavy misfortune has struck have put the question: am I, then, more guilty than others? And many have answered: I am conscious of no guilt. Why, then, is it hitting me in particular? And others have answered: I am as guilty as all others, not more and not less. Why am I punished more than the others? And yet others have answered: yes, I am especially guilty, because I could have better understood and was blinded and led into destruction. Countless people in the German nation will swing to and fro among these three answers. The superficial ones will exonerate themselves of any complicity in the evil. The deeper ones will grasp that there is a collective guilt, and the finest and best in the nation will lay the greatest blame on themselves. They will say to themselves and to others among themselves: if we had been stronger and braver and wiser, we could have prevented the destroyers of the German nation from having won power over it.

Perhaps you are surprised that such a question is raised in a political address. Perhaps you think that this is a religious problem that everyone has to sort out for themselves or about which something can be said in sermons. But this is not so. The question of guilt always was, and is today as well, not only a question that concerns individuals. It is a question that is put to nations and that must be answered by nations. There is something like collective guilt in which everyone shares, even if the doom that follows the guilt does not strike everyone in the same way. I want to speak to you about this collective guilt today. The attitude of the German nation toward this question is of crucial significance for the decisions it has to make in the next months, and for its entire historical future.

You will remember the numerous discussions that were led concerning war guilt during the First World War and after it. In the Treaty of Versailles was the famous war-guilt paragraph that provoked so much bitterness. In the treaty was the demand that the war criminals be handed over—a demand that was never exacted. What is the meaning of this rhetoric about guilt, completely apart from the political appropriateness or inappropriateness of those guilt paragraphs of the peace treaty? Clearly, all of that expresses a feeling that there is, in the life of nations as well, something like guilt, a collective guilt in which everyone shares, even if he is not in a responsible position. It forms a part of the finest traits in the character sketch of the British and the Americans that many among them felt a sense of guilt over the treatment of Germany after the First World War. And it forms a part of the tragic events of our time that Hitler and his diplomatic representatives could use this feeling of the most decent people among the former enemies of Germany in order to prepare for attack on them. Hitler played on the conscience of the world in order to be able to arm, undisturbed, for his attack on the world. As a result, he had successes in the beginning. But then the conscience of the world reacted with tremendous force and pronounced guilty the one who had so shamefully misused this genuine sense of guilt. And the conscience of the world is pronouncing the German nation to be an accessory, because it has been led astray. And this conscience of the world is also speaking through the best people in the German nation. Yes, it is speaking through them most authentically, because it is unclouded by national passion. You, my German friends, who hear these words and inwardly agree with me and acknowledge your share of the guilt in the fate of this time, are the purest expression of the world's conscience. Your voice, your confession of complicity is fundamental to the shaping of the future Germany and of future humanity.

There is a collective guilt of humanity in every disaster that strikes humanity, in wartime as in peacetime. Only fools and hypocrites exclude themselves from this collective guilt, which is acknowledged by all sages and saints and prophets. The misery that a wicked social order brings to the masses of people is a collective sin in the same way as the misery that war brings to two nations. And the misfortune that the world wars of the twentieth century have brought to all of humanity is a collective sin in the same way as the indigence and desperation of the unemployed in all the world, which was one of the most important causes for the emergence of dictatorships. No one in the whole world should be brought by political propaganda and nationalist blindness to where he acquits himself of this collective guilt and lays all the blame on others. Whoever does this only creates the conditions for the next disaster that will come upon the nations.

But least of all should you, my German friends, acquit yourselves of the collective guilt, and I believe—indeed, I know—that you are not doing so. Because on the basis of humanity's collective guilt, the particular guilt of the individual nation rises up. And here the most difficult question occurs in accordance with the ethical guilt of all nations. When we look into the past, we find powerful words by prophets and seers about the guilt of their own nation or foreign nations. We also speak of national decay, national errors, national sins. There is something like that; and only those nations can live whose leaders are able to acknowledge the guilt of their own nation. A nation that persists in national self-righteousness is preparing for its downfall. Hard national fates have the significance of showing a nation where its ethical dangers lie and in what it has been guilty. Britain experienced a rebirth under the German bombs. Will Germany experience a rebirth beneath the British bombs? A nation can be reborn only if it perceives its guilt and has parted with it. The guilt of the German nation is that it has permitted the National Socialists to become masters over it. Surely, it is due to the collective guilt of humanity that it could come to this, and the honest and decent people in other countries acknowledge that. But it still took place not in the other countries but in Germany, and for this reason, in the midst of the collective guilt of the nations, there is still a particular German guilt. Hitler was long seen coming, and many who inwardly despised National Socialism supported it because they all believed they could do business with it and then get rid of it. And thus, they became guilty. All Germans have heard of the horrible crimes that have taken place in the concentration camps. But they hardened their hearts and did nothing and, as a result, made themselves culpable. Every German knew of the extermination campaign against Jewish people. Everyone knew Jewish people about whom he felt sorry, but no protest arose. Not once did the churches take their place with the persecuted of the nation from which Christ came; and thus, they all became culpable. The entire army saw, and keeps seeing, what is occurring in the occupied regions through the Gestapo's henchmen. Generals and soldiers know about it and turn their eyes away, often in shame, but never with an action that could save Germany from this disgrace. And so they have become culpable. The masses of the nation suffer because of the dictatorship that has come over them, but they give way, even now when the war has given the weapons into their hands to drive away the tyrants and to call the criminals to account. And thus, they all became culpable. That is the guilt of the German people. That is what has brought this fate on Germany. That is what answers the question: why us, of all people?

There is a collective guilt of the world to have such a social order from which the Thirty Years War of the twentieth century could develop. And all the world is struck by the consequences of this guilt. There is a particular guilt of the German nation, namely, to have turned itself into the tool of the National Socialist criminals. And the German nation will be struck the hardest by the consequences of its particular guilt. But finally, there are those National Socialist criminals themselves through whose action the guilt of humanity and the guilt of the German nation has become a reality, and who will not escape the fate of the criminal.

Why is this happening to us; why our generation? So ask the people in all nations. And the answer is: because they all share in collective guilt. Why is this happening to us, to those of us from Germany, to those of us from Hamburg, to our families, to me? So ask the people in Germany. And the answer is: because all Germans share in a particular guilt, namely, to have given power to those who have brought doom on Germany and the world.

38.
GUILT—
ATONEMENT—EXPIATION

MY GERMAN FRIENDS!

We have spoken of collective guilt in this war, of the collective guilt of humanity in which every nation shares, and of the particular guilt of the German nation in which every German shares. We have come to realize that the fate which has come upon humanity is a consequence of this collective guilt, and that the fate which is now working itself out throughout Germany is a consequence of German guilt. Where there is guilt, there is an atonement. No one escapes this eternal law of all life. Humanity does not escape it, and the German nation does not escape it. When millions of Germans — women, children, and old people — must leave their homes because a rain of fire can at any moment break out of the dark clouds that hang over German cities; when the rural population must take the wretched masses of the large cities into their cramped dwellings; when families are separated, and many do not know whether the people closest to them are buried beneath ruins or are sitting exhausted on some country road; when all of that is now occurring and will occur on a larger and larger scale, then this is atonement for the guilt of the preceding years. The ruins in Hamburg, Cologne, Nuremberg, and Essen are the atonement for the ruins in Madrid, Warsaw, Rotterdam, and London. The migration out of the German industrial cities is atonement for the migration out of the Belgian villages, when a nation at peace was suddenly caught beneath the rain of German shrapnel — bombed by German pilots — and was seeking to escape the battle front. It is an atonement for the wrong that was perpetrated by the Fascists and National Socialists together on the German South Tyrolese,[60] when they were forced to migrate into strange, northern lands. And today, when the trains with Germans who are fleeing from the cities roll from west to east, this is an atonement for the death trains that, filled with Jewish women and children and old people, drove out of all German cities from west to east to certain death. The German cities slept when the death trains rolled through their train stations with their burden of indescribable misery. Now they are awoken by the fire from heaven; now their inhabitants themselves are filling the trains of misery. We must look all of that in the eye. And I know that you who hear these words have looked at all of this for a long time. I recall that even in the first months of the Hitler dictatorship, Germans with sensitive feelings said, "All of this injustice that is now occurring will come upon us and our children!" Now it has come and will come further. The law of guilt and atonement will work itself out further in all who are accessories to the world disaster, in all who are accessories to the German fate.

Permit me to say a word to you, in this context, concerning the punishment of the war criminals that is being so urgently demanded by the Allies. It is not a need for revenge that drives the leaders of these nations to such a demand. It is more likely the opposite: they want to prevent, as much as is possible, the feelings of hatred and revenge that have arisen in the hearts of the oppressed, exploited, maltreated masses of the conquered lands from manifesting themselves in a disorderly and unjust way. The punishment of the war criminals should be a refuge for the many Germans who, admittedly, share in the collective guilt, but not as leaders and instigators. Simple lust for revenge would not make such a distinction. It would seek to destroy everything that is German. The seducers and those seduced, the criminals and those who have permitted the crimes to occur would be struck in the same way by the blindness for revenge. For that reason, the work of atonement should be put into the hands of people who do not want revenge themselves but rather want to help the law of guilt and atonement to achieve victory in a conspicuous way. They want justice exercised even in relation to those who have trampled all justice underfoot. They want to strike the first guilty parties, after the accomplices—the entire nation—are themselves struck by the war. And now I ask you: isn't that your wish also? The crimes of the Nazi leaders and their henchmen cry out to heaven. The torment and blood of the innocent—those intentionally tortured and murdered in Germany and in all lands under Nazi rule—cry out to heaven. Shall they cry out in vain forever? Shall the most frightful crimes committed in centuries remain without a distinct, visible atonement? You yourselves will not want that! No respectable German will want that. But you will want—wherever possible—yourselves to be those who wash off, through atonement, the shame that the National Socialist criminals have brought on the German name.

It is understandable that you want this, and in many—yes, in most—cases it will be possible; but not in all. When crimes have occurred in occupied countries against the population of these countries, there is a precept of justice to leave the atonement to the judges of these countries. And it would be good if those among you who acknowledge the law of guilt and atonement would say that as clearly as possible, just as, for example, the representatives of the German prisoner of war camps have publicly said it. That is not contrary to the honor of the German nation. It is, rather, the single way to restore the German honor that is trampled through the mud by the Nazis.

But ultimately, it will be the same whoever passes judgment on the war criminals. And it would be best by far if the German nation today exercised judgment on those who have made it guilty and have then driven it into misfortune. This would be the first and decisive step toward expiation, toward the rebirth of the German nation, and toward a new beginning. The law of guilt and atonement is an inviolable law. But it is not the only law, and not the highest law in human life. Over it stands the law of atonement and expiation. As it is in the life of an individual, so it is in the life of nations. Just as there is a collective guilt and a collective atonement, so there is a collective expiation. And just as, in the life of the individual, the meaning of atonement is that one parts with that through which one has become guilty, so also in the life of nations the meaning of atonement is that a nation separates from that through which it has become guilty. The disaster that has now occurred across the German nation has the significance of separating the German nation from those who have drawn the disaster near. The atonement for the guilt into which the Nazis have misled the German nation has the significance of separating the German nation from its seducers. When that has occurred, atonement has turned into expiation. And it is that for which all who love Germany and who hope for a German future are now waiting. Only those who do not love Germany will be pleased if Nazi rule continues to last for long. Because the longer the German people allow themselves to be the instruments of Nazi criminals, the more the disaster will have its effects and the more difficult the distinction of the seduced from the seducers will be. Whoever wants to destroy Germany grants to it the continuation of Nazi rule until complete collapse. Whoever wants to make the complicity of the German nation in Nazi crimes more and more serious is glad about each further day in which Germans put up with Nazi rule. There are such German-haters in all lands! You serve them, my German friends, in every hour in which you refrain from separating from the Nazis. But above all, in that way you serve the Nazis themselves, who want precisely the same things that the German-haters on the outside want: to allow the German nation to become guilty. It is the clear policy of the National Socialists to create a solidarity of guilt, since they sense that their end is drawing near. They want the entire German nation to carry out so many crimes, to entangle it so deeply in its own guilt, that no further separation is possible. You must reckon with this policy, my German friends. You must see through this policy and thwart it. The Nazis inside and the German-haters outside have a silent agreement: they want to allow the German nation to sink deeper and deeper into guilt, the German-haters in order to destroy it, the National Socialists in order to be indiscriminately destroyed with it when there is no further escape. Don't be driven further on this path! Separate yourselves from those who have misled you and have turned you into the instrument of their crimes! Show that the expiation of the German nation has begun, that you are determined to separate from that which has made you guilty, the spirit and reality of National Socialism! Exercise the retribution yourselves on those who can no longer escape retribution!

The German-haters are still not in the position where the future of Germany is decided. The responsible leaders of the Allies still distinguish between National Socialists and Germans, between those who are directly responsible for the crimes and the nation that—partly out of ignorance, partly out of fear, partly out of lethargy—has permitted this monstrous thing to occur. But every day in which the separation of the German nation from the National Socialists is postponed makes the position of the German-friends in all countries of the world more difficult, and the German future more dark.

And what is almost more serious: the later, the nearer to the collapse, that you separate yourselves from the Nazis, the less value it has for the inner condition of the German nation, the less expiating force it has, the less hope there is for a rebirth. Whoever says that he wants to separate himself from the Nazis only on the day of defeat is not believed, with good reason. If the German nation turns away from National Socialism only in the last hour, then it will not be expiated, not even by every disaster that it has undergone. Then a new disaster will brew for Germany and for the world in the womb of an unexpiated nation.

39.
EGYPTIAN PLAGUES AND GERMAN PLAGUES

SEPTEMBER 1943

MY GERMAN FRIENDS!

Most of you know the ancient story of the exodus of the children of Israel from Egypt. Before Pharaoh, the god-king of Egypt, permitted the exodus, his people were afflicted with plagues, the most serious of which was the death of the firstborn in all Egyptian families.[61] Whoever lives in Germany today can appreciate what that ancient story means. He knows what it means when a nation is plunged from one misfortune into another through the guilt of its leaders. He can speak of our time in terms of the plagues that, as a result of the callousness and arrogance of his ruler, have struck a modern nation. For the sake of Hitler's blasphemous self-confidence and for the sake of the hardening of his heart, when one considers the suffering of his and many other nations, indeed, one Egyptian plague after the other has come upon the German nation: the icy cold of the Russian winter, the heat of the African desert, malnutrition and a shortage of everything extending for years, everyone's fear of offending the rulers by saying the truth, the rain of fire over the cities, the defeats on all fronts, and the slow approach of the crushing enemy armies; but above all, just as in Egypt, the passing away of the firstborn and many of those born afterward in German families. The Egyptian plagues have come upon Germany for the same reason that they did upon Pharaoh's Egypt: because of the arrogance and callousness of the ruler! And the significance of the plagues on present-day Germany is the same as the significance of the plagues with which ancient Egypt was smitten: to free the oppressed, to break the arrogance of the ruler, to take the godlike brilliance from him, and to expose him in his total wretchedness and guilt.

Many among you who have heard or read the tale of the Egyptian plagues in past years may have asked: why did the people suffer for the callousness of Pharaoh? All of these plagues struck the entire nation, and yet, according to the story, not the nation but rather the ruler was guilty. Isn't that divine caprice and injustice? And undoubtedly, similar questions will now be asked in Germany: why is the calamity that the National Socialists have brought about striking us? Why has my son, my husband, my father been killed when I never took part in the crimes of the Nazis? Why is it that the very cities in which the present rulers had the fewest supporters—such as Hamburg, Cologne, Münster—are being destroyed? Why do we all have to atone for the guilt of the one who committed crimes not only against other nations but against us? Why are we, his first victims, being smitten so much more by the angel of death than all others? For we, the German people, were Hitler's first victim.

But the history of nations shows that nations always suffer for what their rulers do. And history shows that nations have to be struck so that the rulers are struck. So it was in ancient Egypt. The firstborn of all Egyptian families had to be struck in order that Pharaoh be struck. So it was in Napoleonic France: French youth had to die on the snowy fields of Russia so that Napoleon could be deprived of his power over Europe. So it was in prerevolutionary Russia: millions of Russian men had to die in order that the enslaving system of czarist rule could be broken. So it now is in Germany. "Seven" and more plagues have passed through Germany so that it can be freed from the iron grip of its National Socialist tyrants. The victims of these tyrants, the German people, are being tormented more each day by those who want to free them from their tyrants. For the sake of Hitler's guilt, mothers are dying with their infants under the wreckage of their homes. For the sake of Hitler's guilt, the angel of death is carrying away German men. To break the chains in which he has bound, first, the German nation and, then, many other nations, the happiness of nearly every German family must be sacrificed. You all are aware of that now, as you stand before an incomprehensible enigma.

The callousness of Pharaoh brings the plagues upon Egypt. The crimes of Hitler are bringing destruction upon Germany.

There is a mysterious connection between nation and ruler that is not so very obvious! When a ruler has power over a nation, at that time the nation also has a joint responsibility, even if it hasn't elected the ruler. It has not elected him, but it has tolerated him. In Napoleon's France and in Hitler's Germany, the rulers were not only tolerated but also hailed by many and welcomed by many. You who feel wronged today for suffering beneath Hitler's guilt, ask yourselves whether once you didn't welcome him, even if hesitantly, when he destroyed the republic that you didn't love. Ask yourselves whether once you weren't completely content when he suppressed your political opponents. Ask yourselves whether you didn't feel some satisfaction within you when the Jews were being eliminated. Do you still think about the secret pride, which you didn't want to admit, when German weapons seemed to be invincible and when they subjugated Europe? I'm not asking those who benefited from National Socialism or were united with it. They were participants in its crimes and are justifiably being struck by the consequences that are now so dreadfully displaying themselves. But rather, I am asking those who didn't like National Socialism, who were hostile to it for reasons of the spirit and humanism, and yet who took pleasure in their development of power. I am speaking to those who forgot all the dreadfulness that was being done by the minions of National Socialism on account of a new German victory. I am speaking to those who shut their ears to the misery of Hitler's victims, in order to be able to see in it the instrument of German greatness. A few, themselves among the refugees who had to leave Germany for the sake of Hitler, will be able to absolve themselves completely of such sentiments. These sentiments are what made an effective resistance against the National Socialist Party impossible. They are what kept Hitler in power. These sentiments of secret acquiescence and of unacknowledged pride over Hitler's power are what has brought the plagues of Egypt upon the German nation. That is the bond between ruler and nation: the crimes of the ruler are blamed on the nation because the nation is never without guilt when it puts up with a criminal as its leader.

The ancient story from which we proceeded displays a double ending. Pharaoh gives in. The burden of national misfortune is too great. He can't withstand it. He permits the exodus, and the plagues cease. And then, in newly won confidence, he revokes what was wrung from him: he seeks to lead the tribe setting off back into slavery again and, in this way, produces his own destruction and that of his armies in the rising tide of the Red Sea.

Suppose that the present situation were to conclude in a peace in which the pharaoh of the German people, who has brought all the present misfortune, were to make all possible concessions, and the plagues of war stopped. It would not go the way it did in Egypt: Hitler and his instruments would again attempt to conquer, step by step, what they had to give up. And with this attempt, he would bring the German misfortune to completion. Nothing would be worse for the German people than a peace in which Hitler remains. It would be the true and ultimate downfall of Germany.

For this reason, Hitler must now be removed from the German people, not only outwardly but also inwardly. His spirit must be banished from the German spirit. The power that he has won over the souls of the youth must be broken. The dreams of German greatness in which he appeared must cease to be dreamed. Only when that takes place will the plagues that have struck the German people cease. Whoever thinks about the end of National Socialism with a secret regret has become guilty anew. He is responsible for the growing calamity that has come upon the German people. The meaning of all the plagues that are now striking you is the separation of the German people from National Socialism. The meaning of the destroyed cities is the removal of the tyranny for which you yourselves had turned into an instrument. The meaning of the death of millions is the decontamination of the German soul from the frightful poison that has laid hold of it. The meaning of the defeats, which are becoming more and more threatening, is the practical experience that whoever violates the moral order of the world draws down on himself the plagues that will destroy him and his nation.

It is infinitely important for the German future that this experience be gained soon, that it be experienced deeply and completely. Even those most powerful, in the long run, can do nothing up against what is fundamental to humanity. And a nation that has had itself misused for the oppression of human beings must share the guilt of its rulers until it has broken away from them.

It is meaningless to say that a nation has to bear the plagues that follow from the presumption, callousness, and criminal will of its leaders. There are plagues that can and must be borne, plagues that are genuine afflictions of steadfastness. But such plagues have one feature: they come upon one possessing good conscience. No one is perfect, but there are moments when a nation has this sense: what we are now experiencing is an affliction that we have to withstand and, with good conscience, can withstand. And there are other moments in the life of a nation when it has this knowledge: what we are now experiencing is the result of a tragic error, a guilt that we have fallen into, a doom that our rulers have brought upon us and that they could bring upon us because we were too weak to resist. Today, the German nation senses this; and for that reason, all efforts of the Nazis to summon up steadfastness are to no avail. The sense of error and guilt rests too deeply. No Nazi propaganda can remove it. The doom that rages on all fronts and everywhere throughout Germany can be banished only by separating from the one who has brought it upon the German people, the leader and misleader, the tyrant and corrupter of Germany.

40.
PUPPETS
AND PUPPET MASTERS
SEPTEMBER 20, 1943

MY GERMAN FRIENDS!

Instead of any reports of victory, you are compelled to hear ad nauseum the story of Mussolini's liberation. A skillful, daring coup has been overblown into a world-historical event. But it is not a world-historical event, because Mussolini has ceased to be world history. He is no longer the "Duce," the leader, but rather something completely different: he is a puppet. The trick that freed Mussolini and for which German soldiers were sacrificed has had one result: it has increased the number of German political puppets by one — a very important one. That is what has happened. And everything that will come out of the mouth of this puppet will come not from the puppet itself but from the one who is speaking through it. A speaking puppet is sitting at the radio at various places, telling Italians and Germans whatever is being said to it beforehand. Mussolini had long been turned into an instrument of the Germans but not yet into a puppet. He still had some trumps in his hand. He could still say no to some things that were conveyed to him. Now he can no longer do even that. He is the perfect puppet in German hands and will be used by them as long as they believe that he can be of use. And then he will be thrown away by them, just as a child throws away a puppet of which it has grown tired.

Mussolini is an example of many other political puppets that National Socialism has made use of and is still making use of. The first who was turned into a puppet because he was too old to defend himself was Hitler's predecessor, old Reichs-President Hindenburg. They turned him into their instrument; they had him sign decrees whose meaning he no longer understood. Even after his death, they had him take responsibility for a testament that did not come from him. The German nation knew what was going on, but it was too weak to rise up against this abuse by its highest officeholders. From the hand of a puppet it received its fate. And the next puppet that National Socialism created for itself was the so-called German Reichstag, this assembly of paid yes-men who came together to receive declarations, to shout cheers, and to disperse beneath the singing of the Nazi hymn. It was a particularly miserable puppet. Any good manufacturer would have been able to make it a better and richer puppet theater. Even the German churches were obliged to receive a puppet. It created the position of reichs-bishop, prevented a personality from being chosen for it, and instead appointed a puppet, Reichs-Bishop Müller. Admittedly, the churches were less patient than the rest of the nation in hearing the chatter of puppets. They forced the chatter to stop, and the reichs-bishop puppet was forced into the corner where it still stands today, while the dust falls on the memory of it. In the universities, puppet rectors were appointed, not men who were obliged to defend the intrinsic value of science and the belief in truth but rather puppets of the propaganda minister, who were obliged to see to it that every scientific truth was distorted through the addition of a propaganda lie. Those are only some of the German puppets that National Socialism has manufactured and through which it has caused to be said what it wanted to say. The number of those who have surrendered themselves to such a puppet existence, although they were destined for something better, is great. The more puppets, the easier the administration. With living people, it is difficult to administrate. They bring something of their own to it that often goes beyond the scope of the whole. But one can give puppets any face. One can make them say anything and make them perform any movement, if only the machine is well oiled and the wires are correctly drawn. And in that respect, the Nazis were masters.

But at times, they still had difficulties transforming people who were once living into talking and moving machines. Sometimes it didn't work out right. And so they began to do something that belongs to the most terrible and most dreadful things that are done to the German people by their tyrants. They began to mold people from their youth for puppet existence. They replaced the free will that every person brings with them into the world by nature with an artificially created and controlled fanaticism. People were created whose every movement could be calculated, who—if the right button was pushed—would kill without asking whom and why; who—if another button is pushed—would go to their own death, without asking and without hesitating. In this way, armor-plated puppets have been created, possessing a frightful force of destruction when they are properly guided but without the ability to form and interpret themselves and their lives in freedom. They are puppets from an inhuman world, incapable of hearing when one speaks sensibly to them—for example, when—as prisoners-of-war—they are supposed to be raised to a human level in their treatment. The machine goes on just as it is regulated or breaks into pieces. They are puppets, molded for puppet existence from youth onward, and incapable of becoming human beings again.

And when, after that, the armed puppets were let loose on the nations of Europe, there was no resistance to them. That was something new: machines driven by human machines, just as hard and soulless as the steel of their weapons. But there were not many of them, and the region was large that they conquered. And so another form of puppets had to be created, taken from the occupied territories and appointed as puppet regents of their own nations. There has been something else like that. Even before the start of this war, the Japanese appointed puppets in Manchuria and in conquered China. They are allowed to say nothing and to do nothing that is not dictated to them by their masters. A wire drawn in Tokyo determines every movement of the puppet regents. Europe was organized according to this pattern. Wherever it was possible, puppet governments were appointed. The Norwegian puppet became the most famous. It gave its name to all the others: Quisling. In this way Laval was appointed in France, the one who turned the aged Pétain into exactly the same puppet as Hitler did the aged Hindenburg. So it was done in the Balkans, and so it was attempted everywhere. Even in the foreign churches, the Russian and the Norwegian, they sought to impose puppet bishops, with not much better success than in Germany. And even politically the puppet game was constantly disrupted, and in many lands, such as Russia and the Netherlands, it could not be started at all. Puppets that did not function were withdrawn.

Leaders who did not allow themselves to be turned into puppets were imprisoned or murdered. Nothing was more sought after in Europe in the last three years than human puppets, who allowed their humanity to be taken and themselves to be demeaned into becoming the speaking and writing machines of the Nazis.

What a stroke of luck, therefore, when such a valuable puppet as Mussolini was found, after the demand for useful puppets had so far exceeded the supply. Don't be deceived, my German friends. What is now being pursued with Mussolini is only a continuation of the old puppet game, perhaps in such a way that a similar puppet has been secretly appointed for this wounded puppet and is now speaking for it.

Something profound and horrifying lies behind this National Socialist puppet game. It is a frightfully serious game, a game with everything that is human—above all, with that which turns a human being into a human being: his freedom. If everything were to be taken from each German person after the war but that which is human in each person were to be returned, he would not have lost through the defeat but rather won! He would be liberated from a dominion that has to turn people into puppets in order to be able to use them. It was the goal of National Socialist education to rob the entire German nation of its human freedom, step by step, to turn it into a nation of wire-drawn puppets. It is the goal of National Socialist policy to create puppets in all lands that would dance by means of its wires. In many cases, it has succeeded at that. In most, it has not. A storm fed by the forces of human dignity and freedom has risen against the National Socialist puppeteers in which they are now breaking into pieces.

And you, the German nation? Have the forces remained living in you that have resisted being transformed into machines of National Socialist dehumanization and puppet creation? I am convinced that these forces are still there. So permit them to come alive, free yourselves from the wires that are drawing you, and crush those who want to transform an entire nation into puppets.

And who are these wire-drawers, the puppet masters, who prepare and drive human machines? Look at them just once, first with a sense of shock that they have been able to deceive you for so long and then with triumph! Because if you should look carefully, you would discover that at the deepest human point, these puppeteers of National Socialism are themselves puppets. Behind them stand not human beings but rather dark, sub- and superhuman forces by which they are driven. These forces are everything that is dark, distorted, and desperate in the German soul and that has embodied itself within them. Look at them, how small and hollow they are as people, as personalities, how little they are free of the basest humanity quality! And then see how strong they are as impersonal, dark powers driven by a demonic will, destroying whatever steps into their path, and in the end, destroying themselves. They are masks behind which the powers of destruction hide, puppets on which the darkest substrata of life draw and which must, for that reason, turn all others into puppets. Pull off the mask! End the puppet show of darkness that has plunged you and the world into the greatest of all tragedies. Let humanity and freedom triumph over the puppets and masks of darkness. Tear apart the entire nightmare that lies over you, that lies over the German nation. Rise up from the awful dreams of the last ten years! Drive the National Socialist phantoms into the abyss from which they have come.

41.
TO WHOM
HAS GERMANY SURRENDERED?

SEPTEMBER 24, 1943

MY GERMAN FRIENDS!

A famous passage is found in Goethe's *Faust*. Faust comes with Mephisto, the representative of demonic power, into Gretchen's dungeon cell in order to free the victim of his tempter's art. Gretchen suddenly recognizes the devil behind the mask of Mephisto and calls out, "To you I have surrendered myself!"—to you, that is, to the demonic, destructive powers. And she prefers to go to her death and to save her soul than to have herself freed by him and thereby bring her soul to destruction.

Germany has been driven to the brink of the abyss by the Nazis. It has had itself turned into the instrument of the dark powers that are at work behind the National Socialist mask of the Nazis. When will the German people come to the recognition of Gretchen in the dungeon and cry out with horror and disgust, "To you I have surrendered myself!" When will the eyes of the German people be opened, perhaps in a sudden inspiration, so that it turns its back on its seducers and calls out, "Even if you were in the position to save me, I wouldn't have myself saved, because I don't want to sell my soul to you any longer!" At this moment, many are waiting who love Germany, in all lands and most of all in Germany itself. But still the eyes of the German people as a whole, and the eyes of many military leaders, are not yet opened. They still want to have themselves saved by those who brought them into misfortune and are driving them further into misfortune each day. The demon in the tale perhaps could have saved his unfortunate victim in the dungeon—but only to save her for a much worse doom. The demonic forces behind the Nazi masks are not even in a condition to keep their promise that they will save you. They can delay the collapse for a short time. But they can't save you from it. And this postponement means only that the collapse will be all the more frightful.

"I've surrendered myself to you," says Gretchen when she recognizes the demonic power with which Faust has enticed her. "I've surrendered myself to you," the German people will say when they have seen through the demonic forces with which the Nazis have enticed them.

Permit me to give you a couple of pictures of what the Nazis are and of what they have done and are continuing to do. There is much that no longer needs to be said. You know it yourselves; and it has been reported often enough to you, whenever voices from the outside reach you. But there remain ever new things to report, things that you would have never held to be possible, not because they are too horrible but because they are too dishonorable. You knew information about the completely ruthless brutality of the Nazis toward each of their victims before they had come to power. But what you didn't yet know, and perhaps even today still don't know, is that they are, in the same way, completely ruthless thieves and robbers. Tyrants like Robespierre, who brought thousands to the scaffold, were personally extremely respectable.[62] They distinguished clearly between state necessities, in which they believed, and personal gain, which they never permitted. They were horrifying in their policies but honorable in the use of their power. The National Socialists aren't even that. From the very beginning, they have misused their political power in a dishonorable way. They misused it for petty revenge on their political opponents. There was nothing noble in them, neither in the Führer nor in the large or small tyrants with whom he tormented the German people. Each one carried out his private revenge on what preceded; the great ones set the example and the small ones followed. But what was worse was that all became rich through the power that they had seized. Immense wealth was amassed by many leaders. They lived in luxury and extravagance, at the expense of a nation that was becoming more and more impoverished. They took countless paths to carry out their thefts, not as petty thieves who are hanged but as thieves of millions who are adorned with medals and into whose hands the fate of a nation is given. Robbery against the

Jews ordained for extermination, acceptance of large or small gifts of bribes, shady transactions of which only they as rulers could know, works of art taken into their possession on loan that belong to the nation as a whole and that are never again returned, palaces built above and beneath the earth at state cost—in all these ways, their own nation was being robbed by them.

And then came the conquering of European countries, and a raid began without equal in the history of the world. Everything was taken from the defeated: first, their means of subsistence—to the verge of starvation—then their machinery—so that all production for daily life ceased—then their labor force—so that slave labor was put in place of free labor. All of that took place in the name of war necessity, even the enforced supplying of German soldiers' brothels in the east with Polish, Russian, and Jewish girls. But the raid went further: the indigenous industries, particularly of the western countries, were bought up, in truth, stolen. They gave German currency a rate of exchange far beyond its value and forced them, at the same time, to sell for their true value. And large German concerns rushed for what was bought, concerns that captured all of life in their nets like giant spiders. It was a theft without equal, and it worked for the good of German big business at a time when Nazi propaganda took the field against Western capitalism. But with that, the raid had not ended: they went for the opulent art treasures of the conquered lands. German museum directors took part in exchanging insignificant German works of art of the nineteenth century for the valuable treasures of the past in Paris and Brussels and Amsterdam. Hitler wanted to build a supermuseum in the remote small town of Graz and fill it with the spoils from the conquered lands. What was robbed from private holdings is incalculable. No one knows where all the stolen goods of the European past will go to rest. Thieves and robbers have carried off what the centuries have preserved and collected. And you, the German people, have submitted yourselves to these thieves and robbers. When you hear this, aren't you compelled to utter the cry of horror with the captive Gretchen, "I have surrendered myself to you!" Honorable German soldiers, officers, civil servants, and laborers, aren't you alarmed about the moral abyss to which you are being led?

The Nazis were thieves and robbers from the very beginning. But now, they are becoming something else that there has not been since the horrific times of the Thirty Years War: people deliberately organized to set the earth aflame! They have even proclaimed that they would do this. In a premonition of the end that is unavoidably coming, at some time or other, one of the leaders has said: someday, when we are forced to exit the scene, we will shut the door in such a way that the world will long remember it. And another has said that when the Nazis perish, they will drag all of Europe into their ruin at the same time. Something like that sounds heroic, and if an individual does something like that, it may be understandable, although it certainly doesn't testify to greatness. But when the responsible leaders of a nation speak in this way, it is devilry or insanity that is speaking. Because everything that they are doing to others is being done simultaneously to the German people, and one day, when they can no longer do anything to others, what they have done will lie as a centuries-long curse over the German people.

For it is frightful what they are doing to the cities and villages that they have to surrender: plundering, burning, and murder mark their path in the east just as in the south and will mark it in the west when the attack begins there. The reports out of the parts of Italy conquered by the Allies rival in horror the reports from the regions reconquered by the Russians. Every distinction between belligerent armies and civilian population is set aside. Human life counts for nothing. The retreating army steps with the same indifference over human fortune as it does over the ruins of plundered homes. Europe is being laid to ruin where the German armies are passing through. Europe's curse follows closely on their heels and will accompany them and their children and grandchildren into the distant future.

And why shall Europe as a whole turn into a desert? Do you really want that, German soldiers, officers, laborers, and peasants? Are you infected by that demonic madness which says that because you are heading for a catastrophe—which, as you know, is unavoidable—the entire world must perish? And what is the world in which your children shall live? Shall they be dragged along into the abyss into which the Nazis want to plunge Europe? When the desperate insanity of self-destruction and the destruction of the world seizes you, hold up the pictures of your children before your eyes! Perhaps your eyes will then be opened. And perhaps you will then cry out to the Nazis, "I have surrendered myself to you," and will turn away from them with uttermost disgust. And even more, you will not only turn away from them, you will turn against them and drive them out of the prison into which they have brought you, just as the perceptive eye of Gretchen drove out Mephisto.

You know that you no longer live in a fortress but, indeed, in a prison. From all sides the walls have closed around you, and they are coming closer and closer. How can you believe in the promises of your seducers that they can liberate you? Only you can liberate yourselves, by freeing yourselves from them and thereby saving your soul and the future of your nation. You are prisoners of the Allied nations. You can be freed, not immediately and not without much suffering. But you can be freed by them. You cannot be freed by your seducers and corrupters. Not now and not ever! For that reason, recognize to whom you have surrendered and break the demonic spell. Save your children and the future of your nation.

42.
JUSTICE
RATHER THAN VENGEANCE
NOVEMBER 9, 1943

MY GERMAN FRIENDS!

You have heard much in the last weeks of the Moscow resolutions. You know now what they mean for Germany, politically and militarily. They mean that there will be no separate peace and that war will be carried out until the total defeat of the Germans.[63] That is the one thing that emerged absolutely clearly from the Moscow declarations of the three world powers. No one who is now being sacrificed for the prolongation of the war and for the National Socialist government can change anything in terms of the result of the war. From now on, only meaningless sacrifices are being offered. And the guilt of those who are prolonging these sacrifices is growing beyond measure. For them to survive a few months, they are sacrificing one part of the German future after the other. That is now certain. And neither propaganda nor distortion of the facts can any longer place that in doubt. Keep thinking about that! Every sacrifice that is now being offered is in vain. Every sacrifice is a monstrous crime against the German nation.

But there is still something else in the Moscow declarations, something that was never read in the bloody documents of war history: it is the declaration of the leaders of the three world powers about the atrocities of the Nazis and of those who followed them into the occupied territories. Their words do not sound like a diplomatic text, written under the pressure of many different considerations. They do not sound like a carefully weighed compromise solution. Rather, these words about the acts of the Nazis sound like prophetic speech, like words in which the conscience of the world is speaking.

First, the inconceivable crimes are pointed to, crimes that are now being committed against the inhabitants of the liberated regions by the German armies that are streaming back out. What the Russians are recounting—who are crawling out of the holes of their destroyed cities or out of their hiding places in forests and swamps—must drive every person in the whole world to utter a cry of outrage—even every German, as well, who is not still infected by the poison of Nazi devilry. Whoever still possesses a human feeling will join in this worldwide cry of human outrage over inconceivable dehumanization.

In the second part of the declaration of the three statesmen, the following is said: "At the time when an armistice is concluded with any sort of government which will then be in power in Germany, all German officers and soldiers and Nazis who were responsible for these horrors, slaughters and executions, or who have taken part in them, shall be brought into the countries in which their abominable acts have occurred. And there they shall be tried and punished according to the laws of these lands." That is not simply a wish, not one paragraph out of a long peace treaty. That is a solemn declaration of intent that no self-respecting government could take back or allow not to be carried out. And even if the governments did not want to carry it out, the tormented, bleeding, robbed, and starved nations would force it to occur and take revenge into their own hands.

Do you doubt that it is so, my German friends? Perhaps you do not believe that the horrors that are being spoken of here have actually occurred? That would be possible only if you had never heard and seen what the Nazis did to the innocents in their own nation! But indeed, you have heard and seen. You know what has been and is still taking place in the concentration camps and Nazi prisons. You know of the shipments of Jews to Poland, of the carrying off of the civilian population into slavery in Germany, of the shooting of hostages, of the robbing of all conquered lands. You hear and see something of all of that every day. That is not enemy propaganda. That is truth, which you yourselves can verify. Of course, daily and hourly, infinitely much more is taking place than what you know, than what any individual person knows. Just as it is said in the declaration of the heads of states, the desperation of defeat has doubled the savageness and the terror of the Nazis. You are experiencing that now in your own body. You can imagine how much more savage and dreadful the terror against foreign nations is!

And then follows a section in the declaration of the three world powers that reads like this: "Those who, up to now, have not stained their hands with innocent blood ought to be on their guard, that they do not enter into the ranks of the guilty. Because the three Allied powers will pursue them, with irreversible certainty, into the furthest ends of the world and hand them over to their prosecutors, so that justice is done." There are two serious warnings here. The one is to all neutral countries: there will be no places of refuge for Nazi criminals. No country, no desert, and no ocean can grant them asylum. Nowhere will they remain unpursued. And those who say this have the power to translate their words into action. Toward world criminals, there will be no neutrality. Against the breach of justice, a sword of justice is rising up that reaches to the ends of the earth. Up to now, only prophets have spoken like this, and only when they spoke in the name of God. It will be the first time that human justice encompasses the globe and pursues those who offend everything that is called human in the name of humanity. It is ultimately immaterial if a few criminals, more or less, are called to account. But what is not immaterial is that the crimes against humanity are designated as crimes and are prosecuted by humanity as crimes. That this has taken place through them, against their will and against their knowledge, is what the Nazis have contributed to the development of humanity. They created the crime against humanity and its prosecution by humanity. They created a fragment of human justice and human consciousness, precisely because they wanted to destroy humanity.

Yet another warning lies in the words of the declaration against those committing crimes against humanity, a warning to the Germans who have remained innocent. It is said that lists are being drawn up of every individual, that everything is being gathered that can be found in terms of evidence, so that the guilty are caught and the innocent go unpunished. And that means something quite great: it means that justice, and not revenge, shall be exercised. And that, my German friends, means the protection of the innocent in Germany. It means the protection of the German nation. And truly, the German nation requires this protection. A boundless hatred has built up against everything that is called

German, because the German nation permitted itself to be turned into the instrument of Hitler and because many Germans permitted themselves to be turned into accomplices in his crimes. The German soldiers in the conquered lands sense this hatred to the point of insanity or suicide. The German army command staff senses this hatred in the self-sacrificial battles of the guerrillas behind the German front. The German nation senses this hatred through the walls of its isolation from all the world as the eerie reality that is coming nearer and nearer. They all know that when hatred and revenge operate freely, there is no longer any distinction between the guilty and the innocent. And now think, just once, about the declaration of the world powers in the face of the ocean of hatred that surrounds Germany from all sides. It differentiates guilty ones and innocent ones. It doesn't want revenge. It wants justice to occur. It wants to protect all Germans who were not accessories in the crimes of the Nazis, in the face of the understandable hatred of the liberated nations. It wants to give this hatred the target that belongs to it: the criminals, and not the innocent.

That is the meaning of the warning to those who have kept themselves undefiled by innocent blood up to now. It is, even today, the greater part of the German nation to which that applies.

And now, my German friends, permit me to ask you: is this not the only thing that can be done and one of the most urgent things that must be done? Does your conscience not agree with that? And if not your conscience, then, nevertheless, your political sense. For a moment, imagine if the criminals and the tyrants who maltreated first you and then Europe and drove the world into one of the most horrible catastrophes should go on living unpunished, their hands stained with the blood of the innocent, their souls stained with the memory of acts of inhumanity. Imagine if they would live among you and brag about those things, poisoning the souls of your children and existing as the living image of the deepest German disgrace for you! When you imagine that, does it not give you some sense of liberation to think that this collection of all that is bad in the human soul shall be eradicated from Germany? Is it not like a word of cleansing, what has been stated by the leaders of the three world powers in their declaration?

No false national feeling should bring you to join forces with criminals who were the ones committing crimes against you to start with. To the contrary: you will become their first judges! And you will judge them as they have deserved to be judged, by you and by humanity! To the extent to which you yourselves use the sword of justice against those committing crimes against humanity, you prove before all the world that your hands are spotless and that there is still a German nation that can hear the voice of justice.

43.
RETRIBUTION UNPARALLELED

MY GERMAN FRIENDS!

The mass of destruction that is occurring in the world in these years is inconceivable. No one can estimate how much of what has been erected over centuries will remain after this time of destruction. Never has humanity possessed such dreadful weapons of destruction. Never was there more human work that could fall prey to destruction. When one of the famous cities of antiquity sank into ruins in an ancient battle, it was but a fraction of what is being destroyed in one night today. When entire areas were devastated in the Thirty Years War, this wasteland was a fruit garden in comparison to what an army that is rolling back leaves behind today. When refugees with their rescued belongings appeared in earlier wars, it was an easy thing to provide them with a roof over their head, food, and clothing. Today, there are millions in all parts of the earth who can barely manage to save their lives and who wander through the land, homeless, starving, and freezing. Everyone has adopted superhuman measures. Only the imagination of the ancient seers was able to portray the end of the world as we are now experiencing it. And even their most glaring colors are dull when compared to what is taking place everywhere today.

Perhaps many of you have seen copies of a famous picture that shows the destruction of a Spanish village by a German bombing attack in the Spanish Civil War.[64] The picture was painted even before the beginning of the Second World War. But everyone who saw it could foresee in it all the horrible things that were bound to come over the greatest part of humanity in the following years: the rubble of people's homes, the bodies of children torn to pieces, the confused eyes of mothers, the torment and the boundless terror on all faces. People looked at this as an interesting picture at that time and were inspired by the great skill of the painter. People empathized with the victims and were gripped by the fate of these people. But they knew of that from such a distance. Certainly, most believed that their lives were far away from that village. Only some, more deeply seeing people suspected that their own fate was described by it, that this picture was a final warning for people — a warning to which they did not listen. Soon after that, Warsaw and Rotterdam sank into rubble. Soon after that, Coventry and the center of London burned. Soon after that, European Russia was devastated. Soon after that, Cologne and Hamburg went to ruin. Soon after that, wide sections of Berlin went up in smoke — a smoke that darkened the sun and rose a kilometer high toward heaven. And among these great signposts on the route of destruction lie the ruins of all the innumerable places that no one, for the time being, can name. It is as if everything that humanity created was made to be fuel for the flames that are ignited by this same humanity. It began in those days when the small Spanish city, full of defenseless and innocent victims, was attacked and destroyed by National Socialist and Fascist pilots, just as on a drill ground and as a test, so to speak. There it became clear what power is given to humanity to destroy what it has built, and there it became clear how certain groups of people intended to use this power. And then these groups, the National Socialists and Fascists and Japanese militarists, began their war against the rest of the world. They trusted the weapons in which such a force of destruction was embodied. They were the first to have these weapons, and they believed that no one could resist those who first used the weapons of total destruction. They were almost right in the end. But they found a resistance with which they had not reckoned: the resistance of people for whom everything and anything they had was destroyed but who did not give up their opposition. And then they became unsure and acted in a way that gave those whom they had first attacked the time and possibility of turning the weapons of destruction against the destroyers. And that is what is now taking place. And it is taking place with double, triple, and ten times the strength: for every city destroyed by the Germans, a German city sinks into ruins. How was it when the inhabitants of Coventry and

London's working-class district came out of their ruins? Didn't the National Socialists and their friends sit together and celebrate the victory, brutally, arrogantly, boasting about their own security, promising stronger and stronger attacks, ever worse devastation? And then they waited, and nothing decisive happened. Instead of this, millions died in the frozen waste of Russia and ten thousand in the sandy desert of Africa. And one night, they no longer sat up and celebrated victories and boasted about their unassailability, but instead they gathered in their hideouts, doing the very thing that they had recounted triumphantly about their opponents only a year before. And gradually, even the hideouts became insecure, and houses and cities burned above them. The weapons of destruction had turned against them! What they had done to the others was now being done to them tenfold. Destruction struck the destroyers!

That is what is happening today: a retribution unparalleled in the history of the world; a retribution like that found only in the divine words of wrath spoken by the prophets concerning guilty nations. These words of wrath became true: desert sands now cover the formerly thriving cities against which they were spoken. And the words of wrath are becoming true today, just as then: ruins are covering the splendor and beauty of the German cities and all the wealth that was stored up in them. For Germany had become guilty when it first took up the weapons of destruction, attacked weak nations, and finally, in blind arrogance, attacked the strongest nations. For the sake of this guilt, the German cities must lie desolate; the heart must be burned out of the capital of Germany; the forges and workshops of German prosperity must turn to ruins. Indeed, they had ceased being tools for the creation of human prosperity long before. They had long since become tools for the creation of human misery. They had turned into forges of death, and now death is returning to them and killing them.

You will ask: are we the only guilty ones, then? Certainly not! In the divine words of wrath there is never only one guilty party. All are partly to blame. All suffered then and all suffer today beneath their shared guilt. But all are not equally guilty. There are chief offenders, against whom the divine word of wrath is more specifically directed, today just as then. And no one in the whole world, no one even in Germany, can in all seriousness have doubts about who the chief offenders are in the present-day self-destruction of humanity: those who first forged the weapons of extermination and first used them. For the sake of their guilt, for the sake of the guilt of the National Socialists, fire from heaven is raining day and night on the German cities and is burning the guilty and the innocent.

It is in this light, my German friends, that you should see what is occurring today. In this light you should show it to the German people. It is meaningless to counter the enormous events of a world's end with petty thoughts. It is not a question of a few successful counterattacks that delay the inexorably approaching fate for a little bit. It is not a question of individual people who are a little more or a little less guilty. It is not a question of diplomatic tricks in order for leaders to pull themselves out of the noose that is becoming tighter and tighter. It is a question of recognizing what is truly going on: a divine judgment on human guilt, on the guilt of a nation that—as a whole—has allowed itself to be made guilty, and the destruction of those who preached destruction and practiced it to an extent never before possible.

If you understand the present fate of Germany in this way, then you will bear what must be borne; but at the same time, you will turn away from that which has made you guilty! There is no call for you to remain jointly liable in the guilt. Whoever has recognized that another has made him guilty has to free himself from the other in order to keep from becoming guilty any further. All who hope for a resurrection of Germany out of its ruins are waiting with impatience for the moment when the German people will free themselves from National Socialism. As long as it does not do that, the destruction will go on, and with it, countless innocent people will die. For whoever supports the guilty becomes guilty himself and perishes with him. But whoever breaks free from the one who has made him guilty can be saved, even if through the midst of fire. Divine words of wrath are now coming true in the German nation. Yet behind the words of wrath stand words of salvation, today as at the time of the prophets. For the German nation as well, a salvation is available! And the sooner it understands what is happening to it in the horror of these days, the sooner it will be saved.

44.
BREAKING THE PACT
WITH THE NAZIS
NOVEMBER 30, 1943

MY GERMAN FRIENDS!

One German city after the other is sinking into ruins. And those who sit upon the ruins are asking themselves: who has brought this? Why did it have to befall us, particularly us? Didn't we suffer enough in the First World War, its hunger and its millionfold deaths? Didn't we suffer enough in the inflation,[65] when everything that we possessed vanished? Haven't we suffered enough in the four years of this war and everything that preceded it, in terms of want and oppression? Are our people, above all others, predestined for suffering and misfortune? So many may ask who look upon the ruins of their cities, beneath which not only all of their property but many of their closest people are buried. Who could avoid asking such questions—questions such as those struck by misfortune have asked again and again, like those asked and answered in incomparably marvelous ways in the book of Job?

But when those of you on the ruins of the capital city and many other cities ask, "Why did this have to strike us, particularly us?" then perhaps you will hear a voice that repeats this question, a voice from the land of the dead, a voice composed of the despairing voices of hundreds of thousands of Jewish women and children and old people. And what this voice asks is like an echo of your question: are our people, above all others, predestined for suffering and misfortune? They are asking what you are asking, precisely the same question with precisely the same despair.

But when you ask, "Who has brought us this?" then there is a pause, and the voice from the land of the dead doesn't repeat this question but rather it gives the answer: you have brought us to this! You silenced the voice of your conscience when we were led like cattle through your cities to the places of struggle in the east. You looked away when our property was being smashed into ruins. You didn't lift a finger when our men were being tortured and killed in concentration camps. You brought that on us when you had yourselves turned into instruments of evil, which in our generation bears the name National Socialism! So speak the voices from the land of the dead to you, the voices of the Jewish children and women and old people murdered by the Nazis under your noses. And when you ask where this voice of the dead is speaking to you, you yourselves know the answer: it is the voice of your own conscience through which they are calling and asking, "Who has brought us this?" Your conscience is testifying to you that the blood shed by these innocent people is now coming upon you and your children. You can no longer silence this voice within yourselves. When you indict that which is now laying more of your cities to dust and ash, day by day, at the same time you hear an indictment against yourselves! You hear the indictment of those whose fortune and whose bodies have disintegrated into dust through the crimes of your leaders and through the inability of an entire nation to resist evil.

For this reason, when you ask, "Who has brought us this?" you have to give two answers: one says, "Our leaders," and the other says, "We ourselves!" And when you ask, "With what have we deserved that, are we more evil than others?" a double answer is again necessary: we are not more evil than others, we haven't deserved it for that reason! But we have had ourselves turned into the instrument of evil, of the greatest evil of our time. And for that reason we have had to endure what almost exceeds human strength to endure. We have become the victims not of our own wickedness but of the wickedness of those who first led us astray, then enslaved us, and then misused us for everything evil. That we shared in guilt, that is our guilt. And for the sake of this guilt, our husbands and sons are dying, and our houses are collapsing upon us and burying us and our children! For that reason, the question that you have to ask is actually the question: how could we bring this on ourselves? How could we have had ourselves turned into the instruments of the greatest of evil? How was it possible that the German nation carried out no resistance to a doctrine that was contrary to everything, divine and human, in which its history so abounds? How was it possible that the German nation subjugated itself to people whose vision and works and actions characterized them, from the very beginning, as an accumulation of everything ignoble? How was it possible that noble Germans fell victim to the diabolical spell of these people? How was it possible that the German nation sank to this depth of self-abasement?

When you ask yourselves these questions today, you don't want to know what external conditions have contributed to them. You aren't asking about the economic causes for the Nazis' victory. No one can doubt them. You also aren't asking about the unfavorability of the political situation, about the struggle of parties and worldviews, which helped the Nazis gain victory. No one disputes that. Rather, you are asking: how was it possible that these external circumstances brought about such a downfall for the German people? How was it possible that an entire nation, under the pressure of temporary difficulties, sold itself to the power of evil?

Didn't you know that a pact with the powers of evil first brings what is asked for, and that evil then insists on its right, the right to destroy the one with whom it has concluded a pact? This experience is as old as humanity, and countless sayings, stories, and poems — in the German language as well — bear it out. Evil demands its due after it has fulfilled its followers' many wishes. The German people are experiencing this now. First, the National Socialists gave the Germans much of what their heart desired: the end of unemployment, the restoration of the armed forces, the spread of the German Empire, an unbroken series of victories, and dominion over Europe. Evil seemed to keep all of its promises. And the misery of victims in Germany and all conquered lands didn't count in comparison to such gifts. The idleness of the hearts of even good Germans in the face of innocent suffering allowed the power of evil to govern freely; and the brilliance of its successes outshone the dreadful shadows that necessarily follow evil, and which National Socialism wasn't even attempting to conceal. But the evil with which the German people had come to terms ultimately demanded its share, namely, the German people themselves. So it always is when people sell themselves out to evil: the price that they have to pay is their very selves. A lower price isn't accepted. And this price is demanded sooner or later. It is now being demanded of the German people.

There were Germans who saw all of that from the outset. But their mouths were closed. Others saw it and closed their eyes because they couldn't bear it, and finally, they forgot it. Others, perhaps the majority, were blinded and didn't see to whom the German people had surrendered themselves. They didn't see that they had made a pact with evil. Others finally did suspect what was occurring, but because they shared in the gifts that were first distributed, they accepted bribes and silenced the warning voice. Now they have all awoken and seen what has happened: that the power of evil has become visible in its ultimate depth and is demanding its victims, the German people! When you shared in the gifts of this power and, at the same time, watched the suffering of innocent victims of persecution, then you sealed the pact with the powers that have ultimately brought on you what you are now experiencing. When the torment of the tortured didn't move your heart so that you preferred death at the hands of the hangmen to sharing in guilt, then you permitted the clouds to gather from which the destructive lightning is now traveling down. Evil is collecting its payment. That is what is taking place today.

But perhaps something different is occurring at the same time, full of depth and sincerity: the liberation of the German people from the power of evil to which it had surrendered. Catastrophes such as those that are now coming upon the German cities and the entire German nation are calls to renounce and to turn back. There are no stronger calls than those that are now being issued to the German nation in the hellfire of the burning cities and in the daily deaths on the front. Will the German nation listen to this call? Will those of you who know what this call means be able to make it audible to the German nation? Even today, it is not too late for renunciation and turning back. But one thing is required: that the German nation's renunciation of the powers of evil with which it has made a pact be a total one. What is required is that National Socialism be eradicated, "with all of its works and all of its essence." Because it is the power of evil that the German nation has to "renounce"—just as all of you promised in your confirmation vows. You have surrendered yourselves to it. You have been enslaved by it. You have been led by it into crime. Now you know what it is. Now—through the fate that it has brought upon you—you have become ready to turn away from it! Not in an outward aversion that is beneficial for the moment, but rather an inner reversal that saves the future of yourselves and your children.

45.
A SOLDIER'S REVEALING LETTER
DECEMBER 27, 1943

MY GERMAN FRIENDS!

On the morning of the second day of Christmas, I read the translation of a German soldier's letter that had fallen into the hands of the Allies. I have seldom read something that so strongly expresses the unimaginable horrors of the Second World War as this letter does. It is written by a noncommissioned officer by the name of Karl Peters to a woman, a purely personal letter. The writer did not suspect that, instead of the woman to whom it was addressed, hundreds of thousands in enemy countries would read it. He did not suspect that blood would be brought to a hate-filled boil in hundreds of thousands through what he harmlessly communicated in his letter! He did not know that many people would paint for themselves a picture of "the German soldier" according to the words of this letter—paint it, and place a curse beneath it!

The letter reads this way: "Indeed, when we abandon a city, we lay it to ruin: explosions left, explosions right, explosions behind us! The houses are leveled to the ground. The fire spares only the chimneys, and the whole thing looks like a stone forest. Masses of houses sink as a result of a well-executed blast. Tremendous fires transform the night into day. Believe me, no English bomb can cause such destruction. When we have to return to the border, the Russians will not find a single city, a single village between the Volga and the German border. Indeed, total war in the highest and most complete form rules here. What is occurring here is something unknown in the history of the world. I know that you at home must live through many terrible minutes, because of the heavy air raids. But believe me, it is much worse when the enemy is in your land. There is no escape for the civilian population here. Without a roof, they must starve and freeze to death. We are about to burn up more of their land. Your Karl."

So reads a German soldier's letter from the year 1943. The terrible thing about it is the objective way with which something terrible is being communicated. No human outcry against the monstrous thing that is being done to innocent people in regions the size of Germany! Not once a word of passion against the hated enemy on whom one bestows all of this. Nothing of that: nothing human in the good and nothing human in the evil; complete inhumanity, destruction as an event that is as natural as a flood or a prairie fire. Nazism has brought the German people to this depth of dehumanization!

It should not be said that these things are a military necessity! It is a military necessity to bombard and to reduce places to rubble in which the enemy is entrenched. It is a military necessity to destroy factories, bridges, and depots on a forced retreat. But it is not a military necessity to make a wasteland out of a country, to drive the inhabitants before you, or to leave them for dead. It is not a necessity to wipe out the enemy nation or, if that is impossible, to annihilate parts of it with house and home and livestock and workshop from the face of the earth. It is not a military necessity to massacre millions of women and children and old people, directly or indirectly! But that is what is taking place. That is what is reported with complete indifference in that German soldier's letter.

The letter calls this campaign of extermination against an entire nation "total" war. But originally, this word meant only that every individual in a nation takes part in the overall effort for victory. Total war means that the people behind the front are also comrades in arms, because survival at the front depends on them. In this sense, all nations are today engaged in total war. But the National Socialists have made something different out of the phrase "total war": total war for them is war with the aim of total extermination of the opponent. And the German noncommissioned officer who describes the method of extermination in his letter shows what that means.

In the entire history of civilized Europe there has not been anything of this kind. To be sure, in the Thirty Years War, villages were burned and vanished forever from the earth. Indeed, a city such as Magdeburg was destroyed and many of its inhabitants murdered. But that was an isolated case and aroused the abhorrence of civilized Europeans even then. And soon thereafter came times in which soldiers fought only with soldiers, and noncombatants were protected by treaties of every sort. Up to the First World War that was so, and the German armies kept to this principle as well. One must go back much further into history to find that which is being done today by the Nazis: the war of annihilation. There are examples of that in antiquity, in the battles of primitive tribes, in the ideas of barbaric hordes. The German nation has sunk back to that under the leadership of the Nazis. There is only one difference: the modern war of annihilation is more thorough, more effective, and more total than any earlier one was. The means of destruction are so much more powerful, the affected areas so much more extensive, the possibility of escaping so much less that only now has a total war of annihilation become possible. And the Nazis have recognized and made use of this possibility. They have introduced the total war of annihilation into history, and they are carrying it out day by day, hour by hour.

German soldiers who hear these words, German officers and civil servants who still have a memory of Christian and European civilization: do you consent to this recurrence and perfection of ancient barbarity in the Nazi conduct of the war? Do you consent to the annihilation of large parts of the Russian nation, to the complete devastation of a great land with an ancient culture and splendid monuments of a thousand-year-long past? Is it that which the German West has to bring to the Eastern nations? Can you stand by and watch that or at all take part in that yourselves? Can you offer support when the fate that is now being brought on the Russians strikes your western and southern neighbors? Do you want to create hundreds of miles of wasteland and death on the other side of your borders? Are the German people willing to be used by the Nazis for that?

Have you once thought about what that means for the future of Germany? The enemy armies are approaching the German borders, having seen the wasteland of their own country beforehand. Their cities, their churches, houses, and stables, have vanished from the earth. Their friends and relatives are dead or taken away. Nothing has remained other than the crushed earth of their homeland and the wind that sweeps through the dead cities. And now, they are coming into the land whose occupants have done all that to them. There, as well, there are destroyed cities. But between them lie countless villages and farms, smaller and larger cities to which nothing has happened. The trees are still standing. The fields are still producing. The women and children and old people are still living. What feelings do you believe this will arouse in them? Their superiors will keep them from repaying annihilation with annihilation. The Nazis have still not succeeded in pulling their enemies down to the level of inhumanity on which they themselves stand. But it will become more and more difficult for the leaders of the victorious nations to hold back their people. There are crimes that are so great and dreadful that they drown out the voice of wisdom and restraint within everyone who has witnessed them. Such crimes are being committed today in the name of the German army and of the German people, day after day, and more serious ones are in preparation. How long do you want to continue to conceal this?

Why don't you think about your future and that of your children? One day, those wastelands that the German armies have created on the orders of the Nazis will again be built up. People will live and work there. But from one generation to another, the story of the desolation of the land by the Germans will be told. And for many lifetimes, the guilt of the Nazis will be a burden on the German nation! Can you desire that? Could you desire it, even if a small military advantage, a delay of the defeat for a few days, were connected with it? Not even that is the case, but even if it were, isn't this short delaying of the end too expensively purchased with a centuries-long curse over the German people?

My German friends! Do you really know what sort of an abyss the Nazis have dragged you into? Do you know what a war of annihilation means, that sooner or later it always means the annihilation of both sides? Or have you resolved to comply with the wish of the Nazis and to pull Europe down with Germany into the abyss? Have you resolved, for the sake of the Nazis, to permit not only Europe but also Germany and its future to die? It has been said to the German nation that it shall not be enslaved. But it has to meet one prerequisite for that: it must separate itself from the Nazis, inwardly and outwardly. It must refuse to become further guilty in the crime of the war of annihilation that the Nazis are conducting and want to go on conducting. "We will continue to burn," says the German soldier's letter. The German people, the German laborers and soldiers, should answer the Nazis, "We will not burn any further, except you and everything for which you stand!"

1944

Tillich wrote his radio speeches for the first five months of 1944 while the Allies steadily pushed back the Japanese and German forces. To his European listeners, he now spoke of the painful passion of Germany and the end of Nazism; themes of liberation dominated his lectures. The ending of his speeches coincided with his founding of the Council for a Democratic Germany. Author Thomas Mann, who originally had worked with Tillich on the council, withdrew from the organization. Tillich led the organization until it broke up in 1946, due to the tensions of the cold war.

German Americans seeking to reach an understanding of policy for a postwar Germany often met in Tillich's apartment at Union Theological Seminary. The themes of the council were echoes of Tillich's radio speeches: defeat and punish the Nazis, conserve German economic power within a European economic system, allow the democratic forces in Germany to cleanse Germany of Nazi influences, and ensure that Germans themselves reform of German education. The council's basic opposition to extreme measures of punishment for Germany was criticized, and for a short time, Tillich was blacklisted by the U.S. Army and excluded from democratization projects for postwar Germany. The FBI files on Paul Tillich reveal more entries on the council, which included German democrats, socialists, and Communists, than on any of his many other wartime activities—which included the presidency of the organization of Self-Help for Emigrés from Central Europe before, during, and after the war. This activity proved more satisfying to Tillich than his work with the short-lived council.

United States forces continued their difficult but unrelenting movement to liberate the Pacific islands. In the early months of the year, they made gains in New Guinea, New Britain, and the Marshall Islands. In March, they repulsed a Japanese attack on the Solomon Islands. By the spring of 1944, U.S. fleets were dominating the Pacific.

In Europe, the Soviets continued their major advances from the east. By the end of January, the two-year siege of Leningrad ended. With the Germans in retreat, Soviet forces retook Yalta by mid-April and drove the Nazis from the Crimean port of Sevastopol in May.

From the west, British and American bombers continued their efforts against German targets. Late February was the occasion of what became known as the Big Week raids on sites throughout Germany. While pounding Germany, the Allies also suffered significant losses in the air war. Winston Churchill reported to Parliament that up to that point in the war, the British had lost more than thirty-eight thousand pilots and crewmen and over ten thousand aircraft. The Allies continued their planning and practicing for the June invasion of Europe while deceiving the Germans on the place and time.

Anti-Nazi partisan activities increased in German-ruled areas, as did the German responses to these actions. Retributive atrocities continued against local communities, especially in the Balkans. One village, Drvar, suffered because it protected Tito until his rescue by the Allies in May. While beaten down, the Yugoslav partisans were inspired to continue their struggle against their Nazi oppressors.

Tillich wrote his final Voice of America speech the second week of May. This was less than a month before D day and ten weeks before the most serious act of resistance during the Nazi period, Colonel Claus von Stauffenberg's July 20, 1944, assassination attempt on Hitler. The speeches of 1944 went beyond merely encouraging the German people to resist and to work for the defeat of their homeland, as if their fate rested in their own hands. Their destiny was now in the hands of the Allies. Tillich's message had become an urgent exhortation that they face their guilt courageously and accept honestly the consequences of Nazism's colossal folly.

46.
JUDGMENT
AS REDEMPTION

JANUARY 31, 1944

MY GERMAN FRIENDS!

Two kinds of news about Germany are stirring the souls of everyone who loves both Germany and humanity. One group of reports tells of the misery that the Germans are suffering, and the other tells of the misery that the Germans are causing. In the same newspaper, we read of the hell into which the Russian cities have been transformed by the German occupying force. Simultaneously, we read about the millions of homeless Germans, whose homes and possessions were destroyed by fire, and of the millions of slave workers who are deported to Germany from the cities and villages of Europe. We hear of the growing lack of clothing and food and all the necessities of daily life in Germany, and at the same time, we hear of the gradual starvation of the subjugated nations, particularly their children, for the benefit of the German people. And I could continue in this way: every calamity that comes upon the German nation corresponds to a calamity that Germany is bringing on other nations. If the reports about what the Germans are committing awaken horror, anger, and the demand for revenge, the reports about what the Germans are experiencing stimulate compassion, concern, and the desire to help Germany. But when this desire, this concern, this compassion is awakened, then, in the next moment, one is again called back to the desire for revenge, anger, and horror. Today, everyone lives in this sense of conflict who feels something for the German people and who knows, at the same time, what Germany has done and is continuing to do to humankind and human nature and human dignity as the instrument of the Nazis.

There is only one explanation for this conflict between anger over Germany and compassion for the German people. And that is an ancient, deeply human, and at the same time mysteriously divine explanation. What the German people are now experiencing is judgment. But as judgment, it is a path to salvation.

I will never forget how, already in 1933, after the Nazis were in power a few months, deeper-seeing Germans foresaw the judgment that is now passing. Although they were opposed to National Socialism in a friendly way, even at that time they spoke of the blood of the persecuted that would come upon them and of the fate that was brewing for every German, even for themselves. A part of their character saw clearly into the future. Another part, determined by inertia and fear, obscured this view again. And so they continued, carrying out absolutely no resistance or only weak resistance, and now they are drawn into the judgment that the better part within them had foreseen. At some point, the day will come when many Germans openly indict themselves because they did not speak out and because they did not translate into action what their innermost selves said to them. An astonishingly large number of Germans will tell of the nightmare that has weighed heavily on them since the Nazi seizure of power. Not only the individual but also a nation senses when it has surrendered itself to the power of destruction. But just as the individual wants to suppress this feeling and not acknowledge it, so also with entire nations. The German nation knew, and yet did not want to know, into whose hands it had fallen when it was turned into the instrument of the Nazis. It knew that it was bringing a debt on itself that became greater with every new act of the Nazis and that, as the collective guilt of the German nation, could not be shaken off of it. The German nation knew that it was heading for a new judgment that would fall on everyone. It knew— but it did not want to know. And now the judgment has begun and is taking its unrelenting and unalterable course. It has come more quickly than anyone would have thought, because it has been directly defied through blind arrogance. Now it is present and is erupting more fearfully with every day upon the German nation. It is as if the ancient biblical words of judgment about the destruction of the nations—all descriptions of the end—had come to pass in what is coming upon the Germans. When, in coming times, stories of guilt and judgment among the nations are told, the account concerning the short span of the Third Reich's rule in Germany will make the greatest impression of all stories. Seldom have guilt and judgment so quickly and so completely followed one after the other. Seldom has an attack on the moral world order so quickly been turned into an event of growing destruction by the ethical world. Are the German people ready not only to see this but also to desire to see this? Are the German people today broken to the point that they now acknowledge and accept with complete clarity that which they always knew in dark foreboding? Everything depends on their doing that. Because then, the judgment will be salvation.

Don't misunderstand me. Neither I nor anybody who feels sympathy for the German nation says that it is more wicked than other nations and, for that reason, must suffer even more. If a person says that about another person, then people call him self-righteous and find it more difficult to help the self-righteous than the unjust. If one nation says of another that the other is more wicked than itself, then the self-righteous nation is in greater danger than the unjust one. We don't speak of the judgment that is now passing on the German people out of self-righteousness but rather because we look at it as a visible example of the world's moral order, which asserts itself against anyone who violates it, more quickly or more slowly but with unrelenting power. When a nation recognizes that, then it is no longer under judgment; then salvation has already begun. It is a frequent event in the world's history that a nation which recognizes its guilt and takes the judgment on itself develops strengths that more fortunate nations lack. Often enough, something has come into being in the depth of a historical catastrophe through which a nation has become great. Of course, that is not always so. The catastrophe of the First World War led only small circles inside Germany into the depth. The nation as a whole did not take the catastrophe for the warning that it was. It did not discern the threat of judgment that it was. The German nation deceived itself after the First World War with the claim that it was not even partly to blame for the war, that it was never actually defeated, that certain political factions were to blame for the defeat. And when those who thought like that got power into their hands, the German nation was defrauded of the blessing of its defeat. It had hardened itself against the word of judgment that was spoken to it in the misfortune of the First

World War. And so, with little resistance, it was driven into the guilt and judgment of the Second World War. Had the German people listened to the First World War's threat of judgment, it would have been able to avoid the judgment of the Second World War.

And that means that if it does not acknowledge the judgment of the Second World War, it will bring on itself total destruction. But I want to conclude not with these threats but rather with the great, ancient truth that judgment is salvation when it is accepted as judgment.

If what is being experienced today on the front and in German cities purges the German people of the things that turned them into the obliging instruments of the Nazis, then they are on the path of salvation. When the German nation ceases to swing to-and-fro between an outrageous arrogance and an absurd sense of inferiority, then a new Germany will be born. If the German nation, through the judgment that is passing on it, is healed of sometimes falling on its knees before power-without-spirit, sometimes fleeing into a thin, feeble spirituality, then greatness will have come to pass for it. If the German nation learns that it is not alone in the world and that it has something essential to contribute to the life of the human race, then all the immense suffering of these days has not been in vain. Then the path of judgment has become the path of salvation. Then the German people will have been not only outwardly freed of National Socialism but also inwardly liberated from it; and that is the only thing that matters!

47.
COMMUNITY IN THE SERVICE OF POWER
FEBRUARY 15, 1944

MY GERMAN FRIENDS!

When I spoke to you the last time, I challenged you to cast off the so-called German faith as heresy and to struggle through to an ancient, genuine "faith of the Germans." Indeed, faith creates something without which people cannot live with one another: faith creates community. Even the word *community* has been very misused. People spoke of national community and meant the rule of one class or group. People spoke of familial community and meant the tyranny of the father. People spoke of human community and meant the balance of great powers. The weak were invited into community so that the strong could rule. No one will want to deny the misuse of this word *community*. It is just as it is with all great matters: they can be turned into a facade behind which small and evil things take place. We know that even divine matters are not safe from this misuse. Indeed, perhaps we can say that the greater an idea is, the more defenseless it is to distortion and dishonest use. So it is with the great idea of community. No one can protect it from being used as an instrument of power. But just as nothing great stops being great for that reason, so also for the idea of community. Let it be placed into the service of power a thousand times, and it will liberate itself a thousand times from its bondage, because humanity cannot live without community. A nation cannot live without community. And we know today, better than any earlier generation, that even the human race cannot live without community.

Community can be demanded for the sake of power. That is possible because community needs power to be able to live. That is so with all living entities; also with the life of a national community. It needs power to keep from decaying. It needs power to keep from being destroyed. It needs internal and external power. Every community of living cells within a body requires a power that holds the cells together, directs their growth, and protects them against harmful influences from without. A community of human cells, a national community, also needs such a uniting, directing, and protecting power. But on the human level there can occur what never takes place in nature, that power doesn't serve community but, rather, community is forced into the service of power. So it has happened in Germany: even before the Nazis, there were groups who cried, "Community, community," and meant, "Power, power," that is, the power of their class. But under the Nazis, German national community has been transformed into a machine whose sole purpose it is to produce power, and more and more power, for the ruling Nazi party and Nazi bureaucracy. What was called German national community has become an instrument for the generation of power. And the community that should have been created has been weakened with every increase in Nazi power and has been brought to the verge of disintegration. Is there still a German national community today? I believe there is, but I believe it exists only in secret, underground, with those who are fighting for Germany against the Nazis. They are invisible. National community is living only within the feelings of those who hate the Nazis for the sake of Germany and who yearn for the liberation of the German nation from them. But there is no longer a visible national community in Germany. The power that it wanted to serve has destroyed it.

Community requires three things: a common destiny, mutual trust, and the same goals. We want to make this threefold reality clear, first, in the community of the German family. How is it going today with the German familial community? Certainly, there is, even today, a common destiny in German families. That they are torn apart by military work and military service does not need to destroy their community. It can deepen it. And still, we must ask: in reality, is there still a community in most German families? Isn't this community split into three parts by the war machine: first, the men, who have their particular destiny in the army for years — an army that is not an army of the people but rather an army of the state, an enormous technical machine that has inter-

1944

twined the person and community in the same way? And does that not apply to the women who are placed in the workforce — an army that is also not a people's army but rather a state's army, also an enormous technical machine in which individuals and communities are able to last only with resistance? And does not the same apply to the children, who, from early on, find their particular destiny in the party — a destiny that has little or nothing to do with the destiny of the family; that casts the children into the struggle of life early on, exposing them to all the dangers of this struggle; that shapes young men into war machines and young women into incubators? And what is perhaps even worse: not only has the state split the community of the family, it has also sown distrust between the parts. Particularly frightfully, that expresses itself in the mistrust between parents and children. What is more destructive of community than the parents' fear of a report by their children, than the fact that fathers and mothers are sitting in concentration camps because their children have turned against them, that young boys have received the power to watch and to arrest their parents and teachers?

And with common destiny and mutual trust, the third characteristic of community has also disappeared from the German family: the same goals. All goals are absorbed by the state. There is no other goal than the state and its power. There are no goals for individuals besides the power goals of the state; and there are no goals for the family besides the goals of the war, labor, and incubating machines into which the entire German nation is converted. There is no longer any German familial community.

But perhaps you will say that there is all the more national community now. No, and once more, no! As surely as a machine creates no community of its parts, just as little can the German state machine — of which every individual is a part — create a German national community. On the contrary: with every day longer, with every improvement of the state machine, the national community is being further dissolved. But doesn't the German nation have a common destiny, you will ask, especially since the point at which the war turned against Germany? Outwardly, it appears to be so. Even many good, Nazi-hating Germans are deceived by this observation. In actuality, it is completely otherwise: there is no community of destiny between the Nazis and the masses of the German nation. There will be none as long as they have the power and the German nation is nothing but a tool of their will-to-power, inside and outside. And there will be none when their power has broken to pieces, first outside, then inside. The German people will live when the Nazis have come to an end. When they turned the German people into an instrument of their insane will-to-power, without taking the well-being of the German people into consideration, at that time they separated their destiny from that of the German people; at that time they broke the national community from themselves outwardly. And they have broken it wherever they have seized control: they have shattered marriages and families, friendships and neighborhoods, youth associations and church communities. German national community lives today only in the struggle with the National Socialists. Everywhere else is distrust and hatred. One Nazi leader distrusts the other and seeks to become more powerful at his expense. The army distrusts the party and the party the army. And within the army, one general distrusts the other and one officer the other. The laborers distrust the civil servants; and among laborers and civil servants, each one watches the others to see whether he is being plunged into misfortune by them. Neighbors distrust whether neighbors are not secret agents of the terror. Friends close their mouths before those whom they'd hitherto considered friends. So it looks with German national community. The Nazis have turned it into that. And they have given the people no common goal: power for the sake of power, namely, for the sake of their power; that is all. But in truth, that is nothing. There is community among the German people only where the people secretly, silently, and resolutely come together for the battle against their tempters and oppressors, against the destroyers of German community. Today, German community is community in the freedom struggle against National Socialism.

48.
REBELLION AND LOYALTY
MARCH 21, 1944

MY GERMAN FRIENDS!

You are living in a conflict that is more difficult to bear than much of the difficulty that touches you daily. I mean the conflict between your knowledge about Germany's approaching catastrophe and your sense of duty, which calls you to prevent this catastrophe. You know that the war is lost, but you don't allow yourselves to act as if you know it. You know that all further resistance is useless, but you cannot make up your minds to give up the resistance. You are pulled back and forth between the feeling that calls you to rebellion against Germany's rulers and the feeling that drives you to continue to serve them against the foreign enemies. I want to speak to you today about this conflict.

First, I want to stress that every German senses, today, that Germany has lost the war. But there are different forms of this feeling. Some know it because they have knowledge of the military situation: the military leaders and the upper strata of National Socialism. They know that the war, under all circumstances, is lost militarily. Even if the defense of borders in the east and the west is possible for a while, at some time or other it has to break down. That isn't a question of foresight but rather a question of simple calculation. If one side becomes weaker and weaker, without being able to replace its lost strength, and the other side becomes stronger and stronger, and its every loss can be easily compensated for twofold or threefold, then it is inevitable that in the not-so-distant future, the one side will have lost. The German military personnel and the Nazis are good at arithmetic. They are continually miscalculating, to be sure, when it concerns spiritual things, because they know nothing about the soul. But they don't even slightly miscalculate when it concerns numbers and material. And they have long since calculated when the numbers and the material of others will be so great that they can suppress any resistance. German leaders know that, but they don't say it, because if they were to say it, the German people would put the question before them: then why go on fighting? And their days would be numbered.

There is still another group in Germany that knows about the coming defeat of Germany. They are those whose mind tells them that the catastrophe is unavoidable. But they don't dare admit it to themselves. Their feelings are fighting with their reason. They cannot psychologically bear what was admitted intellectually by them long ago as unavoidable. Perhaps this is the attitude of the great majority of Germans. It is what they normally call the head-in-the-sand policy: they turn their eyes away from the coming disaster, and thereby, they have the momentary fantasy that the disaster does not exist. In these moments, their imagination operates and believes it sees paths where there are none and escapes where, in reality, only chasms await. They listen to the words of hope that come from the mouths of the Nazis, and in which the Nazis themselves do not believe. They follow them when they call for resistance because they say to themselves: who knows whether something unexpected will yet happen that will prevent total defeat? They ask, "Who knows?" as if they did not know. But in reality they know and only wish they did not know. Feelings suppress the better judgment. And so they continue to dream, although they have long ago awakened. And so they continue to hope, although they know there is nothing to hope in the direction in which they had hoped. And so they make fools of themselves and turn the German people into victims—contrary to their better judgment.

There is still a third group in the German nation who truly don't know that catastrophe is at hand. It is not alive enough intellectually to look around. Their thinking is not sharp enough to be perceptive. Their field of vision is too narrow to look beyond that which is nearest to that which is farther and which is laden with disaster. And so they believe what the newspaper or radio tells them. They sense an uneasiness, to be sure, but it has not become conscious. They certainly have doubts in the Nazi propaganda, but the doubts are not strong enough to break through the spell. And so they live from day to day in comfortable ignorance, willing to believe what is said to them and to do what is commanded of them. They have not yet awakened. When the awakening comes, it will be frightful for them—much worse than for the other two groups among the German people; much worse than for the Nazis, who long ago prepared themselves, inwardly and outwardly, for defeat; much worse than for those who have awakened but do not yet want to admit their knowledge to themselves, continuing instead to forestall the coming disaster with their minds. They are not entirely prepared. But those who continue to sleep today and who cannot see will experience a painful awakening.

We have spoken about three groups among the German people: those who know about the approaching defeat and aren't fooling themselves but don't say it; those who see the approaching defeat but who do not want to admit it to themselves, since they cannot bear it; and those who cannot see and will confront an evil awakening. When we keep these three groups in view, it is not difficult to say why the German people go on fighting today. The Nazi powers have to go on fighting, although they know that the battle is hopeless, because every day in which it continues to be fought is a day that they add to their rule and often, even, to their life. And even if they lose their life in the battle, that is still better than if they lose it in the escape from the avengers of their tyranny and inhumanity. They have to go on fighting, although they know that at the end of this battle stands their destruction.

And those who, in general, know nothing, whose eyes are closed, go on blindly fighting. They do not see that it is a lost battle, at whose end stands catastrophe. And yet, I believe something is going on with them as well. They are in that state between sleeping and waking where bad dreams come. I believe that the majority of those who have still not awoken in Germany are suffering from bad dreams. In their deepest soul, they support what will come, but it has still not come to full realization. In dark foreboding, it is pressing to the surface, but it is still not admitted. Of this group among the German people, one can only hope that their dreams become more and more burdensome and that they awaken before the catastrophe itself is here.

But most important are the broad masses of those who know and yet don't want to know. To them it should be said: stop pursuing this desperate game any longer. Look at what you have already seen, acknowledge what you have recognized. Don't avoid it because you believe you can't bear it. Don't hide yourselves from the face of what you know will still find you: defeat and catastrophe. You have the feeling that you must go on fighting out of loyalty to Germany. You know that the Nazis have led Germany into ruin. You don't love them. Perhaps you hate and despise them. But you feel bound to them because you believe that Germany's destiny is bound to them. You are loyal to them because you want to be loyal to Germany. And yet you are certainly not comparable to those who are sleeping, who know nothing. You surely know what kind of destiny the Nazis are leading Germany to. You have certainly seen that the end is the abyss and that there is no escape. Why, then, do you support them? What sort of responsibility do you have? A responsibility for Germany? Undoubtedly. But that surely means a responsibility over against the Nazis. Because it is they, indeed, who are making any German future impossible. It is your responsibility to get rid of the Nazis for the sake of Germany. You who know and yet don't want to know are the majority of the nation. Its fate depends on you. If you know, then do what your knowledge tells you you must do. For the sake of your responsibility for Germany, take the responsibility on yourselves over against the Nazis. There is no loyalty toward those who knowingly allow German people to bleed to death for the sake of their power. Give up this war. It is no longer yours. It is no longer Germany's war. It is the Nazis' war, their war alone, and Germany and you, my German friends, are their instruments and their victims.

49.
A German
Good Friday

March 28, 1944

MY GERMAN FRIENDS!

With this Sunday, Palm Sunday, the week has begun in which Christendom remembers the suffering and death of Jesus. It is the holiest week of the entire church year, and even those not on close terms with anything having to do with the church or Christianity sense something of the inner greatness of this Passion. There are probably few people whose hearts are so hardened that they don't kneel before the majesty of the man on the cross. Why is that so? Why, for two millennia, has the picture of the Passion been the most deeply distressing of all pictures of human greatness, human humiliation, and human triumph? And what does this picture have to say to us who are going through the years of a passion suffered by all of humanity? What does it have to say to you, as Germans, who are going more and more deeply into darkness and suffering?

Why, in fact, does the suffering of this man, Jesus of Nazareth, have such greatness? Why has it become more important than the suffering of all other people and nations? Certainly, first of all, because it is innocent suffering, or more precisely, the suffering of the innocent one. There is much suffering for which we can show no guilt. Countless people have been killed for crimes that they never committed. Countless people have become victims of great catastrophes and have asked themselves: why us, of all people, why our particular generation? Surely, there are few in today's Germany who don't ask: why me, of all people, why my generation? Am I, are we, especially guilty? No one can answer that "Yes, you are guilty, woman who has lost a husband, child who has lost his father, man who wanders as a cripple through the destroyed streets of your homeland." No, you are not especially guilty. But are you, for that reason, innocent, just as the crucified one is innocent? Who would risk answering yes? No, everyone is guilty and innocent at the same time. Not one of us is only guilty; not one of us is only innocent. For this reason, there is only one complete picture of innocent suffering: the picture of Good Friday.

But there is still something else that people have always sensed in this picture: precisely because it is the picture of the innocent one, it points beyond itself. It has a helping, saving force for everyone who is grasped by it. It displays, to perfection, the radiating, reconciling power that innocent suffering has when it is borne with inner greatness. It gives us the feeling that we do not have to despair, that within all the guilt and self-destruction of people, something has remained in which life can come to a reconciliation with itself.

And now we want to ask ourselves: what does the gripping picture of Good Friday mean for the German people in the year 1944? Where do the German people stand in this Passion Week? With whom in the Good Friday story can they be compared?

When I put this question, my thoughts go back to the year 1919. It was the first Good Friday after the German collapse. The preacher in a large Berlin church compared the German nation with the crucified. Germany, for him, was the innocent sufferer, hung on the cross by the victors in the world war on the one side and by the victors in the German revolution on the other side. That is all I remembered, but it was enough to awaken within me the foreboding that a nation which agrees with such speeches is reeling toward its next disaster. The suffering of the German people is not the suffering of the innocent one. It wasn't this after the First World War. But it is also not the suffering of the only guilty party: it isn't that now, and it wasn't that in the First World War. The German people are guilty and innocent at the same time. And when they look to the cross in this Passiontide, they can see themselves as those who crucified and as those who are crucified at the same time. The German people are on the cross and with those who raised up the cross at the same time.

We all know that the German nation has brought infinite suffering on other nations, that it allowed itself to be turned into the instrument of one of the most dreadful powers of all time, and that it has, in that way, become the cause of the most frightful war. Even if the extermination of the Jewish people had not taken place, even if the countless atrocities of the Gestapo had not filled the whole world with horror, even then, the extent of innocent suffering that Germany has brought on other nations would be incredible. Millions have been nailed to the cross of the most profound suffering and the most agonizing death by the henchmen of National Socialism. And the German people stood by and looked on, just as in the old pictures of the crucifixion. No one became outraged over the suffering of the innocents. No German seized the German torturers by the arm. Only a few grasped what was taking place, and they had to look on silently as the innocents were slain and as a blood guilt was building up that, sooner or later, had to burst forth over the murderers, as well as over the spectators who were their accessories. They resemble the disciples and women who stood powerless and despairing beneath the cross.[66] A few suspected what was happening. The masses permitted it to occur with indifference, and the murderers triumphed. That was the German nation beneath the cross. The German people should see itself in this way on Good Friday. It should recognize its own conduct in the mirror of the passion story. It should grasp that it belongs to those who are doing the crucifying. It should see the curse that it has brought on itself in that way. It should listen to the words of indictment and condemnation that are directed at it in hatred, in all parts of the world, in hatred and distress, in earnestness and just wrath. "We have been crucified by you," cry out innocent people from all over the world to the German people. And only very few among them have the greatness of the innocent one to ask forgiveness for those who are killing them. From the mouths of most of the victims of the Germans come not the word of forgiveness but the word of curse.

And yet, that is not everything that the German people must say to themselves on Good Friday. They are also allowed to see the other side: they can see themselves on the cross together with their countless victims. The German people are not only guilty, and they are not alone in their guilt. And if, at the beginning of this war, the German people were almost exclusively among those who crucified, they are now, with every day, themselves moving closer to the cross. And they have already experienced something of that which they brought to others in suffering and death. And more and more of this is coming upon the German nation. And soon it will completely hang on the cross to which it has nailed the others. And then it will not be only guilty. It will also shine forth a beam of innocence out of the darkness of its guilt. And then its suffering will also have something reconciling for the other nations. It will have done something which has a propitiating impact upon itself: namely, when its suffering is borne with the dignity with which the innocent one bore it on the cross.

My German friends, when you sense, and when many within the German nation sense with you, that your suffering must be borne not with bitterness but with greatness, then you will reconcile the nations to you. And if you are reconciled to your fate, which is guilty and innocent suffering at the same time, then you can reconcile that fate to yourselves. But if you grumble, just like one of those crucified on Good Friday,[67] if you amass bitterness, hatred, and a desire for retribution within yourselves, then your suffering will have just as little reconciling power as the suffering the German people had after the First World War. Then the true Good Friday has not come for the German people. Then you will again proceed among those who crucify others, and the end of this war will be a suffering without reconciliation and a death without resurrection.

50.
THE ANCIENT AND ETERNAL MESSAGE OF EASTER

APRIL 4, 1944

MY GERMAN FRIENDS!

The fifth war Easter has come. It follows on the fifth war Passiontide. In countless churches, the Easter bells have become silent this year. They lie buried beneath the wreckage of their steeples, from which they allowed the message of life to ring out over populated streets on Easter morning in previous years. The streets are fields of ruins. The people have fled. The bells have become silent. In the vast steppes of Russia, bells have long ago turned into a memory of past years. And even though Easter bells still ring here and there in German villages, in the occupied territories, on the hasty retreats of the east and behind the bloody lines of defense of the south, they have a different tone than in past years. They are no longer bells of celebration. Nothing of the joy of reawakened life forces, in nature and in human life, vibrates in them any longer. It is as if all of those were memories of a period of life long since past. For the present, it no longer has any meaning. And even when Easter bells still ring here and there today, an undertone of pain and despair is in them that reminds one more of Good Friday than of Easter. It is as if the somber peal of the bells of Good Friday does not permit the bright, exultant tones of Easter to prevail this year. It is as if Passiontide, which normally ends on Easter morn, will never, ever cease. But when you listen more carefully, you can distinguish the other tone in the sounds of the Easter bells, their true tone: that death is not the end, even when it appears to have triumphed. The ancient, triumphant message that death is swallowed up in victory has not lost its meaning even in this year of horror and death, 1944. It has also not lost its meaning for the German people. That death is swallowed up in victory also applies to the German people, but not in the victory of German weapons. Such victories do not prevail over death. They only lead new victims to it, among both conquerors and the conquered. And the German people have now come to know, for the second time in a generation, what it means to be victorious unto death. Each ever-so-great victory was only the first step to an even much greater defeat. The victory of weapons is not the victory in which death is swallowed up. It isn't so for the German people. It isn't, in the long run, for any people. It isn't for the dead on the battlefields of this war and the previous war or any war. No victory of weapons gives life. The incredibly large hosts of the dead in this war, even the dead of the German nation, will not rise from the dead through the victory of one side or the other. And if Germany had reached all the goals that Hitler set for it, and if Germany had conquered the whole world, death would not have raised its dead. It would not have conquered through the victory of weapons.

Easter does not speak of the victory of weapons; it doesn't speak of the defeat of death through national power seizures and political concentrations of power. The victory over death does not happen in the palace of Augustus, who had united the world. It doesn't happen in the victorious battles of the Romans, who made this unification possible. Not once does it happen through the power and position of the high priests and the splendor of their temple. The victory over death occurs where no one expects it, where no one can hope for it. Easter becomes living where a genuine Passiontide, a genuine Good Friday, has preceded it. And for this reason there can be Easter in Germany today better than in the days when it was only a spring festival or pleasant custom. Because there is a genuine Good Friday in Germany today, there is also a genuine Easter. Because Germany can no longer hope in whatever comes from itself, it can hope only in one thing: the eternal law of death and life, the law that Easter follows Good Friday. Germany stands under this law; and it doesn't stand there alone but together with the many nations from which it has led many to the Place of the Skull, such as Jews and Poles, Serbs and Russians, Frenchmen and Norwegians. They all continue to stand within their Good Friday, and they all anticipate their Easter. And with them are the masses of the German people, whom no one can completely exonerate from the crucifixion of the other nations and who now themselves anticipate their Easter on the cross of endless suffering. For what kind of Easter do the nations wait, for themselves as nations and for their dead? What does the law of death and resurrection mean for a nation? It does not mean the victory of weapons, neither temporarily nor ultimately; perhaps it means defeat, temporarily or ultimately. But no doubt it means the strength to endure defeat and still live, perhaps in new forms, within a greater unity, but to live and not to have oneself destroyed or to destroy oneself. When the German nation, in the year 1919 and thereafter, fell under the temptation of those who whispered to it that it had not been defeated at all, then it evaded the law of death and life. When many in the German nation began to think and say that they had not been defeated, the German nation shirked acknowledgment of its Passiontide, its Good Friday, its death. And for this reason, in the period between the wars it reached neither Eastertide nor resurrection nor new life. It acted as if it had lost the war by accident, as if the defeat had not been history's judgment on its leaders and nation. But such a judgment is emerging today. And if the German nation at that time had acknowledged that its defeat was a true judgment of history, then it could have changed itself and risen from the dead. After the First World War, Germany denied its Good Friday and, for that reason, squandered its Easter. Everything that had led to defeat remained just as it was—the same ideas, the same forces, the same groups. Nothing was altered, nothing was taken into death, and for this reason nothing new could arise. How will it be this time? Will it again be the case that people whisper to you: we haven't been defeated at all; it was an accident, a miscalculation, the evil will of others. Will you listen to it when people speak to you in this way again? Will you deny death once more and thereby lose life? Or after the horrifying thing that has come upon you, will you acknowledge that something within Germany must die so that Germany can rise from the dead? Will you take upon yourselves the cross of defeat this time, so that the sun of a new period of history can summon you from the grave?[68] Or do you want to miss your Easter for the second time? And thereby, perhaps forever, take from yourselves the possibility of a historic resurrection?

My German friends! Today, the German destiny no longer lies where the Nazis would have you seek: in the attempt to escape defeat, in striving for a compromise, in the desire to save what can still be saved—above all themselves. Rather, the German destiny, the possibility of an Easter message for the German people, lies in the elimination of all that has led Germany astray and has deceived her about herself and that is embodied in National Socialism. Someday, peace will come. It will be difficult for the German nation, which had itself turned into the instrument of the destroyers of Europe and into the scourge of the entire world. But whether harder or easier, whether with greater or lesser losses, the German resurrection does not depend on that, nor does it depend on what becomes of Germany. Rather, it depends on whether the German nation becomes a new nation, a people that loves justice and not power, that loves truth and not deceit, that wants not to destroy but to build, and that does not wish to exist unless it does so within the community of nations. The resurrection of such a Germany would be an Easter message for Germany and for the world. And it would be an Easter message even over the death fields in all lands. Admittedly, even a resurrected Germany cannot awaken its dead. But it can give a new meaning to the death of its dead: they died for the sake of the resurrection of their nation, unknowingly or knowingly; and for that reason, they take part in this resurrection. The dead do not appear, but they speak through us. And it lies with us to give their dying meaning. Germany gave no meaning to the dying of their dead of the First World War. We hope that it will give meaning to the dying of their dead of the Second World War and, thereby, of those of the First as well. We hope that Germany will live on as a resurrected Germany. We hope that the eternal meaning of the German people and the eternal meaning of each of its dead will combine into one meaning: the resurrection, the message of Easter.

51.
THE COST OF SURRENDERING FREEDOM

APRIL 18, 1944

MY GERMAN FRIENDS!

Something has gone wrong in Germany—not for the first time today, not for the first time yesterday, not in our generation but rather for a series of generations. Surely, you will all concede that something has gone wrong in this war; that ever since the great turning point in Russia and the victorious appearance of the Allied air force, the war as a whole is destined to be lost; and that, sooner or later, its outcome will mean the collapse of Germany. But you will say: a war is nothing exceptional. Every nation has experienced defeats. And victories can follow defeats. A defeat is nothing conclusive. Certainly not. But if one wants to work one's way out of the consequences of a defeat, one must know why the war was lost. One must ask: has something gone wrong, not for the first time today but even before? Isn't our defeat perhaps the result of a series of mistakes that have been made earlier and that lie much deeper than military errors?

If we ask in this way, then there is no doubt what answer we must give. Something went wrong in Germany long before the war. It wanted to recoup its losses in the First World War and began a policy of attack on everything that was vulnerable. But it forgot that, by doing this, it wasn't simply robbing a couple of nations of their freedom, but it was attempting to overthrow the existing international order. It forgot that it was defeated two decades before by the same world powers that it now attacked once again. It was misled, through political and military successes, into an indescribable self-confidence and turned the world into its enemy for the second time in a generation. But

[245]

world conquest has yet to be granted to any nation up to now. The attempt to achieve this leads necessarily to catastrophe. Germany lives again between two world power groups. It was a false pride to attack both. It has to end badly, just as in the First World War; and if the lunatics are now going underground in order to prepare their third assault on the world powers in the East and the West, they are preparing Germany's third and surely last catastrophe, because it will no longer recover from it. The world is so structured and world history has moved in such a way that when Germany bursts forth beyond its natural borders, it will be thrown back by the remaining powers that world history has fixed: now, then, and in the future as a whole. Great German statesmen knew that and attempted to give Germany security and development within the borders that are set for it. Blind megalomania overstepped these borders and provoked fate. And fate has taken up the provocation and has dashed what has provoked it to the ground. That is what has gone wrong in Germany.

But how has it come to be that such megalomania has come to rule in Germany, and that the possibility of provoking fate against Germany is given to it? There must have been something going wrong in Germany long before. We don't need to seek further what it was. It was the conquest of Germany by the National Socialists. When they had conquered Germany, they made preparations to conquer the world. Today Germany, tomorrow the world. That wasn't only a song, that was a desire, and that became an action, an act of destruction. Had the German people not been defeated by them, the Nazis would never have been able to prepare for world conquest. When the National Socialists subjugated Germany itself, something had gone wrong in Germany. Many in Germany saw that it was wrong. Many resisted. Many were expelled, impoverished, or killed for their resistance. But the German nation as a whole, its leaders and its masses, have not resisted. And that is what went wrong in Germany. Some were too weak to accept the sacrifices of a serious resistance. Others were too apathetic. They didn't know what political power meant, and they allowed themselves to slide into the hands of Germany's destroyers. And still others were too foolish to carry out resistance. They didn't believe that the Nazis would take their own principles seriously. They didn't believe in the seriousness of the propaganda hostile to the Jews, the attacks on the church, the dissolution of political parties, and the preparation for war. They didn't believe in those things until they felt them in their own bodies and until it was too late. And still others saw what was taking place. But they gave money and the means of power into the hands of those whom they would have readily used for their aims but by whom they, in fact, were used. They, above all, are responsible for the fact that something went wrong in Germany. When the Nazis had won victory with the help of all these strengths and weaknesses, it was too late. Then the war, then the defeat, had to come. Then something had gone wrong in Germany that would take a long time to repair.

But, we ask further, how could it come to that? How could such a reign of destruction come to power? When we hear this question, we say to ourselves: something must have gone wrong in the German nation even before the Nazis came. What was it? It was the inability of the German people to tolerate freedom. It had much freedom in the years between the wars, but it could not deal with it. The German people didn't know what they should do with their freedom, and they did only one thing with it: they did everything to lose it again. They undermined everything that the governments elected by the people did. They didn't think about sacrificing private interest for the welfare of the whole. They derided their own representatives and supported all those who fostered hostility toward freedom. Something went wrong in Germany when it had won its freedom: it despised and squandered its freedom and threw itself into the hands of the most evil tyrants. That was what went wrong in Germany.

But, we must continue to ask, if something like that was possible in Germany, if an entire nation followed in its tracks, then something must have occurred even before, something must have gone wrong long before. And so it did. The German people never carried out a great freedom struggle, as most of the great peoples of the earth have done. The German people have never had a genuine revolution like other nations. They've always shown themselves to be submissive to their princes and high rulers, to their teachers and mayors. The German people have never sensed the breath of freedom to be the life-bestowing breath of humanism. They've preferred to submit rather than accept the risk of freedom. That is what went wrong in German history. It is for that reason that Germany could be so easily conquered by the Nazis.

It is for that reason that it is now proceeding toward its catastrophe. While the other nations liberated themselves, the Germans remained subjugated to their rulers. The upper middle class aspired to be noblemen rather than free people. The lower middle class aspired to be upper middle class rather than develop a democracy. The laborers aspired to be lower middle class rather than fight for the liberation of their class. The civil servants preferred to have security rather than the right of free persuasion. The officers preferred human machines to true human beings. That is what went wrong in Germany over the centuries. And when the great German poets and thinkers spoke of freedom, they didn't have in mind the freedom to determine the destiny of one's own people. Rather, they were concerned with the freedom of thought one can have even in chains. And so, the entire German nation could be chained up, first by the nobles, then by the princes, then by the magistrates, then by the property owners, and then by the Nazi authorities. They took consolation in the fact that the spirit was still free even if life remained enslaved. That is what first went wrong in Germany. That is the ultimate foundation of everything else that went wrong. But that also shows how everything can become right: namely, by the German nation's fighting its way to freedom, by throwing off Nazi tyranny and by taking its destiny into its own hand. When will that happen? When will people be able to say: something went right in Germany? When will the disastrous chains of falsehood come to an end? Even the frightful defeat of this war would be a stroke of good fortune if it made Germany dependent on itself, if it were to lead the German people to freedom, and if, after defeat, something would go right in Germany.

52.
UNBEARABLE
WAITING

APRIL 24, 1944

MY GERMAN FRIENDS!

You are now passing through a period of waiting. Great and frightening things are brewing in the east and in the west. Powerful armies are assembling between the North Sea and the Black Sea in order to burst forth, when the moment has come, and break through wherever the German defense has become weak in terms of men, material, and mental strength. And in the west, the British Isles have been converted into a springboard from which the best-equipped armies of the world can and will push off for Europe. The uncertainty about the moment in which the storm will rise up from the east and the west is increasing the anxiety of the period of waiting, turning it—to a mounting degree—into an unbearable ordeal. It is a time of waiting; but during this time of waiting, more is taking place than normally occurs in times of great activity. Destructive work is being carried out to an extent to which people have never performed it or experienced it before. In every war, that which is valued by humanity suffers destruction. From time immemorial, conquered cities have been burned and their inhabitants scattered, but that affected comparatively small places and small numbers. In the twentieth century, by comparison, there are cities of millions that are sinking into ruins and millions of people who have become homeless. And that applies to Germany more than any other land. The destruction in England, with all of its horrors, was an upbeat to the fortissimo of the air raids on Germany and all places that serve the German war effort.

In this way, the ordeal of anticipation combines with the ordeal of daily experience for many Germans. And the yearning for the end to come, no matter what sort of an end, becomes stronger and stronger. Undoubtedly, you have often said that a horror without end is worse than an end with horror. But worse than both is waiting for destruction that will surely come but about which one knows neither when nor where nor how it will come. And in this waiting ordeal you are now experiencing, the soldiers are the first line of defense on whom a fire will rain down from heaven the like of which has never come upon living people. In this waiting ordeal live the women who suspect what is in store for their husbands and sons and who bear only a tiny spark of hope within themselves that their lives can be saved. In this waiting ordeal stand all who think of Germany with love and grief and know that the most distant German future will be determined by the events of the most imminent German future. And finally, in this ordeal—or more precisely, the expectant dread of it—live the Nazi leaders and those seduced by the Nazis, the Nazi beneficiaries and Nazi criminals. They know that their fate is being determined in these months and that it means life or death for them!

But there is one group in Germany that, to be sure, shares in waiting for what is coming with all the nations of the earth but that can be free of the torment and anxiety of such waiting: those in Germany for whom the waiting of these days is the anticipation of the day of liberation. And there are countless of them among the German people: first of all, those who are in actual captivity, the hundreds of thousands of Nazi victims in the prisons and concentration camps for whom what is coming, in spite of everything horrible that is connected with it, means liberation from something even more horrible. And all those who have taken up the underground battle against Nazi tyranny—many for a long, long time—and who anticipate their victory in what is coming await the day of liberation, even if it demands the heaviest sacrifices of themselves and the German nation. And all those who have been forced into the Nazi system without believing in it await the day of liberation—many reluctant ones and ones still not resisting, many who have grasped that the greatest evil for Germany is not defeat but rather Nazi rule. Even if all of them look with suspense into the future, they could still be free of the torment and anxiety of expectation. Because they know that—whatever else will also happen—the worst has already occurred: the moment in which Germany and they themselves fell into the hands of the Nazis. At that moment, the greatest of evils that can befall a person or a nation came, that of which the poet says, "But the greatest of evils is guilt." What is yet to come now is less serious—even if it should be ever so serious—than what happened eleven years ago, at the time when Germany became guilty, more guilty than ever before in its history, when it threw itself into the hands of National Socialism. For all of you who have grasped that, you who have been burdened with the torment of German guilt year by year, this period of waiting is not torment but rather hope. It is certainly no shining hope. It is a hope that exists like a weak light in a great darkness. It is a hope that is mingled with much sorrow, but it is not the anguish of others who must see only darkness. You see the light of a German people liberated from National Socialism and purified of the guilt that it has brought on Germany.

And for still another reason, this period of waiting must not be a period of anguish for you: because you can proceed beyond that which lies immediately before you. Action drives away anguish. The Nazis and their personnel are also taking action. They are acting to counter the overwhelming danger with all means. They are also acting to counter the overwhelming anguish in their inner selves. But this action doesn't help them at all, because it is relevant only to the moment in which the storm breaks loose. And for them, everything depends on the outcome of what is happening in this moment: they cannot look beyond that, for beyond that lies darkness for them. And for this reason, all of their activities are burdened by dread and accompanied and contaminated by the torment of an unbearable suspense. Your action, my German friends, proceeds beyond that moment, reaches into the German future, and sees a light in the night of the "afterward." So take action for the sake of this "afterward" in the days that lie before it and are full of fearful waiting. Take action over and above the imminent. Prepare for the future, and it will be restored with every step with which you progress. When guilty Germany trembles in the torment of waiting, that Germany which has turned itself away from the guilty parties should be silent and should prepare for the day of liberation. I am summoning you to that, and in reality, not I but rather the fate that has led you into these days. Prepare yourselves for the path that proceeds through the fire of purification to the goal: a Germany that is free from those who have permitted it to become guilty. Instead of taking part in the fearful waiting of those who have nothing for which to hope when the storm has crushed their buildings, make yourselves strong through hope. Whatever lies on the path of the future, whatever will be destroyed by the storm that will soon break loose—in terms of those who are innocent and in terms of that which is irreplaceable—turn it into a liberating storm. Whether or not it becomes that depends on you. Show all who now stare anxiously at the imminent future that the imminent future is not Germany's future, that it depends on that which lies beyond this, no matter what horror the imminent future will be filled with. Loose yourselves—loose many others with you—from the grasp of those who are waiting with fear and agonizing suspense. Have the courage, and give others the courage, not to wait for that which is coming but to work for that which you want to come: a Germany freed from those who have enslaved it, cleansed of the guilt that they have brought on it.

53.
WHO STANDS ON
THE SIDE OF JUSTICE?
MAY 2, 1944

MY GERMAN FRIENDS!

In every battle, the best ally is the belief in the cause that one is championing, and in every war, the strongest weapon is the sense that one is on the side of justice. How does it stand with the German people? And how does it stand with the defenders of German power in the fearsome battles that are imminent? We know whose side the greater number and the stronger weapons are on. Certainly, no longer on the German side. For a long time, the German war reports have acknowledged the superiority of the enemy. But do the Germans perhaps have more of that other weapon: the belief in their cause, the certainty of standing on the just side? And are their weapons, perhaps, so strong that Germany can withstand the attack of far superior forces with their help? To put the question means to answer it with a no. Think back to the period when Germany still had the greater numbers and the stronger weapons. How did it then stand with the belief in its cause? How many Germans believed then in the justice of the war begun by Hitler? Perhaps they still sought to justify the surprise attack on Poland as the consequence of the deficiencies of the Peace of Versailles. But when they did that, could they also continue to justify the campaign of extermination against the Polish children? And where was even the appearance of justice in the attack on Norway, in which soldiers were used who, as children, were taken in by the Norwegians after the First World War out of compassion for their starvation? Who can have faith in such a cause? Here, isn't all justice on the one side and all injustice on the other? Justice on the Norwegian and injustice on the German side? What German soldier can look a Dutch or Czech or Greek man in the eye, without feeling shame over the injustice that is being done by Germany in these nations, first through conquest, then through exploitation and enslavement, and then through the starvation and debilitation of an entire generation?

People can silence their consciences, and National Socialism has understood nothing better than to deaden the conscience of the German people and to corrupt its moral judgment. But that is never completely successful. For a human being remains a human being, even when National Socialist education has sought to transform him, from childhood on, into an inhuman creature. Traces of primitive humanity are detectable even in the most fearsome Gestapo executioner and SS murderer, if one only looks deeply enough into his repressed anxiety and secret longing for something human. And what is also true for those outward examples of inhumanity is certainly true for the masses of the German people: the Nazis have not successfully silenced the conscience of the Germans. They have not silenced it everywhere, nor have they silenced it entirely. The German conscience still speaks, and it bears witness to this reality for every German: you are not fighting for a just cause when you fight against the Norwegians and the Dutch, against the Polish and Greek children, against the Czech youth, and against the women and elderly of France and Serbia. Every German soldier whose conscience offers this testimony is robbed of the strongest of all weapons: the belief that he is fighting for a good cause. The German nation as a whole is without the most powerful of all allies: the consciousness of standing on the side of justice. It is difficult to deny that and to maintain that the German cause is the good cause in this war.

And yet, the Nazis attempt to tell you that, to hammer it into you day and night. Are they persuading you? They can't, because their crimes cry out more loudly than their propaganda. And their propaganda consists of more screaming than knowledge. One of the thoughts with which a good conscience is supposed to be given to the German people is the contention that Germany has to protect Europe from Russia. But however one may think about the Russian system of government and economics, two different things are certain: it is certain that the initial attack in the war came from Germany and not from Russia, and that Russia was so insufficiently prepared that its defeat was all but achieved. What brought Hitler's defeat in Russia was the Russian person, who is invincible when he's defending Russian soil but easy to defeat when he's being used for the conquest of foreign soil. There is nothing for Europe to fear from him; and the surprise attack on it, on the Russian nation by Hitler's armies, was certainly nothing that could turn the German cause into a good cause. And something else is certain: Russia wants to protect itself. It wants the European nations to govern themselves and not to be incited by new dictators into new wars with Russia. But Russia doesn't want to conquer the European nations, either from the outside or from within.[69] It knows that it would be frustrated in that, in precisely the same way as Hitler is being frustrated. It doesn't want to repeat Hitler's megalomaniacal experiment. Fear always offers wicked counsel. It conceals that which one should truly be afraid of and is frightened where no fear is necessary. The fear of every German should not be the arrival of the Russians but rather the return of the Nazis. It does the German cause no good to play on the fear of Russia, and it can't pacify the German conscience to appoint the Nazis protectors of humanity in the face of barbarity. Everyone has a sense of where the worst barbarians sit, even when he himself, as a German, doesn't want to admit it. Everyone senses that the true barbarians of our time are found in National Socialism and that no one is called to be the guardians of European culture less than they are. Russia was destined to be turned into a German colony. For that reason, ten million people had to die. That is surely not a good cause but rather the most evil cause conceivable.

On still other grounds they seek to make German people believe they are fighting on the side of justice: they tell them that Hitler has created European unity, which shall now be broken up again by the Western powers. The Nazis are summoning you to the defense of Europe and want to give you a good conscience in this way. But does the defense of plundered lands produce a good conscience? Is the prolongation of the enslavement of entire nations a just cause? Perhaps a European unity could have arisen. And the routed, outwardly weak Germany was certainly an intellectual and economic center of interest between the wars for many from all nations. But that ended at the moment Hitler came to power and the fragile threads of a European unification were severed. Hitler destroyed a voluntary unification of Europe in order to replace it through forced unity. Is that a just cause for which it is worth killing? Isn't the outcry of the enslaved nations, the heroic passion of their resistance against German conquerors, a cause of continuous horror for every German soldier who lives in their midst? And doesn't the sight of twelve million European slave laborers in Germany itself give every German a daily reason for grief, fear, and bad conscience? Does a just cause look like that?

But finally, when all these justifications for the German cause are clearly shown to be invalid, then the Nazis say to the German people: even if everything was unjust, and even if it is an evil cause for which you are fighting, you must continue to fight. Because, so they say, this is about the existence or nonexistence of Germany. Is it truly about that? Isn't it about something completely different? Isn't it about the existence or nonexistence of the Nazis? Isn't it about the existence or nonexistence of the corrupters of Germany? But if the corrupters of Germany perish, isn't that the salvation of Germany? So it is. And for this reason, every German who tears Germany away from the Nazis should have a good conscience, but not the one who fights for them. Don't deceive yourselves, my German friends. Even the battle for an evil cause can be heroic. Even the gang that defends itself to the last has courage, even if the courage of despair. But this courage still doesn't produce a good conscience. It still doesn't make just the cause for which one kills. One cannot fight for the Nazis and at the same time sacrifice Germany and its future with good conscience. One cannot fight for an unjust cause with good conscience. End this battle!

54.
FIGHTING THE
TYRANNY OF FEAR

MAY 9, 1944

MY GERMAN FRIENDS!

Frightful pictures are being painted daily concerning what awaits you when Germany collapses militarily. The Nazis want to squeeze the last blood sacrifices out of you and are doing so by the wild fear that they arouse in you through the visions of horror with which they frighten you. They want to put you into a position in which you can be dragged to the slaughterhouse because you believe that you can escape something different and much worse in that way. Fear makes people incapable of judgment. A deeply frightened nation can no longer see what is being done with it. Against its will, it surrenders to those who want to exploit its fear. This fear has nothing to do with cowardice. One is cowardly who runs away from that which he feared. One is brave who knows what threatens him and stands fast. There is such bravery, even today, everywhere within the German nation, and to the highest degree within the army. Without this bravery of the German soldier in the field and of the German laborer in the factory, there would no longer be any Nazis today. They are building on this bravery. They are dependent on it. Daily, the heroic courage of sacrificed German men and the patience of sacrificed German women is needed to maintain the power of the Nazis. For that reason, they fear nothing more than the fact that these sacrifices will one day stop, that this patience will end, and that this bravery will turn against them. To prevent that, they are painting the frightful pictures of a defeated Germany in gloomy colors, with vague outlines, in which everyone can imagine a particular kind of horror. In many ways, they are making you afraid of the unknown, so that you go to meet that which is known all the more confidently, namely, the hell of the coming battles. As good judges of the human mind, they are creating fear within you in order to make you brave. They create fear of an uncertain future within you in order to take the dread of a more definite present from you. Before the mass attacks of the last world war, it was common to give the attacking regiments strong alcoholic drinks in order to numb the natural fear of even the bravest soldiers. In this war, there is an even better intoxicant: first, the Nazi teaching of the incomparable dignity of death in battle; then, the fanatical, blind, and unquestioning submission to godlike leaders; then, the fascination of great victories and power over foreign nations. Finally, when all these intoxicants run out, they administer the last remedy that is available to the German people and to the German soldier: fear, meaningless fear. And even this drug works, although it tastes bitter and not sweet like the previous ones. Fear bewilders, making one incapable of action. Fear sees the disaster approaching and stares at it as the victim stares at the snake: immovable, incapable of moving, incapable of escaping. So the German people feel, and so the Nazis want them to feel. It is bound to hurl itself into the jaws of the disaster that is approaching nearer and nearer from all sides. Because if this stare of fear were to stop, if soberness would follow the intoxication of fear, then the German people would see what it has to do: not to hurl itself into the deadly jaws of continued war but to slay the sorcerer that has offered it one stupefying drink after the other, and ultimately that of fear.

If the German people would awaken out of its stupor of anxiety, it would ask itself: anxiety? About what? But this question cannot be answered. One can be afraid of something, for instance, of hunger or injury. But one can overcome this fear through courage. Bravery is fear that has been overcome. But one can't conquer anxiety through courage, because anxiety doesn't know what it is anxious about. It is a condition from which one must awaken. Everything depends on the German people awaking from this stupor and the frightening pictures that appear in it. That isn't taking place; thus, they are now being led to the slaughter and bleeding to death. But why can't they still wake up? Isn't the sorcerer who holds them spellbound already undermined in · his power over the German people? Did not the dead and captured of Stalingrad and the Ukraine break the spell of intoxication with the leaders for the first time? Hasn't the rubble of the German cities aroused the most drunken Nazis from their sleep? And can't the prospect of the certain death of further millions of German men in a hopeless battle break the last spell as well, the spell of anxiety about peace? It must be possible, for the sake of the German future. The spell must be broken so that the German people can live. Look at their frightening pictures. Look at them closely. Soon things will lose their terrifying quality and become absurd.

There is one frightening picture, called the enslavement of the German people, with which all Germans are held in fear. No one knows exactly what that means. But precisely because of that, it is suited for creating fear. Of course, everyone can see that it is impossible to enslave 70 million people, without making a new order of Europe and the world impossible from the first. But fear gives bad counsel and doesn't ask for reasons. Surely, you yourselves have learned what kind of burden the enslavement of even a few million foreign laborers is for an entire nation. And now they want to make you believe that the victorious nations will voluntarily impose such a burden, that they will bring their own economies to ruin through slave labor, that they will create an enduring source of hatred and resistance for themselves, just as Hitler has done through his slave laborers? That is senseless and absurd. It is a false fear-phantom.

And there is another fear-phantom, called the Bolshevization of Europe. No one knows how that is supposed to happen if the Allied nations—above all, the nations of Europe—don't want it to happen. But precisely the fact that one doesn't know what it means turns it into the object of fear. It is an empty fear, which is filled with frightening pictures of past revolutions but for which there is no actual ground. For even Russia doesn't want a European Bolshevism. It wants a friendly Europe, not a Europe that would be the cause for a new war. No German should continue to kill for the sake of the fear-phantom of the Bolshevization of Europe.

And there is a third fear-phantom, the progressive deterioration of Germany, the destruction of its economy and hunger, with all of its consequences. It is particularly easy to paint this phantom with the harshest colors. But it is senseless to take this picture to be true. The German people are certainly not alone in the world. It is an important member, and the strongest member, of the European family of nations. An impoverished Germany means impoverishment for Europe as a whole in the long run. A starved Germany means hunger and pestilence for its neighbors. A Germany without industry means the reduction of European industry. No one who is responsible can want that. So this last fear-phantom of the Nazis disintegrates into nothingness as well.

The truth will be hard, but it will have nothing to do with the horror that the Nazis are painting. Don't remove the drunkenness of anxiety from them, you who are still sober. Awaken out of the stupor of anxiety, you who are still seized by it. Embrace the courage to see what is true. This appears to be dark. But it is not darkness without light. There may be much in the future that you will rightly fear. But courage is the master of every frightening matter. One can deal with what one fears. But out of anxiety one must awaken. As long as one is in it, one cannot consider anything further to be true and any further good thing to do. For this reason, awaken from this numbness! Shake off this stupor! When you have freed yourselves from Hitler, there is nothing more that you cannot meet with bravery. Then you are also liberated from the deepest root of anxiety: guilt. Wake up, and see how you are being led to the slaughter. Wake up out of the intoxicant of fear of what will come after war. Proceed toward it soberly, with clarity and bravery. It is the German future.

55.
ONE HUNDRED SPEECHES
ON LIBERATION FROM NAZISM

MARCH 7, 1944

MY GERMAN FRIENDS!

Today is the one hundredth time that I have spoken to you in this way. Two years have past since we pondered over the fate of Germany with one another for the first time. And then, during these two years in which more catastrophic things have occurred than normally occur in decades, we pondered these matters week by week. Things looked considerably different in the spring of 1942 than in the spring of 1944. At that time, the German armies were still advancing toward the Volga and the Caucasus. At that time, there were still no air raids on Germany that were very serious. Instead, U-boats were still at the height of their successes, Africa was still a battlefield with alternating victories, American help for Britain and Russia was still far off, and Japan was conquering an empire in the Pacific Ocean. Today, everything is different. Japan is being driven away from one group of islands after the other. The powerful and superior strength of the Allies is approaching nearer and nearer to Japan itself. Africa and southern Italy are in the hands of the Allies. The U-boat war has lost its sting, and the air squadrons of the Allies are laying ruin to the German cities, nearly unimpeded. In the east, since the catastrophe at Stalingrad, there are only retreats of German troops— slowly to be sure, but unavoidably, and with great sacrifices in material and personnel. Italy has broken away from the Axis. Finland is negotiating openly— Bulgaria, secretly—over the best way to get out of the war. The reversal in these two years is like a tremendous drama that is rushing toward inescapable catastrophe. What I and many others have predicted in these two years has come to pass, step by step, with uncanny certainty: first, the impossibility of a German victory, at a time when that was still not as evident as it is today; then, the change from the offensive to the defensive, at a time when German spokespersons still promised new offensives; then, the change from the defensive to the retreat, which we made known when the German propaganda conceded only a reduction of the front; and now, the retreat that is in full swing, in the air, on the water, on land. It is not difficult to say that sooner or later, out of the retreat collapse will evolve. Today, it no longer takes much bravery and farsightedness to foresee the German catastrophe.

Over a period of two years, week by week, you have heard all of that—some among you from me, many among you from other speakers. You heard it. You didn't want to believe it until it came true. Now I think you are ready to hear, after what we said came true. It is difficult to hear the voice of those who deprive you of the one hope to which you have clung, even when it is a false hope. And it was a false hope that Germany could still be victorious. It was also a false hope that Germany would be able to defend that which was conquered. And it is a false hope if people in Germany still hope to escape total defeat. It is difficult to listen to those who take false hopes from you. But in the end, when they have been correct about everything, is it not intelligent to listen to them, even if they further disentangle the last vestiges of a self-deception that is more welcome? Certainly. For this reason, listen to us, even if what is said is hard. Because what we are saying is true. One thing would, admittedly, justify your closing your ears to us: if we wanted to take away not only the false hopes but also the true hope. But it is not so. What I have attempted, week after week over the last two years, is to lead the German people to a new, genuine hope. We didn't want to plunge you into despair, just as we ourselves—the friends of the German people, although the enemies of National Socialism—don't despair in the German people. We know that there is a hope for Germany. We know about a possible future for Germany. And for the sake of this future, we challenge you to break with the bearers of the disastrous present. What I have said to you and have pondered with you in these two years was the inner preparation for the German future. What came into question was always twofold: the separation from National Socialism and the preparation for a new Germany. Separate yourselves from those who are bringing you to ruin: that tone was missing from none of the speeches. It had to be present because nothing new can be born out of the rubble of the past, if the power of those responsible for this rubble is not broken. We know that such a separation was outwardly impossible during the victories of the German armies. We know that it is still infinitely difficult, even today, during greater and greater defeats. And all the same, it must happen and, indeed, happen soon; because every day sooner that Germany turns its back on its corrupters saves a rock for the construction of the German future, salvaging things, rescuing people, and saving our strength. For that reason, free yourselves, those of you who bear weapons in your hands, in the field, and in the factories. We have told you, and we are telling you again today, with greater urgency than ever before: it means a great deal for the future of Germany that it take place soon.

But just as important and, at the same time, possible is the inner separation from National Socialism, the spiritual liberation of the German people. A great part of all those things that I pondered with you was devoted to the spiritual liberation and transformation of Germany. We've spoken of the betrayal of the great traditions of the German people that the Nazis have committed: the betrayal of Middle Age chivalry, of the Christian idea of love, of the freedom of conscience of the Reformation, of the universality of the German classical poets and philosophers, and of the humanism of all great Germans. We have challenged you to recover all of this and much more that is reviled, distorted, and buried by the Nazis. We haven't counseled you to go backward. Such a suggestion is foolish. But we've counseled you to go forward in the strength of the ancients, namely, in the strength of that which was great in them and which is being trampled into the mud by the Nazis. No future is possible for Germany if the German people do not spiritually separate themselves from the corrupters of the best German legacy. In the last months, that has become a more and more serious decision. The Nazis know that they have lost. And they are preparing themselves for the time when they will disappear from the face of German life and go underground. They want to become invisible in order to come again to the surface at a suitable time. And then everything will depend on whether the German people will be able to resist them or whether they will once again fall victim to them, with every awful thing which that means. This decision is being made now. If the German people will now tear themselves away from National Socialism inwardly and—as soon as possible—outwardly, it will be forever immune from its poison. If it hesitates now any longer or never comes to an inwardly clear spiritual decision against the spirit of National Socialism, then it will remain vulnerable to future poisoning. Then there will be no hope for a new Germany, but rather, the shadows of the present will consume the light of any possible future.

To prevent that is the significance of all that I've said to you in these one hundred addresses. It was a continuous struggle for the liberation of the German people from the enslavement to the Nazi spirit. While the fight to break Nazi power leads from one victory to another on the battlefields, it is for you, my German friends, to fight the battle to break the Nazi spirit with the same triumphant force. To support you in this is the ultimate significance of all that I have spoken to you and will continue to speak to you. Every word of mine that comes across the ocean to you concerns the foundations of a future Germany. The intent of these speeches is not to destroy but to build up. They are spoken for Germany, not against Germany; for a Germany that can live freed of its corrupters and freed of the spirit of corruption that they have brought over the German people.

NOTES

1. Paul Tillich, "Spiritual Problems of Post War Reconstruction," *Christianity and Crisis* 2, 14 (1942), 2–6; reprinted in *Theology of Peace* (Louisville, Ky.: Westminster/John Knox Press, 1990), 62–72.

2. Klaus P. Fischer, *Nazi Germany: A New History* (New York: Continuum, 1995), 474.

3. Isaiah 2:1–4; Micah 6:1–8.

4. Matthew 16:22; Mark 8:32.

5. Gregor Ziemer, *Education for Death: The Making of the Nazi* (1941; reprint, New York: Octagon, 1969, 1972).

6. G. W. F. Hegel, *Reason in History* (1837); Immanuel Kant, *Critique of Pure Reason* (1781); J. G. Fichte, *The Vocation of Man* (1800); Martin Luther, *On Liberty* (1520).

7. Friedrich Schiller, *Don Carlos* (1785), *The Maid of Orleans* (1801), and *William Tell* (1804).

8. Perhaps Tillich refers here to the activities of Pastor Martin Niemöller and theologian Karl Barth (primary author of the Barmen Declaration). Many scholars shared Tillich's concern that the church was predominantly concerned with its own independence in matters of religion but generally apathetic to Nazism's callous and oppressive injustices in society at large. See Theodore S. Hamerow, *On the Road to the Wolf's Lair: German Resistance to Hitler* (Cambridge, Mass.: Harvard University Press, 1997).

9. *Herzog,* meaning, literally, "duke."

10. Michael Kohlhaas is a character in Heinrich von Kleist's story based on the exploits of the early sixteenth-century figure Hans von Kohlhase, ("Michael Kohlhaas," 1808). Kohlhase was launched into a life of crime by injustices he experienced in Saxony.

11. G. W. F. Hegel, *The Philosophy of History.*

12. Amos 2—5.

13. The date of Johann Wolfgang von Goethe's death is March 22, 1832.

NOTES

14. Johann Wolfgang von Goethe, *Wilhelm Meister's Apprenticeship and Travels,* trans. Thomas Carlyle (Boston: Houghton Mifflin Co., 1896), 2: 248–49.

15. *Führer.*

16. *Lebensbezug.*

17. Several Germans who were engaged in activities against the Nazis—whether politicians (Carl Goerdeler), church leaders (Martin Niemöller), or military officers (Claus von Stauffenberg)—both opposed Hitler and sought a path to past values or past European political arrangements. See Anton Gill, *An Honourable Defeat: A History of German Resistance to Hitler, 1933–1945* (New York: Henry Holt, 1994).

18. Yet more recently published documents show that there was real freedom not to participate in atrocities, a freedom exercised with only minor consequences, if any. See Ernst Klee, Willi Dressen, and Volker Riess, *"The Good Old Days": The Holocaust as Seen by Its Perpetrators and Bystanders* (New York: Free Press, 1991).

19. Daniel Jonah Goldhagen's *Hitler's Willing Executioners: Ordinary Germans and the Holocaust* (New York: Alfred A. Knopf, 1996) is a recent contribution to the debate over the depth of the German people's involvement in Nazi crimes.

20. Romans 3:9–11.

21. Helmuth von Moltke, a civilian leader of the German resistance, once conversed with a nurse who worked with former members of the SS whose involvement in Nazi atrocities had driven them insane.

22. Revelation 6:1–8.

23. Tillich may be referring to a picture out of a 1498 set of Albrecht Dürer illustrations for an edition of the Apocalypse of Saint John or to that from a 1522 series of woodcuts by Lucas Cranach the Elder.

24. Cologne was bombed November 7, 1941, and in Operation Millennium on May 30, 1942. Lübeck was struck in late March 1942. In July 1941 and June 1942, Bremen was hit.

25. Matthew 26:47–52; Luke 22:47–53; John 18:1–11.

26. Presumed to be Heinrich Heine, a Jewish poet (1797–1856).

27. Perhaps this refers to the political and economic panic that broke out with the return of the soldiers after World War I in October 1918.

28. Jack Forstman's *Christian Faith in Dark Times* presents the perspectives of those committed to a two kingdom approach, such as Paul Althaus. See Jack Forstman, *Christian Faith in Dark Times* (Louisville, Ky.: Westminster/John Knox Press, 1992), 121–30, 197–202.

29. The Third Annual Conference on Science, Philosophy and Religion in Their Relation to the Democratic Way of Life, held at New York's Columbia University in late August 1942.

30. Hegel, *Reason in History.*

31. Matthew 5:44; Luke 6:27.

32. Hitler's speech was delivered September 30, 1942.

33. Klaus P. Fischer relates the horrific activities of the Einsatz-gruppen, special units that executed groups defined as enemies by Nazism in Eastern Europe following on the heels of the Nazi army's eastern invasions. In Fischer, 500–3; Klee, et al, 276, 279. He comments on the participation of the local civilian population in some of the atrocities. See Fischer, *Nazi Germany,* 500ff.

34. Goldhagen, *Hitler's Willing Executioners.*

35. Rather than permitting its use by the German occupiers, the French naval commanders ordered the fleet at Toulon scuttled in late November 1942.

36. Pierre Laval was the minister of state and vice premier of Vichy France.

37. Tillich uses a nice wordplay here that is missed in translation and that reflects his understanding of the demonic as the distortion of the good: "Whoever follows (*folgt*) National Socialism must persecute (*verfolgen*) the child in the manger. . . . Whoever respects (*achtet*) power above all else must despise (*verachten*) the powerlessness of the child in the manger."

38. Matthew 2:16–18.

39. Daniel 5:27.

40. Leviticus 18:21; 20:2–5.

41. *Abbruch.*

42. See note 11.

43. Amos 5:24, "But let justice roll down like waters . . . ," speaks to the Old Testament theme of justice. John 8:31–2, "If you continue in my word, you are truly my disciples; and you will know the truth, and the truth will make you free," focuses on the New Testament of truth. John 15:12, "This is my commandment, that you love one another as I have loved you," is a classic statement of the New Testament theme of love.

44. In the speeches, Paul Tillich quoted from memory. The period of German classicism he refers to is discussed in Paul Tillich, *A History of Christian Thought,* ed. Carl E. Braaten (New York: Simon and Schuster, 1968), 287–431.

45. Vidkun Quisling was the Nazis' puppet in Norway. His name became a synonym for "traitor."

46. Perhaps Tillich is referring to those involved in the White Rose, whose leaders, Hans and Sophie Scholl, were executed in February 1943.

47. Luke 23:26–31.

48. Tillich is referring to the *Kristallnacht* pogrom of November 8–9, 1938.

49. Johann Wolfgang von Goethe, *Faust: The Original German and a New Translation and Introduction*, tran. Walter Kaufman (New York: Anchor Books, 1961), 420–21.

50. Matthew 28:1–2; Mark 16:3, 4; Luke 24:1–2; John 20:1, 2.

51. The bombing raid occurred on April 18, 1942.

52. Evidently, Tillich was unaware of events such as the execution of Polish officers taken prisoner during the invasion of 1939, as well as the deaths of thousands of Soviet prisoners of war who were victims of the notoriously brutal concentration camp at Plaszow in Poland.

53. The defeat of the Germans in North Africa was officially declared on May 13, 1943.

54. Jeremiah 4—9.

55. Matthew 5:5.

56. July 14, 1789 (Bastille Day), was the day on which the French monarchy was toppled.

57. Marshal H. Philippe Pétain was a World War I hero but also the leader of the government of Vichy France.

58. This was the joint statement of Franklin Roosevelt and Winston Churchill, issued from their meeting in Newfoundland in August 1942.

59. Genesis 19:24.

60. Mussolini had negotiated with Hitler the transfer of citizens of German origin out of the South Tyrol region of Italy into German-occupied regions prior to the war. It was an agreement never fully carried out.

61. Exodus 7:14–12:32.

62. Maximilien Robespierre was one of the leaders of the French revolutionary government after the fall of the monarchy.

63. This commitment was made by the foreign ministers of the Big Three (Great Britain, the United States, and the Soviet Union) at their Moscow meeting of October 18, 1943.

64. Pablo Picasso's *Guernica*.

65. The inflation refers to an inflationary period in the 1920s, which reached its peak in November 1923, at which point the U.S. dollar equaled 4 trillion German marks.

66. Luke 23:34.

67. Luke 23:39.

68. John 11:43.

69. Tillich's great disappointment over the onset of the cold war and its spheres of influence may reveal his second thoughts with respect to the motives of the superpowers, but of the Soviets in particular.

INDEX

INDEX

INDEX